THE BAD BOY

THE BAD BOY

BERT HALL: AVIATOR
AND MERCENARY
OF THE SKIES

BLAINE L. PARDOE

FONTHILL

Dedication

This one is for my good friend and colleague Jean Armstrong. She has almost as much fun doing research on these books as I have writing them.

Fonthill Media Limited
Fonthill Media LLC
www.fonthillmedia.com
office@fonthillmedia.com

First published 2012

British Library Cataloguing in Publication Data:
A catalogue record for this book is available from the British Library

ISBN: 978-1-78155-130-1 (print)
ISBN: 978-1-78155-178-3 (e-book)

Typeset in 10pt on 14pt Sabon LT
Printed and bound in England

Connect with us
 facebook.com/fonthillmedia twitter.com/fonthillmedia

Contents

Foreword

On 30 April 1916, several American pilots serving in France's Service Aeronautique assembled with their two French commanders on their squadron's airfield at Luxeuil, France. These men were the founders of the Lafayette Escadrille, the most famous pursuit squadron of the First World War. Of the seven pilots, five were the scions of millionaires, the sons of powerful and wealthy American families. One was the son of a Baptist minister. And one was the son of a Missouri farmer. Weston Bert Hall, the farmer's son, unlike his comrades on the airfield that day, had never attended an institution of higher learning and sampled the wealth and ease that was the privilege of the sons of America's aristocracy. His comrades survived on remittances. But Bert Hall's meal ticket was his rapid-fire intellect, wit and charm.

I first discovered Bert Hall when I was researching for my book *Lafayette Escadrille Pilot Biographies*. I then learned more about him while working on my subsequent title, *The Lafayette Flying Corps*. Initially, I didn't care for the man. There was a lot to dislike about him. History has shown him to be a liar, cheat, thief, braggart, bigamist and a manipulator par excellence. But despite all his flaws, he had a charm and magnetism that attracted others to him.

Hall had no formal schooling. And yet, he was accepted by and was comfortable in the presence of his squadron comrades from Harvard, Yale and the University of Virginia. He lacked the academic credentials that would elevate him to their intellectual status. But he held a hole card. He had won their respect while fighting beside them in the Foreign Legion and in aerial combat above the lines.

Fellow pilot Kiffin Rockwell, who was killed while Hall was with the Lafayette Squadron, called Bert '...a dastardly blowhard, but the man has skill and a killer's instincts'. He further said '...Hall saved my skin, no doubt about it. Even Kiffin's brother, Paul, who had served with Hall in the Foreign Legion, said of him, 'Bert Hall is an aggressive fighter, unafraid of combat.' Paul

Rockwell would become Hall's implacable critic after the war when Rockwell assumed the mantle of defender of the squadron's honour and legacy.

Blind luck had placed Hall in a squadron of remittance men. And he was well aware of the financial advantages his wealthy comrades presented. But Hall could never play it straight. Devoid of a conscience, he always sought the advantage in any situation, regardless of its effect on those around him. While Bert's performance in the air seemed beyond reproach, it was his activities on the ground that earned the ire of his squadron. Eventually, his comrades wearied of his antics to the degree to which even his bravery could not save him. They grew fed up with his lying, his check kiting and his cheating at poker. Hall pushed too far and in November 1916, they forced him out of the squadron. Of his departure he later wrote, 'I think the Lafayette Escadrille is glad to get rid of me. I don't blame 'em.'

Hall never looked back, but continued to follow his ruthless philosophy: 'Grab what you can when you can and the devil take the hindmost.' If he can be believed, Hall played many roles during a high-octane, peripatetic life: combat aviator in Romania and Russia; circuit lecturer; movie producer and star; aviation instructor for 20th Century Fox; commander of the Nationalist Chinese air force; and aeroplane and small-arms merchant. And there were always the women, at least five wives, which he sometimes married two at a time. Hall felt he could forever scoff at the law, but in 1933, he was arrested for running illegal guns into China and wound up serving two and a half years in a federal penitentiary.

Hall never let the world forget that he had been a founder of the famous Lafayette Escadrille. He frequently used that fact to open many doors of opportunity. The problem for Paul Rockwell and for the squadron's legacy was that Hall managed to outlive the six other founding members. He was a poor representative who sullied the squadron's reputation with his antics as he kept one jump ahead of the law. Upon his death in 1948, *Los Angeles Times* editor Bill Henry wrote of him: 'He had his day and it had been a big one. He lived on it more or less for the rest of his life.'

Blaine Pardoe has done a solid job of research in uncovering much new information about Bert Hall that has lain dormant for decades. He used that information to weave a fascinating account about this inimitable master of reinvention. I sped through the chapters, relishing Pardoe's revelations of the 'lovable old rogue's' escapades. Pardoe has shed new light on the man who will always keep historians guessing and forever asking the question, who is the real Bert Hall?

Dennis Gordon
Montana, US
August 2012

Author's Foreword

Bert Hall was the first in a breed of aviation mercenaries that emerged from the Great War. For years, armchair historians have discounted his role in the Lafayette Escadrille and subsequently in China. It was easy to do. Bert's lies, on the surface, seem so numerous and so contradictory that the thought of anyone seriously attempting to tell his story was too daunting. It would have been much easier to embrace the public perception that Bert was a 'lovable rogue' and simply move on.

I couldn't do that.

When I was working on my book, *Lost Eagles*, about Frederick Zinn, I learned of Zinn's lifelong friendship with Bert Hall and it intrigued me. The men seemed so polar opposite I wanted to understand their relationship, and in turn, Bert Hall. I started doing some digging into Hall's life. I wanted to go back to primary research materials to get as close to the truth as possible. In Bert's case, that was the greatest challenge of this book. What I wrote in this book is as close as I have been able to ascertain is the life story of this man.

In working on this project, I was stunned with Hall's sense of timing. He had a knack for being in the right place at the right time most of his life. He was in Paris in the American community at the outbreak of the Great War. He was in Petrograd at the pinnacle of the Russian Revolution. Hall was in China during the period of the civil wars and when the Japanese invaded. Say what you will, Bert had a knack for being in the right place at the right point in history and took full advantage of them.

Aviation and First World War historians are quick to dismiss Bert's own accounts of the war. Until the writing of this book, there was good reason to do so. Bert's first autobiography, *L'en Air!* (In the Air) was published in 1918 and for the most part did not draw fire for being inaccurate. In fact, the only person that seems to have had issues with Bert's first book was Paul Rockwell, and even those criticisms were minor at best. Rockwell had an almost lifelong axe to grind with Bert and erasing Hall from the official history of the Lafayette Escadrille was one of his life's chief motivations.

It was the second autobiography, *One Man's War*, which he allegedly co-authored with John Jacob Niles, which most historians point to and decry as being more of a work of fiction than reality. This book is often the root of arguments that Hall was a bad liar and not a war hero. Those critics are right in terms of the facts, but wrong in placing the blame. As this book and research will demonstrate, Bert's contributions to this book were little more than turning over his diary to Niles. This was not a case of ghost writing; Bert was not even aware that the book had been written and was on sale at the time. Hall had never seen the manuscript and had contributed nothing to the tales presented in the book. Niles and Niles alone was responsible for the embellishment, outright lies and inconsistencies with Bert's prior autobiography and other historical accounts. Bert's only crime was that his greed overpowered his desire to set the record straight. As such, I have avoided referencing *One Man's War* as a source except when it is supported by other accounts.

In fairness, many authors of the 1910-1930s period often embellished real-life accounts. I'm not justifying Bert's exaggerations, but providing a cultural framing for them. I have only used examples from Bert's own books where they were not gratuitous in nature and can usually be validated from other accounts.

While researching this book, I conducted an exhaustive search for Bert's two movies, *A Romance of the Air* and *The Border Scouts*. Every source I went to said they were lost movies from the silent era. I didn't give up. On my third attempt with the Library of Congress, I was stunned when they said they now had *A Romance of the Air*. Getting a copy cost a lot, but it was well worth it to see Bert on film flying an aeroplane. More importantly, a once lost film featuring a First World War pilot is now out there for those who want to see it.

In writing this book I learned that Bert had an enemy from 1916 to his death: Paul Rockwell. In going through his exhaustive files at Washington and Lee University, it became clear that Rockwell did what he could to remove Hall from the history of the Lafayette Escadrille. He went out of his way to taint historians' perspectives on Bert or to outright discredit him. I like to believe that in writing this book I defeated his efforts once and for all.

Over three years of research went into this book. It took this long for a reason. Bert exaggerated and lied about his past as he reinvented himself during his life. But most of Bert's lies started with a kernel of truth. That meant digging deep with primary research sources to try and pull out those wonderful titbits which made up his story. The story you are about to read is my best effort to get to as close to the truth as possible.

If you know nothing of First World War aviation, I have provided ample background to help you understand Hall's role. If you are a fan of this era, I have provided a history of the Lafayette Escadrille during Bert's time there, centred (for the most part) on Hall. This is not a complete history of the unit, but instead is aimed at providing the context of Bert's important involvement in the unit and her colourful personnel.

I have opted to tell this story in the words of the men that were there. Wherever possible I utilised quotes by the men that were there at the time. In writing this book I leveraged a significant number of newspaper articles and interviews to gain perspective on Hall's life or qualify his activities. While sometimes newspaper accounts are inaccurate, they proved quite useful in this case.

I have used the French ranks, where appropriate. When quoting written accounts I left them in their English form. Hence, Sergeant is Sergent, Corporal is Caporal, etc.

There are things I didn't mention which some historians are likely to spot. For example, Hall had medals in his possession that he claimed he earned. My research indicated that one of those medals, his British one, was not in his possession at the end of the war (was evidenced in *A Romance of the Air* and in several photographs). If you don't see something mentioned it is probably because I could not verify it one way or another. Given Bert's tendency to exaggerate his life story, there is quite a file of these in my records, as you might imagine.

I could have easily spent another three years chasing nuggets of information here and there and adding to this book. Would they have made the book better? Maybe – but by how much? In the end, there's a point where every author has to draw the line and say 'It's time to put this down on paper.'

Having properly prepared you, the time has come to explore this man's incredible life and story. So, brace yourself for the story of a self-made American icon of aviation.

Introduction

Them that love me love me well. Them that don't can go to hell.

– Bert Hall

Fremont, Ohio
6 December 1948

It was just after 6:00 am and Bert Hall was driving his Studebaker Commander[1] west as the sun rose over his shoulder. The area around Fremont where he was driving was flat Ohio farmland that stretched on forever. For Bert that morning, the sky was the limit – just as it had always been for him. Bert was heading that day from his home outside of Sandusky to Cleveland on a sales call for his company. His route that morning was on State Route 6, a road he had driven many times before.

He was just coming up on the property of Charles Hudson when a stabbing pain erupted in his chest. Bert swerved the blue Studebaker hard as the ripples of pain swept his body, driving headlong through a wooden farm fence then slamming into a utility pole. The grinding metallic impact threw him forwards, bruising his head and spider-cracking the windshield.[2] In those last few moments as he slumped in his seat and slid slowly to the floor of the car, Bert Hall must have realised that his luck had finally run out. Bert had been a pioneer military aviator – one of the original members of the famed Lafayette Escadrille. He had cheated death for decades around the world. In the skies over France, he was one of the first Americans to pilot an aeroplane in battle. He had flown on both the Western and Eastern Fronts and had evaded the grim fate of many pilots. In a war where the life expectancy of aviators was three weeks, Bert had survived and endured.

As the fate he had cheated most of his life took him in its grasp, Bert had to have enjoyed the irony that his death had been so simple, so common. A heart attack? After all he had been through in his life, all of the dogfights, he was being taken down by a heart attack? Nothing about Bert's life had been common. He was a hero of the infamous French Foreign Legion at the outbreak of the war, by his own reckoning. Bert had woven himself into the history of the Lafayette Escadrille despite his reputation as a wily scoundrel. He had starred in silent movies and had written two highly popular autobiographies that were a mix of fiction, carefully crafted lies and a hint of reality. As with everything in his life, the truth was elusive and the legend was more entertaining and thrilling.

Bert Hall had created a myth about his life and adventures. He wore the label of 'soldier of fortune' with pride. He was a self-proclaimed Chinese General who had been there to build one of their first air forces. His scheming had landed him in trouble with the Chinese and earned him a new title: convicted criminal. Even that nom de plume had not shaken Bert or the public's view of him. America loves to raise men up on pillars as heroes, thrill when they fall, and cheer them when they redeem themselves. Bert rode that publicity rollercoaster with a certain amount of glee.

In the last moments on the floor of his car, Bert must have known that he was finally joining his former comrades in oblivion. He had defied the odds and outlived all of the original members of the infamous Lafayette Escadrille. He had even managed to outlive all but one of his chief critics. Bert had to have embraced that satisfaction in his last moments of life – that the saga of Bert Hall would survive and surpass him. It was a mythical story that he had created throughout his entire life and it would continue on despite his demise.

One must wonder if he smiled in satisfaction in that last moment of life. Certainly he deserved to.

If it wasn't for the First World War and the formation of the Lafayette Escadrille, Bert Hall most likely would have ended up being a small-time con artist. The Great War defined Bert Hall as it did many young men of that era who survived. As America was born on the world stage in the First World War, Bert Hall rode those coattails to the start of his own myth – that of an American legend. When war broke out in 1914, it was not the horrific stalemated trench warfare that is often associated with the conflict. In fact, the first few months of the war were fluid with armies, namely the Germans, making dashing bold moves on the map, sweeping towards Paris. Only later did the war bog down and turn into an ugly brutal entrenched affair that consumed most of a generation of Europe's men.

The numbers paint a grim picture of the fighting. In just over four years, eight and a half million lay dead with twenty-one million wounded and just under eight million as prisoners of war. The Great War ushered in more new ways for man to kill his fellow men than any other conflict. Poison gas, flamethrowers, rapid-fire artillery, tanks, submarines, and above all, the airplane, all debuted in the conflict.

The Wright Brothers flew at Kitty Hawk in 1903 and just over a decade later, their invention would be turned into a weapon of war. By 1914, all of the major armies had some sort of air force, even if that force was nothing more than a handful of rickety aircraft. The aeroplanes that flew in the Great War were often wooden-framed affairs covered with doped linen wings. Aircraft were little more than flying kites armed with machine guns, engines and packed with fuel. Violent and vicious manoeuvres could shred the wing coverings or tear an aircraft apart. There was no protection for the pilots who flew in open cockpits in freezing conditions. Icy winds would tear at exposed flesh. Combat between aircraft was a brutal dance of death in the skies, fought at deadly point-blank range. It was a personal style of warfare where machine guns were used to kill an enemy who was attempting to do the same to you. If enemy aircraft didn't get you, anti-aircraft fire threw hot shrapnel into the air. A flak hit could ignite the fuel, puncture the pilot or destroy an engine. The planes, whipping in the wind at 60-100 mph, were nothing more than bonfires waiting to erupt. The allied air forces did not provide parachutes to pilots, so any hit could mean a plummet of thousands of feet onto the shell-torn battlefields below.

America did not enter the war until 1917 and really only showed up in force in 1918, the last year of the conflict. These were not the first Americans to fight in the war, however. Just after the outbreak of war in August 1914, forty-three Americans volunteered to join the French Foreign Legion.[3] These men would fight on the Western Front in some of the most brutal early fighting in the conflict.

More importantly, this cadre of men would eventually become the nexus of what would become the US Air Service. Most would be detached from duty in the Foreign Legion in the trenches to form a volunteer American squadron or escadrille. This unit, the Lafayette Escadrille, was really part of a larger fraternity of Americans, the Lafayette Flying Corps. These volunteers flew for the French Air Service (the Aéronautique Militaire) and would become the seeds for the fledgling US Air Service when America finally joined the war effort.

Weston Birch (Bert) Hall was in that initial band of men that joined the Foreign Legion and went on to be one of the first Americans to fly in combat for France. Their exploits were replayed in newspapers around the world making the name 'Bert Hall' widely known. Even if he had never scored a victory in combat, he was a hero for climbing into the cockpit. Young men idolised the daring aviators of the Lafayette Escadrille and Bert was there from the beginning of the unit. He scored three confirmed victories while flying for the escadrille and made sure that the stories of his deeds were well covered by the newspapers. Bert would eventually go on to fly for Russia, Romania and China, but oddly enough he never fought for his own country. Much has been made of the illustrious members of the Lafayette Escadrille. Their own publicity machine contributed to their perception in the eyes of many Americans. They were a group of young playboys from rich families, most having attended Ivy League schools at the outbreak of the war. This added to the mystique of the unit, making the members sound more dashing, more daring. Their stories sounded like those of the knights of old, fighting battles with their foes demonstrating chivalry in their dogfights. They were young and charismatic. Men wanted to be like them and women adored them.

Bert was none of these things and was proud of that. Yet oddly enough he was allowed to become part of their legend. He was the bad boy of the Lafayette Escadrille. Phrases have been used to describe him such as 'lovable old rogue'[4] and 'bad old Bertie'.[5] Even in this early part of his military career, he was acknowledged as being the bad boy of the skies – a role he revelled in. Contradictions were part of Bert Hall. He was short, skinny, almost plain looking. During the war years, he was rarely photographed without a cigarette in his hands and a sullen expression on his face. Yet he managed to attract at least five wives, a sign that he had some charisma, a way with words, or both.

Legends don't just happen, they are created. Even at this stage of his life, Bert understood the value of marketing. He created a highly recognised brand, his own name, and spent the rest of his life leveraging those years flying for France. Even his Nieuport fighter was adorned with his name on one side, 'Bert' and 'treB' on the reverse. His later aeroplane was painted with dollar signs. There would be detractors throughout his life, men that questioned his bravery and exposed his tall tales. Somehow, the wild and incredibly exaggerated version of his life was the one that would prevail in the minds and hearts of people.

While it was the glorified combat missions of the Lafayette Escadrille that would form the heart and soul of the Bert Hall legend, his story began back in the Revolutionary War and the American Civil War, and the military record of his father, George Hall. To understand Bert Hall, you have to go back to the Confederate States of America and the stories that his father told him about the horrors and carnage of war.

CHAPTER ONE

From a Family of Rebels

Soldiers, you have been betrayed. The Generals whom you have trusted have refused to lead you. Let us begin the battle again by a revolution. Lift up the flag that has been cast down dishonoured. Unsheathe the sword that it may remain unsullied and victorious. If you desire it, I will lead...[1]

– General Shelby's speech to the Missouri Cavalry, 1865

To fully understand a man as complex as Bert Hall, you have to understand his family and upbringing. Bert Hall's ancestors were not nearly as flamboyant as him, but they took part in almost all of America's early wars and served with distinction. While Bert Hall's name is often spoken in the same breath as a braggart, few can deny the bravery that flowed through is bloodline. Bert came from a long line of rebellious military men who followed their ideals and hearts, even when the cause was lost.

The Hall family emigrated from Europe early in America's history. The first American member of Bert's bloodline was David Hall, born in 1720 in the Virginia Colony.[2] His son, William Henry Hall, was destined to be the first of the fighting Halls in the United States – a tradition that would carry forward in the family for generations. William was born in 1761 in Henrico County Virginia, outside of Richmond, where he was raised in a farming family. The Halls moved to Caswell County, North Carolina, when he was a boy.

When revolution broke out in the American colonies, young William found himself at the perfect age for enlistment. His loyalties were clearly with the fledgling American colonies. In 1778 at the age of seventeen, young William enlisted in the 4th Regiment of the Continental Line under the command of Colonel James Sanders under General Benjamin Lincoln's command. His first tour of duty fighting the revolution was remarkably unspectacular. After marching up to Halifax Virginia and encamping for several weeks, William Hall was given a six-month furlough. Such furloughs were not uncommon with the Continental Army. These men were farmers and they often needed time off to bring their crops in or to plant in the early spring.[3] As local militia, they could be called up at any time of need as determined by the local officials, and during the American Revolution this happened often.

The southern campaign of the rebellion was conceived by the British as the pivotal theatre of the war. It was based on the assumption that there were strong loyalist support in the southern colonies and that the local population would rise up in support of the crown if supported by British troops. Overambitious and aggressive officers also tipped the scales in favour of the colonial cause. General Banastre Tarleton, a particularly aggressive cavalry officer, allegedly refused to accept the surrender of a group of Virginia Colonial troops, instead slaughtering them in the Waxhaw massacre in 1780. This instance alone galvanised many citizens that were on the fence in terms of their loyalties.

The British also issued proclamations that anyone not pledging loyalty to the king would be considered the enemy. This kind of strategy works when you know how people will respond. However, forcing the Colonists to choose, in an environment where doubts were raised as to the brutality of the British, split the population rather than rallying it to the British cause.[4] It had the opposite of the desired effect, driving some people on the fence to the rebel cause.

The southern campaign was unlike the war in New England in many respects. One of the key differences was that most of the battles that took place in the south were not between the Colonial and British Regulars, but by militia – Loyalist and Colonial. Each state called up militia, but in the southern campaign they could be called up for their side. The fighting in the south often resembled more of a civil war than a war of revolution. Often neighbour battled neighbour in raids and skirmishes often driven by petty rivalries more than true political leanings. The British Army found itself not in a country filled with loyal supporters, but in a rugged countryside where militias whittled away at their time and resources in a bitter civil struggle.

The fighting in the American Revolution was characterised through a blend of fighting styles and forces. The British fielded a seasoned and experienced force of Regulars recognised around the world for their discipline in battle. They were augmented with their local colonist Tory militia. The Americans had a smaller Regular army with relatively green militia. In the southern campaign, where the British favoured traditional line formations for battle, the Colonial militia were often less organised, preferring sniping and hit-and-run attacks. It was a clash of tactics and expertise that was often lopsided to one side or the other depending on the circumstances, commanders and the terrain.

In November, Private Hall returned to service in North Carolina once more when he was called up. He moved into South Carolina along the Santee River, encamping at Charlestown and Savannah Towns. William's first taste of battle took place on the Stono River on 20 June 1779. The British had initiated their infamous 'southern strategy' and were wrecking havoc in the lower colonies in an attempt to shift the epicentre of the war out of New England. The British forces occupied Savannah and American General Benjamin Lincoln wanted it back. To do this, his intention was to build up his forces and to create a cordon around the city from all key access points to compel the British to withdraw. There were several skirmishes between the seasoned British troops and General Lincoln's North Carolina militia reinforced with some Continental Regulars.

The British had been stunned by the speed with which General Lincoln had moved. To cover their crossing of the Stono River, they reinforced a bridgehead on the north side of the river at the Stono Ferry. The British erected three field fortifications of abatis and earthwork redoubts. These were garrisoned by a battalion of Scottish Highlanders, Hessians and Tory Loyalist militia forces from North and South Carolina.

General Lincoln had a large force of over 6,500 men, but could only mobilise around 1,200 for the move against the Stono Ferry. He split his forces into two wings – one composed of militia troops under General Jethro Sumner (which was where William Hall was attached) and the Continental regulars under General Isaac Huger.

Despite outnumbering his more seasoned British opponent, the American force found itself outmatched. The First Highland Scots Battalion was led by the one-armed Colonel Maitland who detected Lincoln's force early in the engagement and were prepared for their attack. The Highlanders held their ground until most of them were killed or wounded. General Lincoln was slow to bring his troops in and press their numerical advantage. Lincoln had eight pieces of artillery but by the time they were brought up, the Hessians and surviving Highlanders had taken positions in their redoubts rendering the artillery almost totally ineffective. After a few hours of fighting, General Lincoln ordered a withdrawal.[5]

William's summary of the fighting was limited. 'We encamped and took up headquarters within five miles of the British forces. The battle on the Stono River was fought to the best of his recollection on Sunday the 19th or 20th of July following. He (William) was then under the command of Colonel Pinkney S. Carr who commanded the infantry. Captain Marcajie Lewis, a regular officer with fifty men, was sent to as a guard to the battle ground and he (William) was one of those fifty.'[6] Since William arrived with his horse, it is assumed that he served in a capacity as a mounted dragoon or cavalryman.

Around 6 August 1779, William was given a written discharge from his duties. Many men might have returned home having served, but William Hall returned to duty in 1780. This time he was a substitute for Bazle Davis who had been called up into the North Carolina militia.[7] The principle of substitutes was commonplace even through the period of the American Civil War. When someone was called up they could have another person go in their place, usually in return of payment. While no one can be sure if money changed hands in the case of Bazle Davis, what is known is that William Hall took his place, mustering into the militia in Caswell County North Carolina under the commands of Captain Wilson, Major Elijah Moore and Colonel William Moore.[8] If he was paid for his service, it was the first recorded time in the family history that a Hall profited from his military service, a tradition that would carry on for several generations.

> Where he (William) was then back and was marched with the troops to Hillsborough, Salisbury, Charlotte and from there to the Mascaw Creek head quarters and there remained until we were verbally discharged by Colonel William Moore. In this time Gus Morgan a Continental officer took a party good number of Tories who were under the command of Col. Rugely at Rugelys [sic] Mill. The Tories were taken to our headquarters and he assigned in guarding them.

The battle at Rugeley's Mill on 15 August 1779 was one of a series of failed manoeuvres by American General Gates against General Cornwallis. Gates marched off to a heavily wooded and swampy region with a relatively small force of which two-thirds were green militia, William Hall being one of them. In the dense forests near Camden, South Carolina, the Americans encountered members of Tarleton's Legion (cavalry) reinforced with the 71st Highlanders. The Caswell Militia were assigned to the centre of the Continental force with the Virginia Militia on their left. As the Continental force moved forwards, the Virginians ran headlong into the Highlanders and being inexperienced, tumbled towards the rear pell-mell. The North Carolina Militia needed little promoting. Seeing the Virginians in rout, their line fared no better and clamoured quickly into the rear. General Gates tried to rally the militia but to no avail. Within a few hours the entire Continental force was scattered, fleeing into the swamps to avoid capture.[9] While William's account of taking prisoners to the rear is possible, the British reported very few prisoners taken in the encounter. This can be seen as simply the first time that a member of the Hall family embellished his military career.

After the fighting outside of Camden, Hall was once more discharged from duty. He volunteered again for duty in 1781 under Colonel William Moore and Captain Dudley Reynolds in the North Carolina militia. It was intended to be a six-week stint that culminated with an engagement against Loyalist Tories near the Haw River in one of the more colourful battles of the southern campaign.[10]

On 24 February 1781, the Tories were Americans loyal to the British crown and at Haw River, they were organised as a cavalry force under Colonel John Pyle while the Continentals were led by Lieutenant Colonel 'Light Horse' Harry Lee. When Lee's skirmishers came onto Pyle's lines, they were mistaken for Tarleton's cavalry since they both worth green uniforms. Lee took advantage of the mistake, thanking the Tory scouts and passing on Colonel Tarleton's compliments.

Lee led his force into the heart of the Tory troops posing as their comrades. When he saw Colonel Pyle, he saluted and rode out to meet him as his force carefully took positions around the Loyalists. When fighting broke out, Pyle unglamorously called out to his own men, 'Stop! Stop! You're killing your own men!' A moment later he was struck by a sword blow. The confusion was so bad that Lee's men had to call out before shooting, often asking 'Whose men are you?' When the response came back, 'The King's!', they would be attacked.[11] After the slaughter, the incident earned the dubious nickname of 'Pyle's Massacre'. Given that Hall was a mounted soldier, chances are pretty strong that he was in the thick of the butchery.

The battle was a decisive victory for the Colonial forces, but was overshadowed by a larger victory a few days later at Guilford Court House. Many would claim that it was this battle that changed the fate of the American Revolution. The Colonial forces outnumbered the British three-to-one and eventually yielded the field of battle. While on paper it was a British victory, their losses were enough to force General Cornwallis to leave the south and head north into Virginia, and to eventual defeat.

William Hall glossed over the engagement and any potential involvement in his own recollections:

> To the best of his (William's) recollection this service lasted about six weeks during the time we had the battle with the Tories near Haw River. There we defeated them and killed nearly the whole of them. A little after this time the Battle of Gilford was fought and he would have been in that battle, but for his horse and was with another solider permitted to go home and get fresh horses. He was about 19 miles from Gilford at the time of the battle.[12]

William was once more discharged but was once more called to duty, this time substituting for Charles Cannon in Virginia.[13] Performing substitutions twice, once out of state, implies that there was indeed money being paid for William to go off and fight. He was mustered in the command of Colonel Peter Rogers and Captain Flemming Bates of Halifax, Virginia.

Hall was marched to old James Town, then Williamsburg, and then to a small port city called 'Little York' or more commonly known as Yorktown.

Yorktown was the culmination of the Continental's fight against the British. Cornwallis' force was trapped and laid siege to by General Washington. William Hall was present at the surrender of the British at York Town and was later tasked with marching British prisoners to Noland's Ferry on the Potomac. Afterwards, the Governor of Virginia offered a proclamation of discharge. Having fulfilled his final term of service, William returned to his farm in North Carolina.

William had served nine months as a soldier in the Continental Line and ten-and-a-half months as a militia soldier. He moved for a short time to South Carolina, Tennessee, then to Montgomery County Missouri, the far west of America where he became a respected member of the community. His son, David Hall, was named after his grandfather. The early part of his life was running a prosperous brick manufacturing company.[14] Later in life, he followed his father's call to service and joined the Missouri Militia in the 67th Regiment, a state militia unit that did not see action when he was in it.[15] David's son, Willis Henry Hall, was born in 1819 and was Bert Hall's grandfather.

Willis Henry Hall was a farmer born in South Carolina when the Hall family resided there. Willis moved to Parkville in Platte County, Missouri, with his wife, Eliza (McFarland) Hall, originally from Kentucky. They had five children together, one of which was George Washington Hall – Bert's father. George Hall was born in 1847, two years after his parents married. His father died while he was a young boy in 1859.[16] His mother became a housekeeper, taking in boarders to help make ends meet.

In the 1820s, Missouri was a farming state with cities that were just becoming formed. Nestled along the western banks of the Mississippi, Missouri was considered 'the west' in the United States. Beyond it were fledgling states and the western territories, largely unsettled and untamed.

Missouri prior to the American Civil War was a state torn down the middle in terms of slavery issues. Most of her initial settlers came from the south, so the state's leanings were heavily in support of slavery. Prior to the outbreak of war, the slavery issue boiled over with neighbouring Kansas. At the time, federal law provided that a slave entering a free state was then a free man. The effect of this law and the proximity of the two states led to a series of border clashes, often referred to as The Border Wars or Bloody Kansas. While the fighting was in Kansas, Missouri was the springboard for border raids terrorising citizens who did not agree on the slavery issue.

The federal ruling in the Dred Scott case reversed the law regarding slaves' freedom, effectively ending the concept of slaves being free once they reached a free state. While this eased the border tensions, it did not eliminate the underlying tensions. While Missouri was initially settled by southerners, an influx in the 1840s and 1850s of Irish and German immigrants changed the political leanings on the slavery issue. When the American Civil War broke out, many Missourians clung to the foolhardy idea that it might remain neutral in the conflict.

Any idyllic thoughts of maintaining neutrality evaporated when the federal arsenal was seized by General Nathaniel Lyon and arms were provided to anti-slavery militia. The pro-slavery governor of Missouri attempted to squash the efforts, but General Lyon surprised and captured their force at Camp Jackson on 10 May 1861. Despite an effort to broker a peace, it became clear that Missouri was not destined to be neutral ground, but instead was going to be one of the focal points of the western theatre of the American Civil War.

Young George Hall was attending the Park College in Platte County at the age of fourteen in 1862 when he decided to go off to war for the Confederate States of America.[17] In Cove Creek, Missouri, in early September 1862, he enlisted in Captain George B. Harper's Company (Company G) of the Second Regiment of the Missouri Cavalry.[18] At the age of fourteen, it would have been a rarity to put him on the firing line. Usually, such young men enlisting in the service during the Civil War were assigned as drummer boys. That was not the case with George Hall. He was made an orderly for General Joseph Shelby that meant carrying orders of the general to the troops in the field, often under fire. His subservient position to General Shelby was a role that was to dominate his life.

General Joseph 'Jo' Shelby was the epitome caricature of a feisty southern general. Shelby was first and foremost a cavalry commander. He called his combined cavalry regiments his 'Iron Brigade' and used them with deadly skill in the western theatre. By the time George Hall had enlisted, Shelby had already earned a reputation for cunning and audacity on the battlefield.

Being posted as an orderly was far from safe work. General Shelby was a general officer that led from the front, often under a hail of lead and hot iron, and orderlies were not only armed but pressed into action when called upon. George Hall took part in what historians would eventually call Shelby's 'Great Raid'. Between September 1862 and October 1863, Shelby led his forces on a 1,500 mile raid through Missouri. Starting in Arkadelphia, Arkansas, with only 800 men in his Iron Brigade, Shelby tore a swath through Missouri and the Union forces attempting to ensnare him. Outnumbered often three-to-one, he claimed to have inflicted over 1,000 casualties in the raid. Shelby would later claim that he had captured or destroyed over two million dollars in federal property. The raid was so stunning and successful that Shelby was promoted to brigadier general for his efforts.

George Hall played a key role as his aide and orderly, relaying orders and was often in the middle of the fighting as a result. Shelby's adjutant and chronicler, John Edwards, said of Hall around the campfire during the raid: 'George Hall – nestling at Shelby's feet – the boy orderly – but fierce as a lion in battle.'[19]

By 1864, the Confederate Army was beginning to reel from a series of blows, both east and west. In February 1864, George Hall deserted for a period of nine months, missing one of Shelby's last major campaigns of the war. Hall's service at this time was described as:

> Participated in most of engagements this company and regiment have been up to the time of his desertion. He deserted in Febry [sic] 15/64. He was a good soldier but induced to desert by others of improper desires.

When he left he did not take a horse, an action that would have garnered a more severe punishment if he had been caught.[20] Where George went during his desertion is not known. At that point in time he had been at war for almost two years and was still a boy at sixteen years old. What is known is that George had a change of heart. He returned to the regiment in January 1864 and was reinstated to his former role.[21] Apparently there were no bad feelings on the part of General Shelby for the young man. Like the prodigal son, he was welcomed back with open arms.

General Shelby's last campaign was in conjunction with General Sterling Price in October 1864 and George Hall was once more at his side. The Army of the West struck out from Arkansas into Missouri, but General Price found himself quickly outnumbered and outmatched. Their force fell into a fighting retreat.[22] Shelby was being relentlessly pursued by Union General E. B. Brown and was driven out of Missouri into Arkansas where he ran afoul of General J. M. Schofield and another Union Army. The Federal forces pressed him back as far as Texas on 26 October 1864.

General Lee surrendered the Army of Northern Virginia at Appomattox Courthouse on 9 April 1865. Many people harbour the illusion that this was the end of the Civil War, but it was not. Some commanders held out hope that Confederate President Jefferson Davis might somehow make his way to the west and rally the surviving elements of the Confederate forces. General Joe Johnston continued to fight and move his army in the Carolinas until 26 April, two weeks after Lee's surrender. Because of the slowness of communications, it took a long time for word of the Lee's surrender to reach the western United States. When the word came, many Confederate commanders were unsure how to respond. The majority eventually followed suit and surrendered their forces rather than pursue a lost cause.

Such was not the case with General Shelby.

As late as 10 May 1865, Shelby received word from General Edmund Kirby Smith that he was to be promoted to the rank of Major General, a futile gesture given that the Confederacy was disintegrating by the hour. The collapse of the Confederate government prohibited the promotion from ever being submitted and confirmed, but it was testimony to the fact that Shelby was still ready to go into action. When word of General Lee's surrender reached him, Shelby refused to lay down his arms and surrender.

The word, however, began to tear at his command. While Shelby refused to succumb to the rising tide of peace, many of his men did. Desertion became commonplace. His force of over a thousand began to dwindle in Texas, eventually dropping as low as 132 men.[23] Shelby realised that if he did nothing, what few men he had would be compelled to return to their families and farms. If that happened, there would be no hope for an eventual Confederate victory, something he still clung on to.

The plan the general devised was to fall back into Mexico. From there, the surviving Confederates could either regroup to take the war back into the United States, or possibly establish a Confederate colony in Mexico until the time was right to return and continue the war.

Shelby was not the first officer or former Confederate governor to consider this course of action, but he was the only one with a military command that was still somewhat intact. Other Confederate leaders not captured fled to places such as Cuba or even England rather than remain under the control of the occupying Federal army.

Mexico was a nation caught in the depths of its own civil war, complicated by European influences. The British, French and Spanish were all owed money by the Mexican government of Benito Juárez. When Mexico refused to pay, they sent in their troops. This did not force the government to pay and soon the Europeans grew weary of occupation duties. Napoleon III's solution was to place a puppet emperor on an imaginary throne in Mexico. He brought in Austrian Archduke Maximilian to assume that role.

The French ploy was a debacle from the start. While their armies had secured the key cities of Mexico, the ground between these cities was uncontrolled and often unpatrolled. This occupation did not weaken President Juárez and gave the Mexican civilians a common enemy. Juárez was able to rally many of his countrymen who saw the seating of Maximilian as outside intervention. Mexico lurched into a civil war, one where Maximilian held little sway with the people he allegedly ruled.

Even worse, the French placing of an Austrian Archduke on a self-created throne in Mexico was a direct violation of the Monroe-Doctrine with Europeans interfering in the American sphere of influence, raising the ire of the United States. While the US had been caught in the throes of its own civil war, little more than protests had been lodged to Mexico and the French. With the civil war in the US over, America was turning its attention to Mexico and diplomatic pressures to oust Maximilian. Rumours circulated freely that the massive Federal army might even push into Mexico to remove Maximilian.

The men that went with General Shelby were either fleeing what they perceived was going to be a punishing occupation by the Federal army in the south, or were enticed by stories of gold and silver mines, and the chance to re-establish a Confederate homeland. Mexico was seen as a chance for a new life without the humiliation of admitting defeat.

When word came of Shelby's plans, a large number of Confederate veterans flooded into his ranks. He gathered considerable supplies: 40,000 rounds of small arms ammunition, ten cannons, thousands of British Enfield muskets and wagons of other sundry supplies. Each man was said to have four pistols and 120 rounds of ammunition.[24] His refugees, men whose wool uniforms were more tatters than clothing, were allowed to refit with new uniforms that had never reached the front line troops, but sat instead in warehouses for a lack of transportation. Much of these arms had been intended to supply the Confederate Army but never reached their destinations as the Union forces tore the Confederacy into shreds.

For all of his vast supplies, Shelby did not have a highly defined plan on where to go and what to do when he entered Mexico. On 4 July 1865, commemorating Independence Day, he crossed the Rio Grande into Mexico at Eagle Pass, Texas. He ordered the Confederate flag to be taken down and placed in the river. Weighed down with rocks, it sank into the muddy river. For the devout Confederates, it was a solemn gesture marking their departure from their former nation. With that gesture, Shelby led his men into Mexico with the ever-faithful George Hall at his side.

Not long after crossing into Mexico, Shelby made contact with representatives of Benito Juárez. The smart thing to do would have been for Shelby to throw in his lot with the ousted president. Juárez's supporters were gaining strength against Maximilian and ultimately he was destined to topple the European puppet... either alone or with the eventual backing of the United States. But Shelby was a stubborn man. He put it up to a vote among the near 1,000 men that had crossed into Mexico with him as to what side should they fight for. Given that the United States was likely to back Juárez, the men felt their best chances were to side with Maximilian. Shelby soon realised that all of his arms were more of a burden than a boon. He opted to sell most of them to the Juárezist supporters for approximately eighty-two dollars per man in his command, paid in Juárezist script: money that would be worthless once he reached Maximilian. Unencumbered, Shelby led his loyal followers on an exodus into the heart of Mexico in search of place where the Confederacy might survive.[25]

As they set out their initial prospects looked good. Shelby's adjutant, Major John Edwards, wrote prose about their march of biblical magnitude to a promised land. However, after a short period the Confederates found themselves once more at war. The vast lands between the villages and towns were patrolled by bands of bandits, some numbering in the hundreds. These were augmented with armed patrols of Juárez supporters who saw the Confederates as foreign invaders that supported their enemies. Ambushes became common for the Confederates to fight against. Each attack not only drew precious blood, but tainted their cause and eroded confidence.

The Confederates turned on each other as well. Squabbles between soldiers became formal duels. Former comrades killed or wounded each other for the sake of honour, more often than not simply because of harsh words between them. Each internal confrontation further eroded Shelby's ability to command his men. Several men heard of an American woman being held hostage in a hacienda not far off the road they marched. These renegades defied Shelby's orders and mounted a rescue mission that resulted in the deaths of numerous men. While they managed to rescue the damsel in distress, it was further proof that Shelby's ability to control his troops eroded each day they marched under the scorching Mexican sun.

Bandit raids increased the further they marched into Mexico. Outside of Parras during a storm, the men sensed their lines were being probed. George Hall was posted with the advance scouts and when they realised they were outnumbered, countermarched back to the main encampment in the dark storm.

In the impenetrable darkness, the men mistook each other. Moreland fired upon George Hall and shot away the collar of his overcoat. Hall recognised his voice and made himself known to him.[26]

The young Hall had barely survived the encounter, almost gunned down by his own men. This incident served to demonstrate just how dangerous and precarious the position was becoming.

The only work that Shelby could secure for his rag-tag band of refugees was that as mercenaries, often providing assistance for French military units that were being withdrawn from the failed Mexican Empire of Maximilian. Shelby led his men outside of San Luis Potosi only to find over 2,000 mounted and armed bandits controlling the ground between the road and the city. They fell back on an abandoned hacienda nearly thirty miles from San Luis Potosi where 600 members of the Foreign Legion were dug in under General Douay. Shelby had been asked to help escort the Legionnaires out of the region. Outnumbered and on uncertain ground, Shelby proposed sending a handful of men to the city to enlist their aid and/or get them on the move out of the city.[27]

Three men were chosen for the dangerous mission. Captain James Kirtley, Thomas Boswell and George Hall. Kirtley, even in the darkness, advanced in skirmishing order. Kirtley took the point, followed by Hall and then Boswell. Between each was a distance of twenty yards. It was necessary to get word through to General Douay and Kirtley argued the less risk taken the greater chance there would be for one of the party getting through. 'We must keep apart,' he said, 'just far enough to succour each other, but not too close to be killed by the discharge of a shot-guns out of a flock of partridges one might kill a bag full. The ride was a silent and grimly tenacious one. Three times they turned from the high road to avoid a scouting party of guerrillas, and once, in going past a little group of four or five huts by the wayside – a place, indeed where mescal is sold, and where, upon all the roads in Mexico huts concentrated for this purpose alone – Kirtley, who had kept his position fixed in front the whole night through, was fired upon from an angle of a house. The bullet missed his left thigh barely, and imbedded through the wall.'[28]

After a harrowing twenty-four hours of marching, hiding and being shot at, they reached General Douay. With a welcome, he offered them a chance to rest and sleep. 'Your pardon one moment General,' said Kirtley, 'while I correct you. We do not need any sleep. As we can sleep as we ride. That was part of our drill. We left our General in danger, and he in turn sent us forward to notify you of the danger to your Colonel. We will take the food, the brandy and the horses, but the sleep, no, General, with many thanks.' The men set off again to return to Shelby.[29]

The Confederate force was under siege when the mounted Legionnaires came in, along with Kirtley, Boswell and Hall to break their blockade. Easily the youngest man on the great exodus into Mexico, George Hall did not shirk from danger during the long march. Shelby and his slowing shrinking command made their way to Mexico City where he hoped to throw his lot in with Maximilian. In his thinking it could be mutually beneficial, an exchange of land for a Confederate colony for military service. But the Austrian archduke was leery of taking the Confederates into his own dwindling military. One of his chief concerns was that taking the Confederates in as a distinct military force would only spurn the United States to step up their threatened activities against him. Shelby and his men had marched into the heart of Mexico only to be told their services were not necessary.

Disheartened, the Confederates were in the middle of a foreign country where more than half of the population saw them as interlopers and trying to side with a false leader. Shelby's nominal control over his troops eroded further. Many men broke ranks and set off on their own to attempt to settle down. Others formed or joined infant colonies, farming land that the Mexicans had already played out decades before. Eventually, even Shelby turned to the role of farmer.

Within four years' time, the great exodus of the Confederacy, the last hope for the rebellion, withered away. Most of the men made their way back to the United States. The records do not document when George Hall returned to the United States, but chances are it was when his beloved general made the trek back in 1867.[30] Shelby was eventually joined by his loyal adjunct John Edwards who settled in Missouri. Young George Hall found himself in New Orleans, penniless and a long way from home.

CHAPTER TWO

The Young Adventurer

He was just an ordinary country boy.

– Neighbour, Rose Slayer[1]

One thing is for certain – he learned to live by his wits at an early age.[2]

New Orleans in the post-Civil War era was beginning its long road of recovery from the war. George Hall had only the clothes on his back and the shattered dreams of a new Confederacy when he arrived there in 1867. While Shelby and others headed to Missouri, George lingered in New Orleans, managing to secure a job working steamboats on the Mississippi River. For two years he made his living as a boat hand working on steamboats carrying goods to a rebuilding of the United States.[3]

There is a period where details of George's life are not fully known. George was known to have developed a talent in raising shorthorn cattle and breeding thoroughbred Jersey cows.[4] In 1876, he moved to Page City where he reconnected with the retired General Shelby. Shelby sold him a parcel of his own farmland to work, just over 100 acres.[5] The former Confederates were a tight community, especially those that had served under Shelby. Major Edwards, Shelby's chronicler and friend, moved only a few miles away. His ties to Shelby were so close that, in 1897 when his beloved general passed away, George Hall was one of four men that were at his side when he drew his last breath.[6]

For a time, George Hall worked as a railroad worker at Page City station for the Missouri Pacific Railway as the depot agent, eventually running the entire depot.[7] He was a respected member of the Lafayette County community serving for several years as the School Director. In 1880, he lived with Georgia Page, a recent widow with four children (Mary, Olive, Estella and Walter). Her husband had recently died and by the end of the year, she and George married.

He was thirty-three years old, five years younger than his wife. Living in the boarding house with them at the time was another railroad worker, twenty-three-year-old Weston Birch.[8]

George and Georgia only had one child born to them during their marriage, Weston Birch Hall, born on the family farm on 7 November 1885. The child took his first and middle name from the young man who boarded with his parents, a peculiar choice at best. Weston was born in Higginsville, Missouri, despite the fact that throughout his life he would claim he was born in Eagle Pass, Texas, and in Bowling Green, Kentucky.[9] The obvious connection of Eagle Pass, Texas, to his family was that it was the place where Shelby sunk his Confederate flag in his father's presence. Where and when he took the nickname 'Bert' was never fully explained, but it was a rare moment when he used his full name. It was as if Bert would spend much of his life altering his past. He would claim to be born in 1880 or 1882 at various points as well.[10]

Bert's childhood is something of a mystery. Even in his two autobiographies he skips his childhood experiences almost entirely. There are no published references to him having any sort of relationship with his step-brothers or sisters. His parents had him as a child relatively late in life which may have had an impact on his upbringing. Of all of the children, he was the youngest and the only one born of his parent's marriage. In the myriad of his interviews and travels, Bert never referenced his step-brothers or sisters, which seems to imply that his relationship with them was thin at best. We do know that his father was a highly respected member of the community. He was postmaster for a few years and considered highly respected among his peers: 'Mr. Hall is popular and obliging.'[11] No doubt that Bert's gregarious character came from his father and his understanding of how military service might be used throughout his life. The influence of Bert's father carried with him his entire life. When asked in an interview about where the big moment of his life came into existence, his mind turned back to his early childhood.

'It was not at the front,' he said thoughtfully, 'nor in the air. I wouldn't say that it occurred when Joffre gave me the Medaille Militaire, nor when I brought a plane down in flames; nor was it at any time in getting in and out of German lines with French spies. None of them. The really big moment broke on me in Higginsville, Missouri, when I was 13 years of age. My dad sprung it on me. He was a Confederate soldier. After the civil war he went with Joe Shelby and one thousand other rebels who declined to surrender and joined Maximilian and Carlotta. After fifteen months of fighting, most of them came back to the States and settled down. The old man picked Higginsville and started a stock farm. He was a just and patient man, kind to a degree and beloved by everybody. But he despised a liar. At the tender age of thirteen I told him a deliberate falsehood. 'Step out in the barn, Bert,' was his sole comment. I walked in ahead of him and watched him close the door.[12]

While impossible to confirm, Bert did relate a story of his childhood that told of his first true fascination with aviation. 'At nine, Bert tried a parachute jump from a barn and broke nine bones, including both arms.'[13] Such a stunt was not entirely uncommon for young boys during that era, even when parachutes were seen a 'new technology.'

The few accounts that do exist of his relationship with his father indicate that they were very close.[14] There is no doubt that he was raised on his father's stories of being a cavalryman serving under General Shelby. The Hall family's rich history of serving in the military and how his father's service had dominated his life must have impressed a great deal on his impressionable mind.

Bert was five-feet, eight-inches tall with a slender frame until later in life. He had high cheekbones and had a hairline that was receding. Several accounts state he had thin lips and a large nose. Bert was not a physically attractive man by any stretch. His posture in photographs almost always has him leaning forwards and backwards and his hands are often stuffed in his front pockets. For what he lacked in physical build he made up with outright charm. Bert was a smooth talker, a man that was highly persuasive... especially with women.

One thing is for sure, young Bert Hall was not destined for small town life despite the closeness he had with his father. Bert told a number of wild stories in regards to his youth, most of which cannot be verified. The ones that can be confirmed do tell of his desire to seek adventure and new challenges. By his own account, he ran away from home. Bert, by his own admission, did not have much use for formal education. Bert would claim that he travelled across America taking on a number of jobs. He claimed for a while to work as a section hand on the Rock Island Railroad, though no records exist of him working on any railroads.[15] Bert claimed that he had worked as a deputy sheriff, though this cannot be validated either. More contemporary accounts claim that during the early 1900s, Bert '...travelled with a woman partner (whose identity has been lost, along with so many of Hall's lady friends) working various Con Games. Eventually, he packed up the financial proceeds and walked out on the lady, leaving her to face the wrath of the law.'[16]

In 1906, he signed on as a member of the Sells-Floto Circus. Bert would claim that his role in the circus was that of a human cannonball.[17] Over the years he confused the facts with even more boastful claims. As with many stories of Bert's colourful life, even his exaggeration has a kernel of truth in it. The circus records has a Bert Hall listed as an employee with a role in 'marketing'. Marketing was a phrase used for individuals who either called people into the shows or put up posters for the circus when the show came into town. While it may have been possible that Bert performed as a human cannonball, it is most likely that he only worked in the circus, and then for only a short time. Per the records he was there for only a few months before leaving.[18] Bert often confused the facts around his boastful lies. At one point his circus story 'evolved' into him being with the Hagenbeck-Wallace Circus in 1914 where he claimed he was a stunt rider and a wild animal trainer.[19] The version of this story changed depending on the audience with Hall. The facts were often the only victims in Bert's versions of events.

In a later interview, Bert would tell interviewer John Wheeler that he was a rodeo rider, a car racer in Europe, a taxi driver, a lawman in both Texas and Missouri, and even a gunman. '…I was a peace officer. When I was a youngster, I had many times on the other side of the law but nothing serious. Before I went to the Yukon to find my fortune, I wore a Colt and a badge, right at the turn of the century, and caught my share of malefactors. I never had to shoot a man until I got to the Yukon.'[20] In another version recounted in a different interview, he and his father went to Alaska where their stake was overtaken by claim jumpers.[21] Later in life, one of his contemporaries said that, 'More likely he was wanted fulltime by lawmen.'[22] According to Paul Rockwell (later the unofficial historian of the Lafayette Escadrille), he recounted discussions with Bert from the Great War period. 'Hall was not always successful in keeping a jump ahead of the law and, on at least one occasion, was arrested and convicted. He allegedly made a daring escape from a moving train while en route to prison.'[23]

Bert's mother passed away at the family home on 27 April 1905 at the age of fifty-nine years. Bert made it back for the funeral on 5 May.[24] His mother had left him a parcel of the family property, presumably property she had owned prior to her marriage to his father. Farmland was of little use to Bert. He returned to Higginsville in 1907 for several months to rid himself of the property. Eventually, Bert sold the land to his father for $450. While in Higginsville, Bert became 'romantically' involved with young Opal McColloch. He and Opal were married on 17 October 1907. Opal was under sixteen years of age and her mother had to sign the marriage certificate for her to be wed.[25] For Bert, this would be his first recorded marriage – the first of many.

Bert took the proceeds of the sale of his property and purchased a train ticket to San Francisco.[26] Bert and Opal had a child, Thelma, born in December 1908. Marriage was not enough to shackle down Bert and his fly-by-night lifestyle. At some point between 1909 and 1910, Opal and Bert divorced. Opal took their daughter back to live with her parents in Missouri.[27] Until she remarried in 1914, both Opal and Thelma retained the Hall surname.[28] By 1910, the twenty-five-year-old Bert was living alone in San Francisco, renting a room as a lodger on Market Street. His occupation was that of a chauffeur.[29] In 1910, such a position was one of respect. Chauffeurs only worked for the rich and they had to have a good understanding of mechanics to keep a car running. Hall left San Francisco and headed east between April and October, eventually arriving in Kansas City.

The reason for Bert to go to Kansas City is unknown. What is known is that he secured a position as chauffer for Casimir John Joseph Michael Welch in Kansas City, Missouri. Welch was a rough-and-tumble good-old-boy southern politician that was a power broker with the democratic political machine in Missouri. His contemporaries included power-politicians such as Thomas Pendergast and Joseph Shannon.[30] Welch was a character straight out of central casting. He dressed flamboyantly, was a wild womaniser and ran his districts in Kansas City as if it were Tammany Hall in New York City. Welch's control of the plumbing union gave him additional muscle to use to control his part of Jefferson County. Welch was like a feudal lord of old. No doubt that Bert learned a lot about dealing with seedy personalities from his association with Welch.

Welch was born in Michigan and moved as a boy to Kansas City. As a paperboy, he enlarged his territory by bullying and beating up his competitors. It was this trademark style that would mark how he managed his political affairs. As a political power broker, he controlled thirty-six precincts on the east side of Kansas City. Welch controlled the political power down to who got what job. Welch was the extreme case of a power-politician, womanising and running illegal schemes on the side. He was a known brawler and often travelled in the company of a band of henchmen. His 'staff' was little more than a group of thugs that applied blunt force to achieve his goals.[31] How Bert infiltrated this tight-knit community is a mystery. The fact that he fit in with a political power broker is not. Bert was the kind of person that was destined to take advantage of the circumstances and opportunities such a job presented.

Bert was Welch's chauffer for at least a year. He was known as one of the few men in town that could handle Welch's Moon motor car. The Moon's innovative 'curtain-pole' steering mechanism was difficult to handle. Bert became a regular fixture at Welch's Fifteenth Street political area. There can be little doubt that his role was two-fold: to act as a driver for the political boss and to be an additional pair of fists in a fight. 'Bert Hall understood a motor as well as 'Cas' his boss understood why a Democrat should be allowed to vote and a Republican run out of a precinct on election day.'[32] Being a chauffeur at the beginning of the twentieth century was not just about driving cars – it was about keeping cars running. Cars were temperamental and paved roads were a rarity around the country. 'Bert learned the 'ins' and 'outs' of a gasoline engine,' per one early account.[33] Understanding such technology was cutting edge in 1910.

In Kansas City, Bert once again found himself drawn to marriage. This time he married Emily Harris Levy. They were wed by the Justice of the Peace in Jackson County Missouri with no witnesses.[34] Bert was five years her senior, demonstrating again his preference for younger women. Why Bert parted company with 'Cas' or his second wife is not known. We do know that by 1910 Bert had secured employment with a Galveston, Texas, cotton broker and banker named D. W. Kempner, again as a chauffeur. Bert served as the driver for Mr and Mrs Kempner for several years. On the weekends he undertook the sport of car racing on the Galveston beaches during the summer of 1911.[35]

Race car driving in 1911 required a combination of mechanical and driving skills. The races on the Galveston beaches were both drag-style and traditional circular lap races on the flat wet sands where locals could bet on potential winners. The stock car races at Galveston were a precursor to the NASCAR races later in the century. The pinnacle of the racing season was the Cotton Carnival in August. These races were not just a test of the men but the machines. For example, in the 1910 races during the carnival, of the dozen competitors only four finished the three-hour race. For Bert, this was a perfect mix of thrills and gambling: two of his passions. While there are no records of Bert taking part in formal track racing events, the weekly beach races were highly popular with the locals and Bert earned a reputation as a strong competitor.

Accounts vary, but it appears that during this job for the Kempners, he was first exposed to the latest technological craze of the era, the aeroplane, though details have been long lost to history.[36] He accompanied the Kempners to Paris, France, in 1912 and while in France left their employment.[37] Two different accounts have surfaced over the years as for the reason of him leaving their employment. The most commonly accepted excuse for his release was, 'drunken brawling,' which was told by Paul Rockwell.[38] According to his employer, while in Europe, Bert quit to join the Bulgarian Army.[39] A check of the archives does not show a Weston or Bert Hall having ever served or contracted for service in the Bulgarian military. It is highly probable that Bert told the Kempners he was leaving to join the army, but in reality pursued other employment.

What is known is that by the summer of 1914, Bert was working in Paris as a taxi driver.[40] The summer of 1914 would be the last summer of the world's innocence. War clouds were brewing around the globe and Paris was one of the cities destined to be in the heart of the conflict. Bert was in the right place at the right time.

CHAPTER THREE

Bert Hall of the French Foreign Legion

We are the famous Legion
That they talk so much about
People lock up everything
Whenever we're about.

We're noted for our pillaging
The nifty way we steal
We'd pinch a baby carriage,
And the infant, for a meal.

As we go marching,
And the band begins to play – Gor'blimee!
You can hear the people shouting,
Lock all the doors, shut up the shop
The Legion's here to-day!

– French Foreign Legion Marching Song[1]

As autumn of 1914 loomed on the horizon, the winds of war whipped across the globe. The roots of the coming war had taken decades to build, a web of alliances and royal relations that connected and divided the governments in Europe. In many respects, Europe was a powder keg waiting to go off – all it lacked was a spark. On 28 June 1914, a Serbian assassin murdered Archduke Franz Ferdinand of Austria, igniting the flame that set the world ablaze for the next four years, consuming millions of lives in the process.

Few people foresaw how events could get out of hand so quickly. Seeking vengeance for the death of the Archduke, the Austro-Hungarian Empire declared war on Serbia at the end of July. Serbia's ally, Russia, mobilised its army as it prepared to defend its ally. Germany, in support of the Austro-Hungarians, declared war on Russia. The French Army mobilised in response to the threat to her Russian allies. France declared support for Russia and Germany declared war on France on 3 August. The world was being drawn into a cauldron of carnage and seemed unable to stop. England, fearing a Europe dominated by Germany, girded her loins for war as well.

The only major world power that shied away from the coming conflict was the United States. Her geographic isolation and the potential profits of providing military arms and supplies was enough to keep America neutral, at least for the time being. August of 1914 in Paris was a time of charged emotions and excitement. France had suffered the loss of Alsace-Lorraine to the Germans in the Franco-Prussian War in 1871. Despite small indecisive wars in the Balkans, the Franco-Prussian War was the last great conflict on the continent. The fighting had been a matter of weeks and had not torn apart entire nations or killed millions. In the minds of most military planners, this was seen as a template for what to expect in a war in 1914.

But much had changed in the decades between the wars. The rise of industrialisation and dramatic changes in technology had provided armies with new untested weapons that were destined to alter tactics and how wars were fought. The introduction of the machine gun and rapid-fire artillery altered the ways armies were to fight on the ground. At sea, the introduction of the dreadnought, massive fast-moving, heavily-armed battlecruisers, was to change the nature of naval warfare. A relatively new technology, the aeroplane, was a wildcard in terms of warfare. No one was sure what role it might play, only that it was likely to play some important function.

In early August, the Parisians were not the only ones in the city of lights that were catching war fever. There were a number of Americans in Paris, some on holiday, some on business. They found themselves intrigued and excited at the prospect of war. The Americans tended to congregate at the Palis Royal Hotel. There, at the hotel bar, they could speak with other Americans about events that were emerging and discuss the war news of the day. The young Americans at the Palis Royal Hotel were, for the most part, college students or recent graduates with a sprinkling of men that were hard-working labourers living in Paris. Many came from wealthy east coast families that could afford for their sons to spend the summer in Paris. Some attended Harvard, Yale or other Ivy League schools. Many, if not the majority, had not performed a hard day's work in their lives. They had lived the life of privilege.

Also in the Palis Royal Hotel bar was another American, a taxicab driver named Bert Hall. He came to associate with fellow Americans, young men with money which he attempted to pry from them with games of cards. While most of the men were in their twenties, Bert stood out as one of the older more experienced men.

The Americans were a colourful lot. Victor Chapman was there, the son of a wealthy New York family. He was in Paris to study at the École des Beaux Arts. David King, a short stocky man from Providence Rhode Island, had been in Paris to take in the sights and work during the summer off from Harvard. The poet Alan Seeger, a former editor of *The Atlantic*, had come to Paris that summer and was suddenly caught up in the turmoil just before the start of the war. Also present was a tough Edward Morlae from San Francisco. He was the most like Bert in that he was in Paris working day labour. A short, wiry, bookish young man named Frederick Zinn was a graduate of the University of Michigan who had come to Europe to travel as a present to himself for graduation, never expecting to arrive as war was about to break out.[2] William Thaw II was there as well, sporting a moustache that made him look more like a stereotypical villain from a silent movie than a dashing college boy. A Yale man, Thaw was a pilot and aviator who was in Paris with his mother, brother and sister to try and interest the French government into purchasing an aircraft stabiliser he had designed.[3] New Orleans native James Bach was also in the crowd of Americans. While he was the same age as Bert, he had graduated from college in Paris and had been a civil engineer working in England before returning to Paris.[4]

Also in the mix was the Rockwell brothers, Paul and Kiffin. Both were from a prosperous family in North Carolina. Kiffin was a student at the prestigious Virginia Military Institute. His brother Paul was an up-and-coming newspaper reporter for the *Atlanta Constitution*. Paul attended one year at Wake Forest University then transferred to Washington and Lee University in Virginia.[5] Paul Rockwell was outgoing and gregarious with his fellow Americans. Like Bert, they came from a Confederate family – both of their grandfathers, Captain Henry Rockwell of North Carolina and Major Enoch Shaw Ayres of South Carolina, fought in the Civil War.[6] Little did Bert realise that the group of Americans gathered at the Palis Royal Hotel bar were to play a pivotal role in his life. Nor could he have imagined how Paul Rockwell would spend a lifetime attempting to erase him from history or to at least discount his contributions.

The talk of the impending war was only heightened when Germany declared war on France. Enlistments were the talk of the day and the French attempted to seduce the Americans to join the French army and fight. The most commonly spoken story relayed by the men in Paris was that the war was going to be short: six to nine months in length. The thought was that the war would be like the last one – fast. The introduction of new technology would make it even shorter than the Franco-Prussian conflict. The French recruiters peppered the young men with talk about Rochambeau and Lafayette who had aided the American Revolution. This was a chance for the young men to pay back that debt. There was more to it than patriotic hype. If a group of well-known young Americans could be recruited to fight for France, it might help sway more Americans to join the war. It was a propaganda coup for the French if they could be enticed to enlist.

The young men were excited at the prospect of going off to the war. After all, it would be quick and they would have grand stories to tell back home. Like many young men, they did not seem to contemplate their vulnerability and mortality. To them, this was an opportunity to take part in an epic adventure. The Americans were intrigued with the idea, but there were risks that seemed insurmountable. Enlistment in the French Army would cost the Americans their US citizenship. A law passed in 1907 stated that any American citizen '... shall been deemed to have expatriated himself when he has been naturalised into any foreign state in conformity with its laws or what he takes an oath of allegiance to any foreign state.'[7] Part of the enlistment in the French Army was to take an oath to France. While the Americans were eager to join, few were willing to risk their citizenship. When President Woodrow Wilson read newspaper accounts of young Americans in Paris possibly enlisting to fight in the coming conflict, he issued a statement to remind them what they would be giving up. Wilson did not want to place at risk America's young neutrality in the coming conflict. The matter fell upon Myron T. Herrick, the US ambassador of France, to convey to the men the implications of such actions.

Ambassador Herrick met with the Americans to try and express the potential risks they were undertaking. 'I got out the law on the duties of neutrals ... read it to them and explained its passages... It was no use. Those young eyes were searching mine, seeking, I am sure, the encouragement they had come in hope of getting. It was more than flesh and blood could stand, and catching fire from their eagerness I brought down my fist on the table saying, 'That is the law, boys, but if I were young and stood in your shoes, by God I know mighty well what I would do.'[8] The men knew they had to find a way to enlist, even if it meant losing their citizenship.

For a few days it appeared a stalemate existed. Then the French discovered a potential loophole: the French Foreign Legion. The Legion was not technically part of the French military infrastructure, despite the fact it fought in every major conflict for France since it had been formed in 1831. It was formed and operated as an almost independent army with its own logistics, recruitment, regulations, etc. When you enlisted in the Legion you did not have to swear an oath to France. Instead, you simply swore an oath of loyalty to the Legion. While a thin technicality at best, a check was made with Herrick. He confirmed for the Americans that if they enlisted in the French Foreign Legion, they would not lose their citizenship.

The Foreign Legion was a military unit that was a mix of myth and reality – a unit that conjured romantic images of desert strongholds and men wearing shaded kepis fighting Arab hoards. It had been formed by King Louis Philippe in March of 1831. The Legion was a unit that was open to volunteers from any country, as long as they were between the ages of eighteen to forty. No paperwork or identification was required to join. More importantly, the Legion was loyal to itself. It had served in every major conflict that France became embroiled in since its founding. In many cases the Legionnaires bore the brunt of battle.

The Legion had its own holidays and traditions that were beyond the normal French military structure. In one battle at Camerone, Hacienda, on 30 April 1863, three officers and sixty-two Legionnaires battled against 2,000 Mexicans. It was a scene eerily reminiscent of the Alamo for the Americans. When presented with a surrender demand, the Legionnaires responded, 'We would rather die than surrender.' When the Legions ranks thinned to five survivors during the siege, rather than succumb, they fixed their bayonets and charged into the centre of the Mexican force. To this day, 30 April is a holiday celebrated by members of the Legion.[9]

The mystique of the Legion added to its romantic image and diabolical reputation. Members of the Legion in some cases were men fleeing from the law, others were simply unable to function in normal society. Legion members were said to be a mix of cutthroats, murderers, robbers and worse. Myth portrayed some members as those that were trying to find a new life for themselves, fleeing from lost loves, etc. Part of that reputation was well deserved. The Legion, while considered elite in the French military, was known to be lenient on regulations dealing with uniforms and regulations. In terms of discipline, the Legion often favoured physical punishment and physical retribution for failing to follow orders. On the flipside, civilians often cringed if the Legion was billeted in a town because they would take what they needed. In battle, Legionnaires were said to be ferocious. German propaganda spread the word to their troops to not surrender to the Foreign Legion. They claimed that the Legionnaires did not take prisoners but killed enemies that were surrendering. The result of such rumours was that members of the Legion who tried to surrender were often shot on sight. As such, Legionnaires fought with brutality, driven by lies and shadows of their own dark reputations.

Enlistment in the Legion may have held its romantic appeal, but the pay was considerably less than the French army. The pay for a private in the Legion was one sou (one cent) a day in 1914. Three of every ten sous were withheld as payment for issued tobacco whether the private smoked tobacco or not. The net effect of this was to turn tobacco into a tradable commodity in the ranks.[10] College students from wealthy families could rely on their parents to augment their pay. Men like Bert Hall who worked for a living had to make do with what they got or devise ways to supplement their pay.

While the French cleared obstacles to find a way to enlist the Americans, the Germans crossed into neutral Belgium executing the Schlieffen Plan. While they were making manoeuvres to indicate a mass assault at the French border, the Germans planned on sweeping through Belgium and along the channel coast. They would then be able to drive south, surround the French army and take Paris. The goal of the plan was to entrap the French army and force a quick surrender so that Germany could divert resources to fight against the inevitable Russian onslaught. It appeared that France's fate was in peril, adding to the excitement in Paris.

On 24 August 1914, the French recruiters had the Americans assemble at the Hotel Des Invalides, the military headquarters, to induct the new troops into the Legion. A total of forty-three Americans went to the headquarters and formally signed their paperwork and took their oaths. The next day, their last as civilians, the Americans rallied at the Palis Royal Hotel and together paraded through the streets of Paris. Alan Seeger and René Phélizot carried the flag as they walked.[11] Large crowds cheered as they marched along the Avenue de l'Opéra, Place de l'Opéra, Rue Auber and other streets. Their story of joining the Legion to fight the invading Germans was carried by almost every newspaper in the United States, including the names of those men that enrolled. Many of the men signed the flag before lining up for their uniforms. Each of the men was interviewed and the men learned that those with prior military service were mustered in as Caporals (Corporals) or Sergents (Sergeants). Many of the men exaggerated their 'experience' in hopes of getting better pay or a chance to lead. Oddly enough, Bert enlisted as a private, either not realising the ploy or not telling a convincing enough story.

The enlistment period with the legion was for '...the duration of the conflict.' In the years that followed, many of the surviving volunteers told stories of fulfilling a patriotic duty. Bert Hall, only two years later, had his own interpretation of the reason for enlisting. 'There was no hands-across-the sea Lafayette stuff about us Americans who joined the Foreign Legion in Paris when the war broke out. We just wanted to get right close and see some of the fun, and we didn't mind taking a few risks, as most of us had led a pretty rough sort of life as long as we could remember.'[12]

Bert and his new Legionnaire colleagues were sent to Rouen for the Legion-equivalent of basic training. 'While waiting there we had our first taste of what was coming later. We were about seven hundred, garrisoned in an old machine shop. We slept on a brick floor, underneath the benches, and, as we had very little straw, the floor seemed pretty hard.'[13] For the most part, the Americans were kept together. This was not driven by regulations but by the commonality of their language. The hope was that the Americans who spoke French could help the ones that did not learn French, especially with military commands. They were in the Second Regiment Etranger, made up almost entirely of recruits except for the officers. They were issued their considerable gear. 'In the barrack room things began to take some sort of order. The capote (great coat) had to be folded and placed first on the shelf above the beds, then the varcuses (shell jackets) and so on, until the pile was some three feet high. The belts, cartridge pouches, bayonets hung on hooks below, and any private belongings had to be hidden in the bed or behind the pile of uniforms.'[14]

Protective helmets were not issued in the Legion in 1914 – simple kepis were worn instead, hardly protection against a bullet or searing piece of jagged shrapnel. The uniforms and trousers were a blue colour (with bright red breeches), making the men stand out against the background. The concept of camouflage would not truly emerge for another year or so. The men of the Legion practiced their marching with a full kit consisting of their uniform, rifle, shovel, pick, canteen, 125 rounds of ammunition, emergency rations, gamel (mess pan) and a wool blanket. The first two weeks they practiced marching ten miles carrying all of their gear in preparation for war.[15]

They spent September in Toulouse where they had been transported to. Their days were filled with drilling – marching, mastering military commands, learning to use their weapons. Most non-students of the First World War think of the stalemate of trench warfare, but that did not fully emerge until after 1915. The first few months of the war were highly mobile with armies moving great distances quickly. The German thrust on Paris resulted in the epic Battle of the Marne on 6-12 September. Only through a last-ditch effort on the part of the French army blunted a German drive only thirty miles from Paris, one that might have ended the war... the 'Miracle of the Marne'. Many of the men of the Legion wondered up until that point if they had joined the losing side or if they would be rushed with almost no training in the maw of the German army.

In October, the men of the Second Regiment Etranger were sent to the front. For most of the Americans, they became aware that the excitement and glory that they had sought in a quick war was going to be deadly conflict and consumed lives. Bert's own recollection of the events were detailed in an account for the *New York Times* several months after the fact. It detailed the Legion's march to Craonne where they would take up position opposite a

German army and where the Americans were destined to shed their blood fighting for France.

It wasn't so bad when we first got there about the beginning of October, as the weather was warmer (though it had already begun to rain and has never stopped since) but we were almost suffocated by the stench from the thousands of corpses laying between the lines – the German trenches were about four hundred yards away – where it wasn't safe for either side to go out and bury them. They were French mostly, result of the first big offensive after the Marne victory, and believe me, that word just expresses it – they were the offensivest proposition in all my experience.

Well, I was saying, we reached the firing line on Oct. 4, after marching up from Toulouse, where they'd move us from Rouen to finish our training. We went down there in a cattle truck at the end of August in a hurry as they expected the Germans at any minute; the journey took sixty hours instead of ten, and was frightfully hot. That was our first experience of what service in the Foreign Legion really meant – just the sordidest, uncomfortablest road to glory ever trodden by American adventurers.

After we'd been at Toulouse about a month they incorporated about two hundred of us recruits, thirty Americans and the rest mostly Britishers, all of whom had seen some sort of service before in the Second Regiment Etranger which had just come over from Africa on its way to the front. They put us all together in one company, which was something to be thankful for, as I'd hate to leave a cur dog among some of the old-timers – you never saw such a lot of scoundrels. I'll bet a hundred dollars they have specimens of every sort of criminal in Europe and what's more, lots of them spoke German, though they claimed to have left seventeen hundred of the real Dutchies behind in Africa. Can you beat it? Going out to fight for France against the Kaiser among a lot of guys that looked and talked like a turn verein [sic] in St. Louis.

Why, one day Thaw and I captured a Dutchie in a wood where we were hunting squirrel – as a necessary addition to our diet – and, believe me, when we brought him into camp he must have thought he was at home for they all began jabbering German to him as friendly as possible and every one of them quite sad when he went off in a train with a lot of other prisoners bound for some fortress in the West of France.

But that was only a detail, and now, I'm telling you about our arrival in the trenches. The last hundred miles we did in five days, which is some of a hurry, but none of the Americans fell out, though we were all mighty tired at the end of the last day's march. Worse still, that country had been fought over and there were no inhabitants left to give us food and drinks as we had

had before at every resting place, which helped us greatly. Along the roadside lots of trees had been smashed by shell fire, there were hundreds of graves with rough crosses or little flags to mark them, and then we passed a broken auto or a dead horse lying in the gutter.[16]

Bert came to the realisation that this was not his father's war, where men faced each other across a battlefield with a hint of honour and a dollop of horror. No, this war brought about quick and seemingly random death from artillery shelling or snipers. 'At the end of the fifth day we got our first sample of war – quite suddenly, without any warning as we didn't know we were near the firing line. We had just entered a devastated village when there came a shrill whistling noise like when a white hot iron is plunged into cold water, then a terrific bang as a shell burst about thirty yards in front of our columns, making a hole in the road about five feet deep and ten in diameter, and sending a hail of shrapnel in all directions. One big splinter hit a man in the second rank and took his head off – I think he was a Norwegian; anyway, that was our first casualty. No one else was injured.'[17] Bert would later comment that his comrade William Thaw would mutter, 'Wish I was home,' when an artillery round came whizzing past.[18] After their brief encounter of artillery fire, the Americans of the Legion quickly adapted.

Our boys took their baptism of fire pretty coolly, though most of us jumped at the bang and ducked involuntarily to dodge the shrapnel, which, by the way, isn't very dangerous at more than thirty yards though it does a lot of harm at shorter range. Personally I wasn't as scared as I expected and most of the others said the same. At first one is too interested to be frightened, and by the time the novelty has worn off one has gotten fairly used to it all – at least that seemed to be our general opinion.

There were no more shells after that one, and we continued to march till nightfall when we camped in an abandoned village. Next morning there were 100 big auto trucks ready to take us to a point about forty miles along the lines and we clambered aboard them and set off at a good speed, all but twenty unlucky lads who were left to pad the hoof as a guard for our mules and baggage. My pal, William Thaw, was among the number; he marched for thirteen hours practically without a stop, and when he reached our camp he lay right down in the mud by the roadside and went straight off to sleep though it was raining like sixty and he was drenched to the skin. But he was all right again in the morning, though it was a man's job to wake him up.

Next day we set off before dawn, having received orders to take our place in the trenches about eight miles away. It soon got light, and after marching about half an hour we were unlucky enough to be seen by a German aeroplane which signalled us to their batteries. The first shell burst near, the second nearer, the third right among us, killing nearly a dozen old-timers, and we were forced to break ranks and take cover until nightfall, as they'd got the range and it would have been suicide to try and go on. Pretty good shooting that at five or six miles distance.

The French talk a lot about their artillery, but, believe me, the Dutchies are mighty fine gunners, especially with their cannon, even the very biggest. Why, one day, when my company was having its usual weekly rest from the trenches there were a couple of hundred of us bunking in a big barn fully eight miles behind our lines. About 3 in the afternoon along came a German aeroplane, and a half an hour later then dropped a couple of shells between the barn and a church some thirty yards further back, just by way of showing what they could do. We thought that was all and settled down comfortably for the night, but not a bit of it. At 10 o'clock sharp a shell dropped plump on to the barn itself and killed five or six and wounded a dozen more, none of them Americans. We got out on the jump, though of course it was raining, and we were wise, for in the next half hour they hit the barn eleven times without a single miss, and at 10:30 there weren't any big enough bits of it left to make matches of. The barn was perhaps thirty yards long by fifteen wide, but remember they were firing at a range of ten miles or so and in pitch darkness. Of course they got their guns trained right in the afternoon and just waiting till night to give us a pleasant surprise. I did hear those were Austrian mortars, not German; anyway, they were good enough for us I can tell you.

We broke ranks and fled to cover and remained in hiding all that day near a ruined farm with shells falling all about, though they didn't do much damage. But our old-timer didn't like it one little bit. They had not been used to that kind of thing in Africa, and then the Germans and Austrians didn't at all fancy the idea of being fired upon by their own people. In our company all of the Sergeants and most of the other non-coms were Austrian – not that they turned out later to be any worse fighters for that. There was one Sergeant named Wiedmann who fought like a lion; he was the bravest man in the regiment. Poor chap, I've just heard he was killed the other day by a hand grenade and I'm sorry. He was a real white man if I ever knew one. Our Lieutenant named Bloch, and only the Captain was a Frenchman. But all this mixture of races led to some curious results, as the following story will show.[19]

This was Bert's first recorded encounter with an aeroplane in war. In his later life he would spread the myth that he had been America's first fighter pilot, but this was the first time he recorded seeing an aeroplane and witnessing its role in battle. In 1914, aeroplanes were considered new technology. They were slow and dangerous machines. Most were not armed: the age of fighters and bombers was still months away. The role that aircraft played in the early months of the war was that of observation, being the aerial eyes for the enemy. From thousands of feet up, enemy troop and artillery positions could be plotted and noted. The movement of armies was impossible to keep secret with observers in the clouds. It was destined to have a profound effect on him in the years to come and would be pivotal in his life.

Bert did not sugar-coat life at the front for the American volunteers. The quixotic image of a dashing member of the Foreign Legion was something that faded quickly against the backdrop of carnage that was unfolding in the war.

> For three or four days we had nothing to do but dodge shrapnel and try and keep warm, as the enemy maintained a constant artillery fire – with a regular interval for luncheon -- starting about 6 a.m.. and stopping towards 5 p.m.; and they got the range. I tell you one lies pretty flat when there's any shrapnel about. Some of the English boys were killed on the second day, but we Americans have been fine and lucky – only one killed the whole time, though we have had some very narrow shaves. For instance, Thaw had his bayonet knocked of his rifle by a 'sniper' while on sentry-go, and another boy named Merlac had his pipe taken clean out of his mouth by a shrapnel ball in the trenches. It didn't hurt him at all, but I never saw anyone look so surprised in my life. Shortly afterward Jimmy Bach... had his head cut by a rifle bullet which just grazed it without doing more than make a deepish scratch. I myself had a close squeak the very day of our arrival in the trenches. A piece of shell weighing three or four pounds smashed to bits the pack on my back – including my best pipe – without so much as bruising me, though it scared me something dreadful.[20]

Life in the trenches fell into routine. At the same time, the Legionnaires struggled with lice and vermin.

> Our company had an eight days 'shift' in the trenches, followed by three days rest at a camp four miles in the rear. During the week's duty it was impossible to wash or take off one's clothes, and we quickly got into a horrible condition of filth. To begin with there was a cake of mud from head to foot about half an inch thick, but what was worse was the vermin which infested our clothes almost immediately and were practically impossible to get rid of. They nearly broke the heart of Lieut. Bloch. He had a wonderful

crop of bright red whiskers, of which he was as proud as a kitten with its first mouse, because he thought they gave him a really warlike appearance, and he was always combing them and squinting at them in a little pocket mirror. Well, one day the lice got into these whiskers and fairly gave him Hades. He bore it for a week, scratching away at his chin until he was tearing out chunks of hair by the roots, but at last he could stand no more and had to have the whole lot shaved off. He was the saddest thing you ever saw after that, with a little chinless face like a pink rabbit, and was so ashamed he hardly dared show himself in daylight.

David King, one of the Americans in the Legion, coined the phrase 'Algerian Cootie Club', discussing how some of the men tried to cope with picking the lice off each other. The phrase commemorated a number of African soldiers which served beside them in the regiment. The Cootie Club was a ritual where the men would pick the lice off of each other in a vain effort to control their infestation.[21]

Like many of the men that enlisted, the Legion provided them a chance to craft a new identity and background for themselves. Bert thrived in such an environment. As King would recount:

> In our off moments we told the stories of our lives – usually mythical – and read our shirts. We had a crude chimney in our dugout and were busy brewing chocolate. Bert, from Kentucky, ex-racing driver and God knows what besides, was going all out. He finished, and there was a moment of awed silence. His sidekick broke the spell:
>
> 'Bert (scratch) (a result of the lice infestation – author) you know that's a damned lie.' (scratch, scratch)
>
> The answer was disarming. 'Well, who the hell said it wasn't!'[22]

Hall's time in the Legion allowed him to hone his skills at reinventing himself, weaving tales about his life and experiences. Testing those tales with the men in the trenches gave him a good feeling for what stories would work and what wouldn't.

> They (lice) are terrible, one cannot rest or sleep a moment. I discovered one remedy that would give relief for a few moments at a time. I had on three shirts and when the to-tos (lice) got well assembled on the inner one I would change it, putting it on the outside. This kept them hustling to make the trip down and up on the inside, during which took them almost an hour. I would sleep during that time.[23]

Bert and the other men learned the harsh realities of battlefield logistics too.

Mud and vermin were only minor worries really; our proper serious troubles were cold and hunger. It's pretty cool in the middle of France toward the end of November, and for some reason – I guess because they were such a lot of infernal thieves at our depot – we never got any of the clothes and warm wraps sent up from Paris for us. It was just throwing money away to try it. My wife mailed me three or four lots of woollen sweaters and underclothes, but I never received a single thing, and the rest of the boys had much the same experience.

That was bad, but the hunger was something fierce. The Foreign Legion is not particularly well fed at any time – coffee and dry bread for breakfast, soup with lumps of meat in it for luncheon, with rice to follow, and the same plus coffee for dinner, and not too much of anything either. But in our case all of the grub had to be brought in buckets from the relief post, four miles away, by squads leaving the trenches at 3 a.m., 10 a.m., and 5 p.m., and a tough job it was, what with the darkness and the mud and the shell holes and the German cannonade, to say nothing of occasional snipers taking pot shots at you with rifles. I got one bullet once right between my legs, which drilled a hole in the next bucket in line and wasted all of our coffee.

As you can imagine, quite a lot of the stuff used to get spilt on the way, and then the boys carrying it used to scrape it up off the ground and put it back again, so that nearly everything one ate was full of gravel and, of course, absolutely cold. More than once when the cannonade was especially violent we got nothing to eat all day but a couple of little old sardines, and, believe me, it takes a mighty strong stomach to stand that sort of treatment for any length of time. As far as we Americans were concerned, who were mostly accustomed to man-sized meals, the net results was literally slow starvation.[24]

Bert's first taste of true battle, where he went forwards with his rifle to engage the enemy, did not end up as he had expected. The proverbial fog of war made for almost comical results.

The second night in the trenches we had an alarm of a night attack. I crept out to a 'funk hole' some thirty yards ahead of our trench with a couple of friends. It was nearly 10 o'clock and there was a thin drizzle. We stared out into the darkness, breathing hard in our excitement. The usual fireworks display of searchlights and rockets over the German trenches was missing – an invariable sign of a contemplated attack, we had been told. Suddenly I glimpsed a line of dim figures advancing closely through the darkness. 'Hold your fire, boys,' I gasped. 'Let them get good and close before you loose off.' They came nearer, stealthily, silently. We raised our rifles. Suddenly my friend on the right rolled over, shaking with noiseless laughter. For a moment we thought he was mad. Then we, too, realised the truth. The approaching column, instead of eager bloodthirsty Germans, was a dozen harmless domestic cows, strays, doubtless, from a deserted farm.[25]

Corporal Morlae was suspicious, wondering if the cows were providing cover for German troops. 'As Morlae approached he was attacked by a gentleman cow in the party and beat a hasty retreat back. The cows were the only enemy we sighted all night.'[26] 'There were considerable casualties among the attacking force, for a week at least the American section of the Foreign Legion had an ample diet.'[27] The next night, Bert was part of a three-man detachment, including his close friend Bill Thaw, once more making their way up to the forward trench.

We were crawling back to the trench about midnight when suddenly we found ourselves under a heavy fire. One bullet went through Thaw's kepi, but we soon saw that instead of coming from the Germans the fire was directed from a section of our own trenches who thought there was an attack. We yelled, but they went on shooting. I was so mad that I shot back at them, but luckily there was no damage done anywhere.

Two nights later there really did come an attack in considerable force. A lot of us crawled out into a hollow in front of our trench and, starting at about forty yards distance, we let them have it hot and heavy. We had our bayonets fixed, but they didn't get near enough to charge. I think we kept up America's reputation for marksmanship; any way, they melted away after about half an hour, and in the morning there were several hundred dead bodies in front of the trench – they had taken the wounded back with them. The bodies were still there when I left, nearly three months later. I crawled out a night or two afterwards and had a look at them, and was lucky enough to get an iron cross as a souvenir off a young officer. He was lying flat on his back with a hole between the eyes, and he had the horriblest grin human face ever wore; his lips were drawn right back of the teeth so that he seemed to be snarling like a wild beast ready to bite.

We took no prisoners at all; in fact, none of them got near enough, and our Colonel didn't think it worth risking a counter-charge. To tell the truth we hardly took any prisoners any time except here and there an occasional straggler. I've heard stories about the Dutchies surrendering easily, but you can take it from me that's all bunk. I used to think that one Irishman could lick seventeen Dutchmen, but, believe me, when they get that old uniform on they are a very different proposition. On one occasion a company of the Legion surrounded a Lieutenant and eleven men. They called on them to surrender but not a bit of it. They held out all day and fought to the last gasp. At last only the Lieutenant and one soldier were left alive, both wounded. Again they refused to give in, and they had to kill the Lieutenant before the last survivor finally threw down his rifle and let them carry him off. I heard he died on the way to the station, and I'm mighty sorry; he was a white man if he was a German.[28]

To the men of the Legion, death was a random thing. They became almost blasé about the loss of lives... something common with men in battle.

...an Englishman, got out of the trench one day to stretch his legs, as he said he was tired of sitting still. Someone called to him to come down and not be a fool, as the Germans were keeping up a constant rifle fire, and after a minute or two he jumped back into the trench. 'They didn't get you did they?' called out someone. 'Oh, no,' he answered, sitting down. Then all of a sudden he just keeled over slowly sideways without a sound, and, believe me, when they went to pick him up he was as dead as David, plugged clean through the heart. He never even felt the shock of it. If they ever get to me, that's the way I hope to die.[29]

War changes men. It is the nature of war to do so. In all of his tall tales about his life prior to the war, Bert never claimed to have killed another man while in the Legion. His time in the trenches in 1914 and early 1915 altered that in the form of a captured German spy.

One remarkable thing about the prisoners we did get was their exceedingly thorough knowledge of everything going on, not only of the war in general, but of all that was taking place behind our trenches. Their spy system is something marvellous. Why, they knew the exact date our reinforcements were coming on one occasion nearly a week beforehand, when the majority of our fellows hadn't even an idea there were any expected.

In some cases they got information from French villagers whom they had bought before they retreated. I saw one such case myself. We were bivouacked in a ruined village, and a lot of us were sleeping in and around a cottage that hadn't been damaged. We were downstairs, while the owner of the cottage and his wife and kid had the upstairs room. One of our boys happened to go outside in the night and, by jingo, he saw the fellow coolly signalling with a lamp behind his curtain. He went along and told the Captain, who was at the schoolhouse, and they came back with a couple of under-officers and arrested them red-handed. He tried to hide under the bed and howled for mercy when they pulled him out. His wife never turned a hair – the Sergeant told me she was glad he'd been caught. They shot him there and then in his own yard, and his wife was around in the morning just as if nothing had happened.

After that we always used to be very suspicious of any house or village that wasn't devastated when everything round had been chewed up; there was nearly always a spy concealed somewhere not far off. To give you a case in point. There was a fine big chateau near Craonelle, where our trenches were, that hadn't been bombarded, though they had stripped most of the furniture and stuff out of it. Well, one fine day the General commanding our section thought it would be a convenient place to hold a big pow-wow. He and his staff had only been seated at the table about ten minutes when a whacking great 310 millimetre shell burst right on top of the darned place, followed by a perfect hail of others. The General and his staff ran for their lives; luckily none of them were badly hurt, though they got the deuce of a scare.

After the bombardment some of us went along to look at was left of the chateau and – will you believe me? – we found a little old Dutch sous-off half choked in the cellar, but still hanging on to the business end of a telephone. I call that the pluckiest thing I've seen in the war, and I can tell you we were mighty sorry to have to shoot him. He never turned a hair, either, and we didn't even suggest bandaging his eyes. He knew what was coming to him from the start; that he was as good as a dead man from the moment he got into the cellar. He told us he had been there about a week, just waiting for some confiding bunch of French officers to come along and hold a meeting.[30]

Some of the men in the Legion survived on their one cent a day. The young college-age men received funds from their families back in the United States. Men like Frederick Zinn sold photographs and stories to magazines back in America so the nation could see the first images of the war engulfing Europe and the world. Paul Rockwell penned articles about the men of the Legion crafting stories to focus on their representing the US in the conflict despite America's neutrality. Bert sold a few stories himself, though his stories stood in contrast to those of Paul Rockwell. Rather than conjure the popular image of the Legionnaire, Bert tended to tell the story as it was – horrific and deadly.

By the start of winter 1914, a few realities were beginning to set in for the men of the Legion. First, all of the bravado and talk of a quick war lasting six to nine months were nothing more than hollow promises. The war showed no sign of ending after five months. Also, the nature of the war was changing as well. Movement of large bodies of troops were still happening, but at a frightening cost in terms of casualties. Artillery and machine gun fire were forcing men to dig trenches to protect themselves. Trench warfare was in its infancy. The men that lived in these cold and muddy holes did not believe that this would eventually lead to a long stalemate. Even the generals still clung to the hope of breakthroughs where mounted cavalry would charge into the enemy's rear wrecking havoc. In an age of machine guns, it was a folly but one that many generals still clung to.

Bert experienced this for himself. He called the trench system of the French lines the Piccadilly Circus.

> It was some network, more complicated than the streets of Paris dare be. You could get lost very easily if you could not see the marks. Afterwards we marked them with names like streets... In a particular trench where Jimmie Bach and myself were, we had a sort of a rise just where we went out. So one day we decided to dig that out. Jimmie got his pick and started to dig. About the second stroke, he picked out part of a human head. So we decided we'd leave it there.[31]

The harsh living conditions took a toll on the Americans.

> From the 17th of October until the middle of December, I never washed my face and hands. I never had my shoes off and no change of clothing of any sort. But I used to shave regularly, as I never could stand whiskers. We had coffee brought up in the morning about 3 a.m. and as I never drank coffee I used mine to make a lather and shave. Some days we had absolutely nothing to eat. There was no drinking water to be had, as there were numerous dead lying all over the country.[32]

Disillusionment had to have gripped the Americans who volunteered five months earlier. By Bert's own estimates, the casualties by December 1914 in the Second Regiment Etranger were approximately forty per cent.[33] Flying over the trenches daily were aeroplanes, now in increasing number. There were stories that accompanied the new technology. Aviators were said to fly for a few hours a day then return to the rear areas, billeting in comfortable homes far from the random death of raining artillery barrages. It was seductive for the men in the trenches.

In December, Bert was wounded. A piece of artillery shrapnel struck him in either side of a leg, naturally, his accounts of this vary. The injury was serious enough for Bert to be sent to Paris to be operated on. He recuperated for two weeks in the City of Lights before being returned to the front.[34] For the first time in months he slept on a real bed with clean clothes in a place where hygiene was not a forgotten concept. In Bert's own words, 'We got a little excitement, though not much, but as for fun – well, if I had to go through it again I'd sooner attend my own funeral. As a sporting proposition, this war game is overrated.'[35] Bert Hall's mind was made up. He was going to find a way to get out of the trenches and transfer to the newest branch of the military – the French Air Service.

CHAPTER FOUR

Into the Air

Altogether I spent nearly three months in the trenches near Craonne, and, believe me, I was mighty glad when they transferred me (with Thaw and Bach, two other Americans who've done some flying) to the Aviation Corps, for all they wouldn't take us when we volunteered at the start because we weren't Frenchmen, and have only done so now because they've lost such a lot of their own men, which isn't a very encouraging reason.

– Bert Hall, 1915.[1]

Bert's close friend in the Legion, William Thaw, had been trying to join the French Air Service before he had enlisted in the Foreign Legion in August 1914. Thaw came from a wealthy family – his father Benjamin was a director on the Pennsylvania Railroad and served as an officer on the boards of several other businesses. William (Bill) had been raised in the lap of luxury. He attended private schools in Pennsylvania and New York and had completed two years at Yale before his enlistment.

Bill's interest in flying had begun back in the US. His father had bought him a Curtis Model E Hydroplane flying boat and Bill had taken lessons in 1913. Flying aircraft in 1913 was tricky enough, but flying boats added a level of complexity to flight that made them more complicated and dangerous. Thaw won acclaim in New York by being the first person to fly under all four of the main bridges on the East River. When he came to France in the early summer of 1914, his family had sent his flying boat with him so he could compete in the Schneider Trophy races and attempt to market an aircraft stabiliser he had designed. The final summer before the war, he and his brother spent in Southern France where he became known as 'The playboy of the Riviera.'[2]

Thaw only joined the Legion as he believed that France was right in fighting and applied and had been turned down to join the French Air Service. He contacted the French and told them of his experience as a pilot, but the French military seemed unimpressed. As they told him, there were plenty of young Frenchmen volunteering to fly the small number of planes the Air Service had. Still wanting to serve, Thaw settled for the next best alternative – the Foreign Legion. This did not mean that his burning desire to get into the skies had faded at all, it simply was held in check by French military bureaucracy at the moment.

As Paul Rockwell would later recount during October 1914 while Thaw was in the Legion near Verzenay, he saw a German aeroplane flying overhead. He commented, 'One day, a squadron of American volunteers will be flying for France.'³ His words were prophetic, but wishful at that point. Thaw was not the kind of man to accept defeat. Later that month, he secured permission for him, Bert Hall and James Bach to visit the aerodrome of Escadrille D 6, some thirty-two kilometres from their trenches. The French escadrilles (squadrons) were numbered with their prefix indicating the type of aircraft they were currently flying: D stood for Deperdussin aircraft; F stood for Farman machines; VB represented Voisin bombers; MS stood for Morane Saulniers; and N represented Nieuport aeroplanes. The technology was so rapidly changing that a French Escadrille might go through three or more changes of prefixes throughout the war as new airplanes were issued.

Escadrille D 6 was commanded by Capitaine de Gorges and he greeted the enthusiastic Legionnaires warmly, giving them a tour of the unit and their machines. Even at this early stage of the war, the Deperdussins were slated for replacement as being obsolete. They were two-seater monoplanes with an 80-hp Gnome motor. The aircraft were primarily used for observation but were poorly designed for the task. The observer sat in front of the pilot directly over the single wing, effectively blocking his view from either side of the aircraft.

The three Americans were excited at the prospect of transferring from the slow grinding death of trench warfare for the aviation service. One of the men they met at Escadrille D 6 was senior pilot Lieutenant Felix Brocard who Thaw had met before the war. Based on their experience in joining the Legion, Bach and Hall both exaggerated their flight histories. In Hall's case it was an outright lie. Thaw didn't have to exaggerate, but did create the impression that he could fly almost any type of aeroplane. Lieutenant Brocard took the time to listen to the Americans and agreed to assist them in their efforts to transfer.⁴

One would have expected Thaw to have been the first to receive a transfer, but it was Bach that received word in November that he could transfer to the Air Service. On 15 November, he left the trenches and went to Saint-Cyr to begin his flight training. Thaw, refusing to be deterred, walked the thirty-two kilometres to Escadrille D 6 to meet with Lieutenant Brocard. The French officer assured him that the paperwork was being processed for both him and

Hall. On 14 December, Bert received word that he was transferred into the French Air Service effective on 28 December. Thaw's orders came through ten days later, with an assignment to Escadrille D 6.[5] Bert was sent to Pau for his flight training.

The French military was highly suspicious of German attempts to infiltrate and spy on their operations, especially the relatively new Air Service. While Thaw and Bach were able to provide paperwork validating their backgrounds (passports, birth certificates, etc.) Bert, however, did not have any identification other than his enlistment records from the Legion – which did not require any verification. While today travel abroad required a passport, it was optional for Americans travelling to Europe until the 1920s. '...I had no papers of any sort. I went directly to the Commander's office and he asked me who I was. So I told him that I was an aviator. He looked through his papers and said he had no record of me. 'It is not my fault. I am here.' 'All right,' he said, and put my name on the books. I was sent out to the store room and rigged out with a complete outfit, which none of the rest of the boys were fortunate enough to get. That is a result of being a fast talker.'[6]

Bluff and bravado were part of Bert's character, qualities that nearly got him killed. Since he claimed he was an aviator, Bert was asked to demonstrate his flying capabilities. Unshaken by the challenge, he climbed into the cockpit. By his own admission, it was the first time he had ever done so. Still wanting to impress his trainers, Bert did the unthinkable. He had them start the motor. 'Off he went, zig-zagging like a drunken duck, actually left the ground, but crashed headlong into the wall of a hanger. The machine was in pieces, but they picked him up unhurt to hear their verdict of his qualifications as a pilot.'[7]

Aside from a scratched knee and a bruised ego, Bert emerged from the wreckage proud of what he had accomplished. The French officer in charge was not happy in the least. 'What went wrong?' 'I don't know,' Bert replied. 'You don't know! Haven't you ever been in a plane before?' 'No.' 'What in God's holy name do you mean – starting off like that?' 'Well, I thought I might be able to fly.'[8] 'You have never even been in an aeroplane,' he barked at Bert, 'but you have guts, that much I will say for you.'[9] They were impressed enough with his daring to not kick him out of flight training, but instead let him continue... from the beginning.

Hall's lying did not entirely endear him to the French officers. The French were wary of foreigners out of fear they might be German spies. In Bert's instance, his lying about being a pilot only seemed to raise eyebrows and heighten their attention. Bert began to tell exaggerated tales of his time in the Foreign Legion. Some of his stories involved fighting 'furious bayonet charges' during battles at Craonne, which the French knew were outright lies. Further attempts to secure his paperwork proved impossible. Matters were probably not helped with the fact that Bert had a tendency to claim that he was born in several different towns in the US.

Interviews with several of the Legionnaires in his old unit only made the situation more suspicious. Bert bragged to his former comrades that he was the object of a three-year search by the Boston police for alleged violations of the Mann Act – a white slavery trafficking law. Bert also bragged, 'The warden of the Rhode Island State Penitentiary badly wants to get his hands on me.'[10] While the Foreign Legion did not care about past criminal acts, the French military (which the Air Service was part of) *did* care. Bach who was quartered with Bert came under similar suspicion, mostly because of the number of aircraft he damaged during training. In the eyes of the French, these two aviators might well be poised to infiltrate the flight school and cause as much damage as possible through sabotage. Rather than call him out on these stories they suspected that Bert was a German agent. They covertly placed two 'sûreté' agents posing as student pilots in his barracks, one assigned to sleep on either side of him. Their hope was to learn his true intentions while his tall tales could be verified or refuted. They kept close scrutiny of Bert's activities during his time in flight school.[11]

Training in the French Air Service was short, intense and sometimes fatal. Students were given ground school learning at first, studying the basics of flight theory, how the motors worked and how the controls of the aeroplane worked. The next step was to pilot a Penguin. These were small monoplanes where the wings were cut to half-length or shorter. With a small 20-hp motor, they were not designed for flight but rather to drive about the grassy airfield. The Penguins gave the students mastery of the basic controls without the risks that gravity presented. 'I was able to make the old thing go in straight lines, and then I felt that I was a sure-enough flyer. It wasn't so easy at that, for it is very difficult for an old hand with these short-winged machines. When a man shows some improvement at this kind of practice he is given a higher-powered machine.'[12]

The next stage of his training was to fly a low-powered aeroplane at low altitudes, fifty feet or less off the ground. Bert moved on to more powerful training aircraft where he was able to fly basic manoeuvres. As he progressed, he made his way to machines that flew at 500 feet where he practiced navigation and more complicated manoeuvres. The next phase of his training was to secure his military licence. The test consisted of several stages to complete. The first was flying to a specific point approximately fifty miles away and return to base. Secondly, he had to fly in a triangle pattern, flying a total of 200 miles unassisted. The next step was to fly for one hour at 7,000 feet. While the last phase does not sound difficult, one must remember that aviators at this stage of the war did not have oxygen and were exposed to the elements in an open cockpit. The temperatures at 7,000 feet were frigid and exposed skin was subject to freezing. Without oxygen, some men got light-headed or developed tunnel vision. The only way to test this was to put men up at that altitude.

The romantic image of the aviator, wearing goggles, padded helmet and a scarf stick in people's minds when they think of the Great War. For the men that flew aeroplanes at the time, it was anything but easy. The dashing leather flying suit was designed to keep the aviator warm in the freezing temperatures. The rotary motors used in many of the French aircraft had a tendency to spray castor oil. The wearing of a scarf was not just to keep their skin from being exposed, but to keep the oil out of their mouths. Several aviators of the period spoke of the effects of swallowing castor oil and how the first thing many a pilot did after landing was rush to the latrine.

The 'typical' French uniform was a light blue blouse shirt and breeches with boots. The men were responsible for securing their own uniforms and a great deal of latitude was given as to what they wore.[13] Bert is often seen in two different uniforms during the First World War. One is the typical light blue uniform coat and trousers. The other is a black engineer's outfit with a kepi. His black uniform often made him stand out in sharp contrast with other aviators.

There were options for aviators in terms of their specialties or branches within the Air Service. First was piloting to regulate artillery fire – performing observation of targets and using signals (and later wireless sets) to help place artillery barrages on target. Next was bombing aircraft. Bombing was a best an inexact military art, relying more on luck than skill to drop bombs on target. Another branch was photographic aircraft. Aerial photography was in its infancy in 1915 but was improving. Some cameras were large wooden contraptions that were bulky and difficult to load and use. Another branch was reconnoitring pilots, those that scouted enemy troop movements, gun emplacements, etc.

The reality of the risks associated with flight training became apparent to Bert early on. '…I saw the horrible sight of an aviator burning in his machine while his wife, far below, was watching him. This occurred at a training camp behind the lines. He had been expecting her to visit and was anxious to demonstrate his prowess, so he had gone up for an exhibition flight. Something went wrong, and the machine burst into flames. He was a flaming torch as he dropped through the air.'[14]

The last aviation branch was the most exciting: piloting fighting machines. These chasse (pursuit) aircraft provided protection to the other branches with the emphasis on targeting enemy aircraft for destruction. This branch was the birthplace of true fighter aircraft and aviators. It was here that Bert Hall studied. Fighter aircraft were still in their infancy due to complexities of firing a machine gun at moving aircraft. In 1915, the issue was that a pilot could not fire through his spinning propeller without shredding his prop. The solutions included mounting machine guns on mounts over the top wing to fire over the propeller; moving the engine to a pushing position so that the pilot/observer could have a machine gun firing forward; or providing the observer with a pivot-mounted machine gun to the rear. Each resolution had their deficiencies and were, at best, cumbersome and often deadly. In late March 1915, Roland Garros concocted a dangerous fix to the problem, mounting metal deflector blades to the propeller that would allow the pilot to fire forwards. The bullets still hit the propeller, some ricocheting dangerously, but others would pass through the spinning blades. Being a fighter pilot in 1915 was becoming increasingly dangerous with each passing month as both sides of the war attempted to make their aircraft more deadly.[15]

Bert passed his military licence tests earning him his military brevet a month after Bach. Hall had been held back for another month due to the suspicions of being a spy. Thaw did not have to go through piloting school since he possessed a flying licence from the United States. Lieutenant Brocard got him assigned to Escadrille D 6 but not as a pilot, instead he was made a soldat-mitrailleur, a machine gunner. Even that title was an exaggeration, many mitrailleurs were armed with rifles or pistols rather than machine guns at this stage of the war. While he got into the air before Bach and Hall, he was not doing what he so desperately desired – flying an aircraft. He remained in Escadrille D 6 for a month and then was able to convince the French that he should be made a pilot. Thaw followed the same model that his two comrades did. He inflated his story...

Thaw was sent to St Cyr in February 1915 where he was slated to prove himself by flying a Caudron aircraft. 'I told them that my name was W. Caudron Thaw, and finally persuaded them to give me a try.' Thaw insisted that he could fly almost any kind of aircraft, a lie but one that had some skill behind it. He had '...never flown on land, never with a rotary motor, never with a propeller in front, and never with that control.'[16] Despite everything working against him, he got the Caudron into the skies and unlike Bert, managed to live up to his lie. By March, he received his brevet and was posted as a pilot to Escadrille C 42 several months before Bach and Hall finished their training.[17] While he flew in C 42, he served under Capitaine Georges Thénault, a man who was to play an important role in the coming months in Thaw's vision of an all-American escadrille.

Thaw had not given up his original vision of the Americans flying for France serving together in an all-American escadrille. His efforts were joined and superseded in early 1915 by Norman Prince. Prince was a scion of a wealthy family from Pride's Crossing, Massachusetts. He, like Thaw, had learned to fly float-planes first. At the Burgess School where he was undergoing his flight training, he proposed the same idea that Bill Thaw had: a vision of an American squadron flying for France. His classmate, Frazier Curtis, had tried to join the Royal Flying Corps but had been rejected as he was American. While Curtis insisted on returning to England to try again, Prince never lost sight of his concept.

Prince travelled to France in January 1915. In Paris, he was able to gain some support for the idea, contacts that helped him navigate the heady bureaucratic waters of the French War Department. Curtis' attempts to enlist in England failed and he joined up with his former classmate. Despite his contacts, Prince was running into a stone wall of resistance on the part of the French. In their minds, there was no need for American volunteers as there were plenty of Frenchmen willing to fly. Prince made contact with another American in Paris, Elliot Cowdin of New York. Cowdin was the son of a wealthy ribbon manufacturer who had joined the American Ambulance Service in 1914. The American Ambulance Service was a humanitarian organisation in France that had attracted a number of volunteers. Cowdin tossed his name onto the list of Americans that wanted to fly for France.[18] Prince made contact with M. Jarousse de Sillac who was sympathetic to the idea of Americans flying for France. He understood the propaganda potential back in the United States and how it might help sway more American support. He sent a letter to Colonel Bouttieaux of the Ministry of War in hopes of pushing forward Prince's concept:

> I beg to transmit to you herewith attached the names of six young men, citizens of the United States of America, who desire to enlist in the French Aviation — an offer which was not accepted by the Minister of War. Permit me to call your attention to this matter, insisting upon its great interest. It appears to me that there might be great advantages in the creation of an American Squadron. The United States would be proud of the fact that certain of her young men, acting as did Lafayette, have come to fight for France and civilization. The resulting sentiment of enthusiasm could have but one effect: to turn the Americans in the direction of the Allies. There is a precedent in the Legion of Garibaldi, which has had an undeniably good influence on Franco-Italian relations. If you approve these considerations, I am confident that it will be possible to accept these young men and to authorise their enlistment in such a manner that they may be grouped under the direction of a French chief. In doing this you will contribute to the happiness of these six Americans.[19]

The names of the men submitted were Norman Prince, Frazier Curtis, William Thaw, Bert Hall, James Bach and Elliot Cowdin. Thaw, Bach and Hall were already in the service at this point, something glossed over in the letter. A few days later, Colonel Bouttieaux responded. 'I think that your candidates will be welcomed. They should contract an engagement in the French Army for the duration of the war, and should agree to fly only the aeroplanes customarily used in the French Aviation Service.'[20] With the support of Colonel Bouttieaux, Cowdin, Prince and Curtis enlisted in the French Air Service. Cowdin went on to training and was assigned to Escadrille VB 108 where he served as a bomber pilot. Prince joined him as well. On 9 July 1915, he was awarded the Croix de Guerre with a Star and then made the transfer to fighter aircraft getting assigned to Bert Hall's Escadrille M 38 in time for the Champagne Offensive in September.[21]

While Thaw had fostered the original idea of an American escadrille, and Prince had pushed the same idea forward, there was another pivotal player that needed to join in on this effort. His name was Dr Edmond L. Gros. He had been an organiser of the American Ambulance Service. Like Thaw and Prince, he independently shared their vision for an American squadron. Curtis had met a number of Americans in the Ambulance Service and sent a letter to Dr Gros that spawned the good doctor into action:

Dear Dr. Gros:

I went to the Ambulance to-day to see if I could find any drivers who wanted to join the French Aviation Service. The Government is willing to train 100 American flyers and to keep them together in one Corps. Men of flying experience would be preferred, but those of apparent aptitude (knowledge of French, gas engines, etc.) will be acceptable. Mr. Fréchon tells me you are keen on getting up a big Corps, so we ought to be able to work together. I would like to introduce you to one of my friends who is pretty much running this enlarged Corps. I am here on sick leave, three accidents having left me pretty well jarred up. I expect to go to the seaside for a good rest in a day or two, but am very anxious to see you first.[22]

Dr. Gros convened a meeting with Curtis, and M. de Sillac to explore the concept further. They formed the nexus of the Franco-American Committee to champion the idea of creating an American flying force. As with everything in the French War Department, the committee faced a daunting task of attempting to get the proper approval. For the summer and autumn of 1915 – many meetings took place and letters drafted in support of the concept. Gros expanded the members of the committee and worked diligently to organise their arguments and thinking. On July 8, 1915, the Chief of French Military Aeronautics, General Auguste Edouard Hirschauer, attended

a luncheon sponsored by the committee at the house of French Senator
Gaston Menier. Gros had rallied a convincing assemblage of Americans and
Frenchmen to lobby for an American escadrille. Backing Dr. Gros's stand was
Colonel Bouttieaux, General Hirschauer, Senator Menier, Léon Bourgeois,
Mr. Robert Bacon, M. de Sillac, Dr. William White, of Philadelphia.

The French had long-maintained that there was no need for an all-American
squadron but the impressive gathering of leaders and their well-conceived
arguments in favour of such an activity were impossible to deflect. By the end
of the luncheon General Hirschauer had been swayed as to the benefits of
such an escadrille and agreed to give orders for the formation of the American
unit – under French command. The working name of the unit was to be the
Escadrille Américaine.[23]

While the decision had finally been made, it would be another six months of
wrangling the French Air Service to make that decision a reality.

Bert Hall was in favour of an American escadrille as well but he was not
one of the architects of the concept. He went to advanced training at Avord
Training School in the summer of 1915 and after completing the course, was
kept on as an instructor.[24] While this may have been testimony to his skill, it
may also be interpreted as the French still not being convinced that he was
not a German saboteur/spy and desiring to keep him from the front. Finally
in mid-August 1915, Bert was assigned to Escadrille MS 38. Escadrille MS 38
had been formed in January 1915. The symbol of their escadrille was a black
thorny, upright thistle plant on a triangular pennant of black and red. The
thistle symbol was painted on the side of their aircraft. Their motto was 'To
it rubs, it stings', characterising their aggressiveness. Their aerodrome was at
Châlons-sur-Marne. Capitaine Marcel Boucher was in command of the unit
and his second in command was Lieutenant d'Harcourt.[25]

Bach had been posted to the unit prior to Bert's arrival giving them some
time to reunite. MS 38 flew the Morane Saulnier Type L and LA monoplanes.
They were called 'parasols' as the wing was a top mount over the pilot and
observer positions like an umbrella with a vertical pole and support wires
spread out to brace the wing. Some models were mounted with a machine
gun on top of the wing to fire over the propeller. On others, a ring-mounted
machine gun was provided for the observer.

Bert's time with his old Legion comrade was cut short. On 23 September
1915, Bach was given a special assignment. Along with another aviator,
Sergent-Pilote Mangeot, they were to carry two soldiers in their machines with
orders to fly over the German lines near Mézières. Their intent was sabotage.
The two aircraft were to land and disembark the soldiers who were armed
with explosive charges. The saboteurs were going to destroy a section of rail

line that ran between Mézières and Hirson. They were also supposed to record as much information on the enemy troop concentrations in the area as well. When they were complete, the soldiers were to make their way to the aircraft and Bach and Mangeot would return them to the safety of the French lines. The mission was especially dangerous as the act of landing agents to perform sabotage made the pilots susceptible to being charged as spies if they were captured. It was the kind of risky flamboyant mission that characterised pilots of the air service.[26]

The pair of saboteurs had been chosen because they knew the area where they would be operating. The problem was that the two men were not aviators. While the field was relatively flat, the ground was rough and covered with brush and small trees. Most landing fields at aerodromes were just that, flat fields of grass. While the landing field was well positioned in terms of concealment and access to the rail line, it was undesirable from an aviators' standpoint as Bach was about to learn.

The flight took place and miraculously the two Morane Saulniers landed and disembarked their occupants. They planted their charges and returned as planned... then things began to go wrong. Bach managed to navigate the rough field, gunned the fuel and made his way into the air. As he glanced back to see how his wingman was doing, he was stunned to see that Mangeot's airplane was nosed-over on the ground. Bach could have returned to his aerodrome, but believed he could carry at least another man back with him. Rather than abandon Mangeot, Bach turned his plane around and managed to land again.[27] Bach managed to squeeze Mangeot into his Morane Saulnier, leaving the remaining saboteur to attempt to make his way back alone. As he built up speed for a take off for a second time, Bach's wing struck a stump, causing him to nose-over and destroying his propeller. His crash removed any chance of the four men to leave German lines via the air. They were fortunate that there were no injuries, despite the fact that Mangeot had been involved in two crashes in just a few short minutes.[28]

To return to the French lines would require stealth, guile and luck. While the men had the first two, luck was against them. The men hid in nearby woods until they thought it was safe to attempt to make their way to freedom. A few hours later they were captured by a German patrol and taken to Laon. Jimmy Bach, Bert's close friend since enlistment in the Foreign Legion, had the distinction of being the first American POW of the war. While the Germans attempted to try him as a spy during two court-martials, he was imprisoned as a enemy combatant. Bach would remain a POW throughout the war.

Escadrille MS 38 flew several missions to drop saboteurs behind enemy lines in the late summer of 1915.[29] In the same month, Bert undertook a mission similar to that of his friend Bach.

I took a spy into the German lines with orders to leave him, and had a narrow escape when I returned for him later. The Germans caught him and forced him to reveal our signals. They were waiting for me to return. When I was about fifty feet from the ground they started firing at me with machine guns, which they had hidden in some trees. My machine was badly punctured and I received a slight wound, but managed to escape and return safely.[30]

Things were going better for Bill Thaw. While flying in Escadrille C 42, his service was so distinguished he was made a Sergent on 18 May. During that same month, he was cited once in divisional and twice in army orders.[31] For Bert, Bach's capture meant that he was alone, at least for the time being, in the escadrille. On the ground, the French were launching their Second Champagne Offensive, which included his old unit, the Second Regiment Etranger. At roughly the same time, the escadrille received the Nieuport 10, considered to be the best fighter of the French Air Service. MS 38 transitioned to its new designation, N 38. The Nieuport 10C.1 was a biplane built for battle. Durable and nimble, it was fast with a maximum speed of 92 mph. It could fly as high as 15,000 feet. It had a reliable 80-hp Le Rhone rotary engine and could remain in the air for two-and-a-half hours. For armament, it was equipped with a Lewis machine gun mounted over the top wing to avoid the propeller.[32]

Bert's own perception of the autumn of 1915 seemed almost blasé, long periods of boredom shattered by moments of sheer terror.

Our work consisted in reconnoitring twice daily; sometimes we went as far as sixty miles back of the German lines, kept tabs on all movements of troops, activity on the railroads, concentration of material and any new earthworks – everything that was going on. We also had two barrages a day to do. That consists of patrolling the lines to keep the German fliers from regulating their artillery fire. This work was very uninteresting, as we found a number of Germans and fixed them plenty. We also did photographing. The artillery fire is regulated by two-seated machines equipped with wireless capable for sending up to seven miles. The machine doing the regulating generally gets over the objective. About the third shot will hit the target after they have received our wireless.'[33]

This reconnoitering work is often very dangerous, and several of my pals were made prisoners while doing it. You go back of the German lines and risk being made prisoner because of possible motor trouble, and also being attacked by German airmen in groups. They try to cut off your retreat. The anti-aircraft guns are shooting at you continually and you are forced to go to certain localities to see if any changes are being made and to note all movements of troops and material. A part of your work is to photography objectives designated by headquarters.[34]

You are given a fixed portion of the front to cover, and receive your orders before leaving, if there are any special points where an attack is going on, you leave your field and climb until you reach the lines. Generally you are 10,000 to 14,000 feet by this time. You continue to climb as you patrol your section of the line; you keep a close watch for Germans above and below.

We generally climb up to 18,000 feet or more, and continued to watch until we were attacked or saw a German below. You slow down your motor, try your gun, and down you go. If there is more than one enemy plane, pick out the nearest and go after him. You continue this for two and a half hours when you return to the French field where you make out a report of all that has passed. Now you are free, you may go where you please, until your next turn. In bad weather we play games, read and gamble. Mostly gamble. Poker and bridge are the two leading pastimes of that kind.[35]

Like many aviators of the war, Bert had his share of victories that were unconfirmed. An aviator needed to receive independent confirmation of a victory. This was difficult if not impossible when an enemy aeroplane went down behind their own lines. Keeping track of victories was important since it became the formal way in which pilots competed with each other. The ace system – the drive to secure five or more victories to earn the title 'ace' – was a powerful motivator. A typical example of an unconfirmed kill was on 10 September. 'Barrage, my mechanic as gunner. Met a German Aviatik over Mourmellon; attacked him and forced him down into his lines.'[36]

On 21 September, he was flying with Captain Boucher as his observer on what should have been a routine reconnaissance mission.

Here we had an exciting adventure. We received a shell (anti-aircraft) very close and we had a piece of it weighting about two pounds stuck in between the elevator and the fixed surface, making it impossible for me to move the commands. Thanks to the wonderful construction of my Nieuport we made a good landing. The duration of this flight was two hours, twelve minutes and our height of 3,600 metres.[37]

Having your controls jammed over enemy territory should have been a frightful situation for any aviator, but Bert seemed to be nonchalant about the risks he was taking. Aviation in the First World War was different than in any other conflict. Aviators painted not only their squadron/escadrille insignia on the aircraft, but they often painted personalised emblems or figures. Pilots on both sides got to know each other on sight. There was an air of chivalry between these men. Yes, they tried to kill each other, but there was a measure of respect for the risks that they took every day. This was personified by Bert's ground encounter with a German aviator. One day, a pilot flew over his aerodrome and accidently dropped one of his thick fur-lined gloves which Bert recovered. The next day, the aviator returned and dropped the other glove, this time with a note stating that the finder might as well have the pair.[38] A few days later, Bert allegedly buzzed the German aerodrome and dropped a note of thanks for the gift.[39]

As the autumn of 1915 continued and the ground war expanded, N 38 flew fewer missions as new escadrilles were made operational. Those missions that Bert did fly were in support of ground operations. At the same time, other members of the Foreign Legion were expressing their interest in taking the fight to the skies rather than the trenches. In May, Legionnaire Kiffin Rockwell had been shot in the thigh and had been hospitalised for a long recovery. While no longer qualified for the infantry, his injury did not prohibit him from being an aviator. His brother Paul Rockwell had been shot in the shoulder and then suffered a flair-up of painful inflammatory rheumatism that kept him hospitalised. When he was well enough to leave the hospital, his ailments prohibited him joining the French Air Service. Bert's other close friend, Frederick Zinn, was also shot and sent back to the United States for a month's leave to recover from his injuries. Alan Seeger, the promising young poet in the Legion, was killed in the brutal fighting.

The Champagne Offensive had been a waste of human lives. The French had advanced a maximum of two-and-a-half miles, most of which they eventually gave up. They had not even fully penetrated the German trenches at a cost of over 145,000 men. The Germans had lost upwards of 80,000 men. In the end of months of battle, the front lines had barely changed.[40] Of the original Americans that had joined the Legion for the 'short war' in 1914, ninety-five per cent of them had been killed or wounded by the end of 1915.[41] Many of those that were alive wanted to get out of the ground war. Bert's old unit suffered greatly. 'Company I Section III on the night of the first day's fighting in Champagne mustered eight men out of the forty-two who had fallen into line that morning. Section IV lost that day more than half of its effectives. Section II lost seventeen out of thirty-eight. War did its work thoroughly with the Legion.'[42] Many of the surviving Americans wanted to follow the path that William Thaw had paved into the French Air Service.

While the efforts to get an American escadrille formed stalled, the Franco-American Committee did make headway in the formation of another organisation – the Franco-American Flying Corps. This 'legion of young aviators'[43] was not a military unit, but more of a fraternity of Americans that were flying for France. They '…wanted to return the politeness that Lafayette and Rochambeau had done us; we wanted to belong to that fine ascrtive [sic] institution, the French Flying Corps, and we thought that the United States ought to aid a republic engaged in a conflict in which the independence of all the nations is at stake.'[44] The goals of the organisation were to provide a social network of sorts for the Americans that were flying for France. The men that were embedded into the French escadrilles were grouped, if possible, together for support. The members of the Flying Corps kept in contact with each other and fulfilled other duties such as contacting family members if a member was injured or killed. Part of the thinking was that such men would be eventually rotated into an all-American escadrille when it was finally formed. In the meantime, the Flying Corps would be a family away from home and provide the committee with the means to recruit and train more Americans.

Members had to meet requirements, both moral and physical. You needed to be in good health, between eighteen and thirty-five years old and not weigh over 160 pounds stripped. 'Good sight in both eyes, sound lungs, and steady nerves' were the physical requirements.[45] Morally: 'You must be of high moral standing not of German extraction on father's or mother's side, able to give testimonials and references from several persons of good standing in your community.'[46] On 19 October 1915, on the roll of forty-two original members proposed to be the founders of the Flying Corps, the name Sergeant Bert Hall appeared. How he met the moral requirements would be matter for debate for years to come. For Bert, 1915 came to an end in battle. 'It was on December 18th, in a fight near Maschalt, that I got eighteen bullets, but the result of it was that I missed that Boche. So, on January 1st, 1916, they sent me to Avord for a rest. I put in my time there as an instructor, but I did more flying than I had at the front.'[47]

Little did Hall realise that the start of the New Year was going to bring about his involvement in an all-American squadron, one that his name would be associated with for generations to come.

CHAPTER FIVE

The Escadrille Américaine – The Lafayette Escadrille

We meet 'neath the sounding rafters,
The walls around us are bare;
They echo the peal of laughter;
It seems that the dead are there.

So stand by your glasses steady,
This world is a web of lies.
Here's a toast to the dead already;
Hurrah for the next man who dies.

Cut off from the land that bore us,
Betrayed by the land that we find,
The good men have gone before us,
And only the dull left behind.

So stand by your glasses steady,
The world is a web of lies.
Then here's to the dead already,
And hurrah for the next man who dies.

– The mess song of the Lafayette Escadrille[1]

Despite the fact that General Hirschauer had agreed to the proposal of the Franco-American Committee to form the Escadrille Américaine, the matter seemed mired in the French War Department. There were factors creating pressure on the Franco-American Committee that forced their hand in the autumn of 1915. One of these factors was the growing number of Americans that wanted to fly for the French. Dudley Hill had joined the French Air Service already, though he was struggling with a problem with one eye that might sideline him as a mechanic. Hill found a way around his eyesight problem: by cheating on the exam when retested. Other men such as Robert Soubiran, William Dugan, Pierre Boal, Frederick Zinn and Marius Rocle had also filed from transfers from their French regiments or the Foreign Legion into the Air Service.[2] Combined with men such as Kiffin Rockwell, Victor Chapman and others, the numbers of Americans exceeded the size of a single escadrille. Yes, there would be casualties, but the numbers were larger than a typical pool of replacements.

The Franco-American Committee had also begun to leverage the press to their cause, especially in the United States. Their vision was to have representation in America as a recruitment arm for their efforts. However, as the newspapers began to spread the story that there was going to be an all-American squadron, a groundswell of volunteers emerged. Airplanes were exciting new technologies and it appeared that America was destined to stay out of the European war. For young men, the Escadrille Américaine represented a chance to learn and master this new technology and perhaps some fame in the process.

The spin that the committee put on it deemphasised the French. 'The American corps – has two objectives – to assist France and to give American airmen experience in war as to fit them to serve as pilots or officers in the American aerial service should the occasion arise. The French military administration is giving the American volunteers every opportunity to gain this experience.'[3] Such words did not sit well with the State Department since the United States was still neutral. The Franco-American Committee's efforts sounded as if they were preparing America for war, something that was against US policy in 1915. All of these efforts and activities required money. The Franco-American Committee wanted to produce a booklet that extolled the virtues of the men in the escadrille as well to serve as a recruitment instrument. There were trips back and forth from France that had to be paid for. The committee also recognised that the volunteers would need uniforms (French aviators were required to purchase their own tailored uniforms) and would need accoutrements, supplies, billeting and other expenditures. The committee also proposed to augment the pay above and beyond what the French Air Service paid its aviators. To do all of this required money, money that the committee did not have.

Dr Gros came up with a solution that was eloquent and added clout to the committee. He contacted William K. Vanderbilt, the wealthy American industrialist who was, at the time, residing outside of Paris. Vanderbilt became enamoured with the idea of young Americans flying for France and agreed to bankroll the majority of their considerable expenses related to the committee and the escadrille.[4] Other investors soon joined suit. Despite this, matters were still moving painfully slow. While the committee had a promise, they did not have an escadrille and with winter setting in along the western front and a slow-down of aviation activity, William Thaw, Elliot Cowdin and Norman Prince formally requested leave to return for the Christmas holiday back to the United States.

The trip was an important lesson for the men on public relations. They went home to their families and granted interviews for newspapers about their exploits. The press and the American people greeted them warmly. At the same time, they learned that their words, taken out of context, could generate concern. 'William Thaw, Norman Prince and Elliot C. Cowdin, American aviators who have been serving with the French army since, the war began, arrived here Thursday, on the steamship <u>Rotterdam</u> on leave-of-absence to spend Christmas with relatives. They said approximately 47 percent of the aviators who have heretofore enlisted have been lost either through death, by capture, or by wounds. As fast as the men drop out however, there are many anxious and willing to take their place.'[5] Such inadvertent comments may have been a way of weeding out those young men who did not realise the risks of aerial combat or was a slip that might drive away would-be candidates. Either way, it exposed the naiveté of the young men in dealing with the press.

The United States was experiencing an economic boom as a result of the war. By remaining neutral, the US sold arms to anyone with cash that was able to dock a ship on the east coast – in other words, England and France. The war was seen as far away. If these young men from prominent families wanted to go and fight… well, that was their business. Their stories made good press and were often page one or two news. They spoke openly about the concept of an all-American escadrille. Thaw, who had been promoted to lieutenant, was the only American at the time that was an officer in the French Air Service, which added to his celebrity.

While the American public drank in the stories of daring and dash by the airmen, the United States Government did not. Senators and representatives that favoured neutralism saw them as an affront to America's official status. The US had a substantial German immigrant population that was less than happy to hear tales of young men from a supposedly neutral nation killing their former countrymen. Letters were sent to Congress complaining, asking how could a country possibly be fielding a squadron in a war while proclaiming to be a neutral player?

Matters became more heated when the German ambassador Count Johann von Bernstorff went to New York and confronted William Thaw in a barbershop. The Count, playing up for the gathered crowd, suggested that the three aviators would be advised to turn themselves over to the authorities and be interned to avoid an international incident. Thaw stormed out.[6] Count Bernstorff contacted Secretary of State Robert Lansing to lodge a protest. He was not alone. As reported in the *New York Times*:

> George Viereck, editor of <u>The Fatherland</u>, yesterday telegraphed Secretary of State Lansing in Washington a request for the immediate arrest of Second Lieutenant William Thaw, Sergeant Elliot Cowdin, and Sergeant Norman Prince of the French Army Aviation Corps, who arrived in New York on Thursday on the Holland-America liner <u>Rotterdam</u>.
>
> Viereck based his request upon international law and Article II of the Peace Convention at the Hague in 1907 which says: 'A neutral power which receives in its territory troops belonging to a belligerent nation shall intern them, as far as possible, at a distance from the theatre of war.'
>
> These men, though of American birth, are officers in active service in the French Army, and it would be a gross violation of American neutrality if they are not detained so as to prevent their return to the front.

Viereck's telegram read:

> In view of the fact that the neutrality of the Administration has been seriously questioned both here and aboard, I trust that you will take immediate action in the case and that you will hold these three officers in confinement, unless they give their parole not to leave American territory without your permission.
>
> Insomuch as you have so ardently championed the rights of neutrals as against the central powers, I feel sure that you will gladly avail yourself of the opportunity to demonstrate to the world that the United States Government is also alive to its neutral duties. In fact, I am advised that we have no choice in the matter unless we regard international conventions as 'scraps of paper'.[7]

While Viereck was known to be an ardent German supporter and an extremist, the article, which ran on Christmas Day, let the aviators know that their stay was not going to be free of controversy. If the article bothered Thaw, he did not let it show. In his father's office, Thaw said:

> The story is too ridiculous to be worth thinking about. I am not giving any thought to it. If there were any possibility of my being held here, or of my two companions, the French government would never have permitted us to go to America.

If there were any legal basis for holding us here, there are hundreds of thousands of aliens in this country who could and should be interned. No, there is nothing in such talk. As I told the New York reporters last night, the German newspaper that started the story may get some free advertising out of it, but that is all.[8]

What was curtailed by the aviators were discussions about aviation and the war. Thaw further added:

I am in a neutral country and I must positively decline to talk about the war. All that I have seen and heard abroad I must regard as confidential, and I can say nothing about it. This is my first leave since I entered the service of the French government, Aug. 24, 1914, and I am gratified to be able to visit the United States, and especially Pittsburgh. I spent most of my time in the east while in this country before the war, but the greater part of the time was taken up in school and college and abroad before I joined the French colours. This is my first visit to Pittsburgh in some years.[9]

One thing was for sure, until the US Government weighed in on the matter, the topic was not going to die down. Two days later, they did. The official word was that no action was to be taken against Thaw, Cowdin or Prince. 'The (State) department probably will take the position that when the three men joined the army forces of a foreign power, they renounced their American citizenship and entered this country as soldiers, unarmed.'[10] For the Americans that were in the French Air Service, this had to have been a stinging rebuke. They had believed that their status in the Foreign Legion had offered them protection of their citizenship. In the case of the three men visiting their homeland, the trip had cost them theirs. While they would claim that political pressure had nothing to do with it, they cut their visit short by a week and headed back to France.

Bert was far from idle in December 1914 and January 1915. Not only was he at Avord as an instructor, but he once more got married. His third wife was Suzanne Tatien who he wed in Paris on 28 December 1915. How he met his third wife is unknown, but Suzanne's existence was something that Bert kept from his squadron mates throughout the war. Perhaps it was due to her young age: she was eighteen years old at the time. While perfectly acceptable by standards of the day, Bert was thirty years old, more than twice her age.[11]

While at Avord, Bert was an instructor for another young American aviator – Victor Chapman.[12] Like Bert, Victor had served in the Foreign Legion. He was six-feet tall with thick black hair and sparking eyes. He was a Harvard

Graduate who, like Hall, had ties to the American Revolution. Victor's great-great-grandfather was John Jay who had signed the Declaration of Independence. Victor had been a student at the Beaux Arts Studio in Paris when war broke out and, like the other volunteers, quickly enlisted.[13]

While Thaw, Prince and Cowdin were in America, French aviators reduced their flying hours due as their fighters were not designed for the bitterly cold winter weather. Also, the flying fields were either unforgiving frozen slabs or muddy swamps that invited crashes and accidents. Bert, like many aviators, was biding their time until spring.

The status of an all-American escadrille changed with the warmth of spring. Colonel Regnier, the Chief of French Aeronautics, wrote a letter to the Franco-American Committee on 14 March 1916 that cleared the final hurdle for the formation of an American escadrille:

> Replying to your letter of March 3, 1916, I have the honour to communicate to you the following information. I had already considered the question of an American squadron, and as early as February 20, 1916, I asked the Commander-in-Chief to advise me of his intentions in this matter. General Headquarters has just replied, informing me that an American squadron will be organised, with the pilots whose names follow: William Thaw, Elliot Cowdin, Kiffin Rockwell, Norman Prince, Charles C. Johnson, Clyde Balsley, Victor Chapman, Laurence Rumsey, and James R. McConnell ... I have every reason to believe that the ... squadron will be constituted rapidly ... and I will keep you posted as to what is done in this matter.

Bert Hall's name was not on the original list. That changed on 16 April when Balsley, Rumsey and Johnson were moved to the replacement list of aviators. They were replaced by more seasoned veterans including Bert and the two French pilots that would serve as commanders of the Escadrille Américaine, Capitaine Georges Thénault and his second in command, Lieutenant Alfred de Laage de Meux.[14] Capitaine Thénault was well known by Bill Thaw, he had been Thaw's commanding officer for the months that Thaw had been assigned to C 42.

The Escadrille Américaine assembled officially on 20 April 1916 at the aviation depot at Le Plessis-Belleville. Its official designation was N 124 and its destination was the Western Front. Prior to Bert's arrival, the Americans celebrated at a dinner in Paris, each of them now proudly wearing their French Air Service insignia. After the dinner and drinking, Prince, Rockwell and McConnell left for Luxeuil-les-Bains where the escadrille was to be initially stationed. A few days later, Bill Thaw, Elliot Cowdin and Bert Hall joined them.

Some of the Americans were relative newcomers to men like Thaw, Cowdin and Hall who had flown for a year. James McConnell was one such novice. Born in Chicago, his parents moved to North Carolina in his youth where McConnell attended several private schools before enrolling at the prestigious University of Virginia. He founded the 'Aero Club' while in college and was a member of one of the university's secret societies – the Hot Feet. The Hot Feet Society was known for their practical jokes on campus. McConnell graduated with a law degree in 1910 and had gone into business with Charles Johnson. When war broke out, McConnell joined the American Ambulance Service, but after long months of seeing the carnage on the ground at the front, sought to transfer to the French Air Service.

When the men arrived at the bath resort of Luxeuil-les-Bains, Capitaine Thénault was waiting for them. The aerodrome was considered one of the best at the Western Front. During training at Pau, the men had walked six miles to collect their laundry. At Luxeuil, cars were provided to shuttle the men from their residence to the aerodrome.

Paul Rockwell, Bert's former comrade from the Legion and Kiffin's brother, had been busy in the background trying to find ways to promote the Escadrille Américaine back in the US. Since his wounding and illness, he had transferred into the French Propaganda Ministry working in public information.[15] The Escadrille Américaine became his pet project. He saw the potential of this unit to draw America closer to the French war effort. He positioned articles about the men of the Foreign Legion and the Air Service in the American newspapers, making their names well known. Rockwell also pushed the French authorities to make sure that the unit was well equipped. If the Escadrille Américaine failed, it would be a public relations disaster for the French back in the United States. As a result, the French had given the young Americans one of their best aerodromes. They were extremely well provisioned. As James McConnell noted:

> The equipment awaiting us at the field was even more impressive than our automobile. Everything was brand-new, from the fifteen Fiat trucks to the office, *magasin*, and rest tents. And the men attached to the *escadrille!* At first sight they seemed to outnumber the Nicaraguan army — mechanicians, chauffeurs, armourers, motor-cyclists, telephonists, wireless operators, Red-Cross stretcher-bearers, clerks! Afterward I learned they totalled seventy-odd, and that all of them were glad to be connected with the American *Escadrille.*[16]

Kiffin Rockwell described the new post in a letter home to his mother:

…it is like a pleasant trip to a resort. This is a resort in time of peace with hot baths and hot water to drink coming up out of the ground… Our captain is a young fellow and one of us. We all eat together at a hotel where wonderfully good meals are served. We occupy a villa that has been requisitioned for us with overlies to wait on us. We go down each day about one hundred yards from here to bathe in a bath-house that is over two hundred years old. The scenery around the town is wonderful and we ride over the surrounding country with our captain and are planning to do a little fishing and hunting, so you can see that it is not much like being at war.[17]

The aviators were assigned barracks adjoining the Luxeuil hot baths, the primary draw of the town before the war erupted. The men were enjoying luxuries and took full advantage of them. For Bert, it seemed that his time in the Air Service was finally starting to pay off. Their excitement was tempered quickly when they met Capitaine Maurice Happe, commander of the Luxeuil bombardment group. They were to work in conjunction with the bomber group in providing air support. After introductions, Capitaine Happe showed the men eight small boxes on a table. 'They contain Croix de Guerre for the families of the men I lost on my last trip,' he told the Americans. 'It's a good thing you're here to go along with us for protection. There are lots of Boches in this sector.'[18]

When the men first arrived there were a number of older model Nieuport 10s in the hangers. These were replaced on 5 May when the first five Nieuport 11s, known as the Bébé (Baby), were delivered. The Bébé was small but an evolutionary step forwards from the Nieuport 10. They were still only equipped with an 80-hp motor and, since the French had not yet mastered the synchronisation techniques necessary to fire a machine gun through a spinning propeller, the Bébé had its machine gun mounted high over the top wing. Bert was assigned aeroplane tail number N.1112.[19]

Capitaine Thénault wasted little time in getting his men into the air. Bert went up a short hop on 6 May with Lieutenant de Laage, Bill Thaw and Kiffin Rockwell. Their Nieuports had not been fitted with machine guns, so the flight was kept on the French side of the lines. Despite lacking a weapon, Rockwell went out looking for Germans and testimony to his aggressive nature.[20]

On 13 May, the escadrille took to the skies under the scrutiny of motion picture cameras to capture the moment as propaganda. Thénault's goals were admirable, to get the men fighting together as a unit. Each of the Americans had either no combat experience coming fresh out of training or, like Bert Hall, Cowdin, Prince and Thaw, had been placed in French escadrilles. They had never flown or fought together. The Capitaine planned a series of sorties designed for the men to familiarise themselves with the front lines they would be patrolling and to learn the key landmarks that might help them make their way back to the aerodrome. McConnell managed on one such sortie to get lost, wandering into Switzerland before making his way back to the aerodrome.

The Escadrille Américaine's first victory came only a few days later on 18 May. Kiffin Rockwell recounted his kill for his brother Paul in a letter.

> This morning I went out over the lines to make a little tour. I was a little the other side of the lines, when my motor began to miss a bit. I turned around to go to a camp near the lines. Just as I started to head for there, I saw a Boche machine about seven hundred metres under me and a little inside of our lines. I immediately reduced my motor, and dived for him. He saw me at the same time, and began to dive towards his lines. It was a machine with a pilot and a mitrailleur, with two mitrilleuses, one facing the front and one the rear that turned on a pivot, so he (the gunner) could fire in any direction. He immediately opened fire on me and my machine was hit, but I didn't pay attention to that and kept going straight for him, until I got within twenty-five or thirty metres of him. Then, just as I was afraid of running into him I fired four or five shots, then swerved my machine to the right to keep from running into him. As I did that I saw the mitrailleur fall back dead on the pilot, the mitrailleuse fell from its position and point straight up in the air, the pilot fall to one side of the machine as he was done for also. The machine itself first fell to one side, then dived vertically towards the ground with a lot of smoke coming out of the rear. I circled around, and three or four minutes later saw a lot of smoke coming up from the ground just beyond the German trenches. I had hoped he would fall in our lines, as it is hard to prove when they fall in German lines. The post of observation signalled seeing the machine fall, and the smoke. The Captain said he would propose me for the Médaille Militaire, but I don't know whether I will get it or not.[21]

For the men of the escadrille the victory was vindication of their prowess and the long, hard work it took to get the unit formed. For the first time in the war, an all-American unit had scored a kill. Kiffin's exploits, spurred on by his brother Paul's efforts, were telegraphed to news agencies back in the US. While Americans had been in the air for over a year, this was news that captivated many US citizens. Paul was living vicariously through his brother Kiffin. Where Paul had been denied an opportunity to fly for France, his brother was a rising American star in the Great War.

Paul Rockwell rushed out from Paris after wiring the word of his brother's success heading to Luxeuil with an eighty-year-old bottle of bourbon to celebrate. He found the men of the escadrille celebrating and Kiffin pulled the cork on the bottle to share the gift with his squadron mates. Before drinks were poured, Victor Chapman offered a suggestion: 'Hey, wait a second. We can get plenty of liquor, but not like this. It's rare stuff. Let's save it for rare occasions. 'What could be rarer than this?' Elliot Cowdin chimed in. Chapman continued. 'Fellows, let's make this a real Bottle of Death. Naturally, Kiffin gets the first drink and from now on every many who brings down a German is entitled to one gone good slug. It'll be something worth working for.' Bill Thaw would take the stewardship of the Bottle of Death from that point forward.[22]

There were other incentives that were brought to bear for the Americans. The Franco-American Committee, funded heavily by Vanderbilt's influx of money, instituted raises for the men and an incentive system. The ace system was designed to spur on competition with aviators, but the Franco-American Committee took it one step further.

It was decided to give a monthly allowance of one hundred francs, later increased to two hundred francs, to each American volunteer. Prizes were distributed as follows:
Francs 1500 ($300) for Legion of Honor
      1000 ($200) for Military Medal
      500 ($100) for War Cross
      200 ($50) for each citation (palm)[23]

The way that a pilot earned medals was by killing the enemy. Not only was the committee augmenting the pay of the aviators, it was instituting a bounty system of sorts against the German Air Service.

On 18 May, the escadrille once again tangled with Germans in a struggle to control the skies.

The American aviators forming the Franco-American flying corps took part in an expedition over the German lines the first time as a separate unit. They sustained particularly heavy shelling as they recrossed the front, but landed safely.

The flotilla, including the craft piloted by Corporal Kiffin Rockwell, of Atlanta; Corporal James Rogers McConnell, of Carthage, N.C.; Sergeant Elliot Cowdin, of New York; Lieutenant William K. Thaw, of Pittsburgh; Sergeant Norman Prince, of Boston; and Sergeant Hall, of Galveston, started at daybreak and spent nearly two hours reconnoitring under a hot fire but encountered no German machines.

Corporal McConnell was flying at a height of 12,000 feet but German shells burst all around him, showing that the range of the German anti-aircraft guns had lengthened. Corporal Victor Chapman's machine was hit and driven out of its course, returning so late to its base as to cause anxiety regarding Chapman's fate. The aeroplane piloted by Lieutenant Thaw lost part of its tail piece and the propeller was damaged by a shell.[24]

For these men it was becoming 'typical' work, but every time they took-off into the skies they were gambling with fate. The escadrille relocated to a new aerodrome at Behonne, near Bar-le-Duc, on 19 May. The only men that did not accompany them initially were James McConnell whose plane had two broken fuselage struts; Norman Prince, who had run out of fuel and wrecked his plane, and Elliot Cowdin.[25]

The Escadrille was poised to provide air support operations to one of the more infamous battles of the First World War, Verdun. The Germans believed that 'France has almost reached the end of her military effort.'[26] The Germans felt if they could seize or destroy the fortress at Verdun, the French will to continue fighting would be shattered. Verdun, in reality, was a series of forts, heavily reinforced and defended. In February, the Germans unleashed more than a million artillery shells over a thirty-nine-kilometre front, just to soften up the French defences. They fed in hundreds of thousands of men into battle, as did the French. Some of the forts surrounding Verdun were lost including Fort Douaumont. In May, the French would attempt to unsuccessfully recapture Douaumont. The result was, at best, inconclusive. All it managed to do was to personify that fighting on the Western Front was a pointless sacrifice of men to gain only a few yards of war-torn ground. Verdun became synonymous with its nicknames 'The Furnace' and 'The Sausage Grinder'.

In the air, the Germans had solved the issue of firing a machine gun through a spinning propeller with an interrupter. This in turn synchronised the firing of the gun so as to stop when the propeller blades passed in front of the gun. On paper, this should have given them an edge in the skies. The French and British doctrine changed during the time that N 124 arrived at the front. Rather than be on the defence in reaction to the German assaults on the ground, they went on a strategic offensive. French escadrilles took the fight over the German sides of the lines. They threw escadrille after escadrille into the fight for the skies. For the first time in the Great War, both sides were putting up large numbers of aircraft at a time, allegedly working together. Aviation, which had been in its infancy only two years earlier, was suddenly coming of age over the cauldron of death at Verdun. Into this maelstrom of battle, the Americans were thrown in.

James McConnell commented in his own letters: '...fights occurred on almost every sortie.'[27] Bert's own recollection of the types of missions he faced during the period:

It was late in the afternoon when we arrived at Verdun, and we were immediately installed in our new quarters at Bar-le-Duc. The escadrille was put into action at once, and I can't say that our first sortie was anything excellent. We all went grouped under Captain Thenault (sic), and I flew next to him, about fifty yards to his right. He had told us not to attack until he gave the signal. Then we were to dive on the Germans. We had passed over three of their machines already, and we continued on into their lines. Just over Etain, some twelve miles inside of the German lines, we saw six or more Boches. The Captain started to dive, and I also went down rapidly and picked out of a German, thinking my comrades were all there. But Captain Thenault had only come down a short distance and pulled up. He signalled to me that the others were not following. So there I was, left alone with Huns, not a very pleasant situation I assure you. I used up my ammunition quickly, as I only had 131 shells, and that didn't last long with a gun shooting 650 per minute. I did all the stunts that I could think of and finally went down as though I was hit. The Germans, thinking that I was going to land, left me for a minute. Then I turned and off I went. With the slight start that I had I managed to escape. We commenced the fight at 12,000 feet and finished at 1,800 feet. I arrived O.K. after one of the closest shaves I ever had.[28]

McConnell summarised another one of Bert's side trips at around the same time. 'At Nancy, Hall left the patrol to make a little tour in the direction of Metz. It wasn't a time for a thing like that. However, he soon found that he was getting lost and decided to follow us again.'[29]

Three days later, the second victory would come to the unit. This time it would be Bert Hall who would be victorious. On 22 May, Bert went out on the morning sortie that proved to be less than stellar. He spotted three German Aviatiks at 4,000 metres and dove in on them, failing to bring any of them down.[30] To take on three German aircraft alone behind enemy lines was an incredibly brave manoeuvre, but Bert was not satisfied. That afternoon, he was at 4,000 metres over the French lines when he spotted a German Aviatik C observation airplane. Hall did not flinch, no doubt still disappointed at not downing an airplane earlier in the day. Now, with the odds even, he dove down on the Aviatik. The German swung about, aiming his machine for the German lines. Bert's machine gun riddled the airplane, killing the pilot and sending the plane in a shallow dive towards the German side of the front. Rather than break away, Bert followed the Aviatik down, his own plane being hit several times as the observer attempted to drive him off of his tail. When he was at a 1,000 metres, he saw the enemy aeroplane smash into the ground. Bert angled his Nieuport back to the friendly side of the lines. His victory was confirmed by a French observation post. Kiffin Rockwell noted in a postcard to his brother that Bert had downed the aeroplane south of Verdun.[31] Kiffin penned a more detailed letter to his brother that day but ended with the note, 'Give Bertie some publicity.'[32]

Based on the aircraft downed, and the vicinity of other patrols that day by the escadrille, it is most likely that Bert downed pilot Gefreiter George Schöpf and observer Leutnant Ludwig Frhr. Von Türcke of FA 206 near Guewenheim.[33]

Kiffin Rockwell summed up the results of his and Hall's victories. 'It is a regular hell here. The worlds has gone crazy. Our activity keeps the Germans out of the air, but flying over the enemy lines we see myriads of gray ants as German soldiers appear from heights. We need sleep badly.'[34] It was an equally important day for Thaw who was promoted to full-Lieutenant for his leadership role in the escadrille.

Paul Rockwell did not hesitate to send out the news of Bert Hall's victory as well, though he was often listed as Bert Hall '...from Bowling Green Kentucky' or '...from the Lone Star State.'[35] Bert stepped forward to take his much deserved drink from the Bottle of Death.

Two days later, the men of N 124 got bloodied badly. While on a morning patrol, Thaw dove on a Fokker E III and brought it down north of Vaux, the third victory of the unit. That afternoon, Capitaine Thénault led sortie consisting of de Laage, Thaw, Chapman and Rockwell. They came across a flight of twelve German aircraft. The ever-impulsive Chapman did not wait for the signal from Capitaine Thénault to attack, instead he dived in on the enemy. Rockwell and Thaw followed him in, mostly to protect their comrade. The dogfight was brutal. Chapman was able to claim downing a Fokker that went unconfirmed. In the process of the melee, he was wounded in the arm. Kiffin Rockwell's Nieuport was struck in the windscreen with an explosive bullet that shattered, cutting his face with glass and hot metal fragments. Thaw also downed a confirmed Fokker though his machine gun jammed in the process. He came under brutal fire from two Aviatiks. In manoeuvring to turn away from them, flying almost totally defensive, one put a bullet through his left elbow and fuel tank. Fuel soaked his legs and feet as he reeled under the agony of his wound.

Pilots feared fire almost more than any other fate. Their aircraft were often made of wood and doped fabric, making them highly liable to burn. French aviators did not wear parachutes. With open cockpits and the wind whipping at a high speed made fire to be an agonising death for those that were so unlucky. Thaw had the presence of mind to kill his engine and glided his Nieuport over the lines, pancaking it near Fort Travennes. He managed to clamour out of the wreckage of his airplane and was sent to a hospital to recover from his wounds.

For the Americans, it was a vicious and visual reminder that this was not a game. Three of them had been wounded in less than twenty minutes. So far none of the Americans had died, but they realised how dangerous aerial combat could be. Arriving that day for posting to the escadrille was Raoul Lufbery as a replacement for William Thaw. If Bill Thaw was the soul of the Escadrille Américaine and Kiffin Rockwell the heart of the unit, Lufbery was destined to be its spirit. His life was even more adventurous than Bert's. He, like Bert, was born in 1885, but in the case of Lufbery, his place of birth was France to French parents. His mother died when he was young and his father immigrated to the US in 1891, leaving him in the care of his French grandmother. At a young age, Raoul travelled the world, from Algiers Tunis Egypt and Constantinople. He crisscrossed Europe and finally visited his father in 1906. After so many years apart it was not hard to image the two men not getting along. In 1912, in Calcutta, Raoul was introduced to aviation at an exhibition of Blériot monoplanes. Lufbery became friends with Marc Pourpe who was demonstrating the aircraft for large crowds and went under his tutelage. Working as Pourpe's mechanic, Raoul learned everything he could about aircraft.

When war broke out, Pourpe enlisted in the Air Service while Lufbery enlisted in the Foreign Legion. Pourpe was killed on 2 December 1914 but this did not deter Raoul's desire to get into the air. He transferred to the Air Service and was assigned to VB 106 flying Voisin bombers for a period. His transfer to the Escadrille Américaine was an interesting choice since Lufbery was a Frenchman in both genetics and upbringing, yet it would be this young man that would be the embodiment of American aviators. The press overlooked his nationality and in most cases he was labelled as an American in newspapers of the time.

Lufbery was not the only reserve pilot rotated into the escadrille. Clyde Balsley, Charles Johnson, Dudley L. Hill and Laurence Rumsey all joined the unit. Hill joined on 9 June. Hailing from Peekskill, New York, his father owned a company that manufactured stoves. Hill had come to France in 1915 to drive ambulances and ended up enlisting in the Foreign Legion as a transfer point to join the French Air Service. The reserved and gentle Balsley came from San Antonio, Texas, and had attended the West Texas Military Academy and one year of collage at the University of Texas in Austin before rushing to France to join the American Ambulance Hospital. Charles Chouteau Johnson received his law degree from the University of Virginia where he had been classmates with Jimmy McConnell and Andrew Courtney Campbell (would would later join N 124). Johnson served in the American Ambulance Service, then enlisted in the Foreign Legion before transferring to the air service. Laurence Rumsey was the scion of a wealthy tannery and railroad tycoon who was best known before the war for his polo playing while he attended Harvard. These replacements were pressed into action quickly.

The constant flying and fighting was taking a toll not just on Hall but on his aeroplane as well. On 28 May, Bert's Nieuport was wrecked upon his return to Bar-le-Duc. 'Prince has smashed completely and Hall as well,' per Kiffin Rockwell.[36] This was further described by James McConnell. 'Prince and Hall broke their machines to splinters.'[37] Either as a result of this accident or shortly thereafter, Bert Hall received a new Nieuport 16 (tail number 1208). The constant strain of war was beginning to show on all of the men. Capitaine Thénault sent Kiffin Rockwell to the Nieuport factory as a pretence to get him some much needed rest and recuperation.[38] Despite the need for down time, Kiffin returned to the unit after a few days away.

In keeping with the tradition of painting their aircraft to personalise and make them identifiable, Bert decorated his new plane as well. The Nieuport 16 was almost identical to the Nieuport 11 except that it was equipped with a more powerful 110-hp Le Rhome rotary motor. Armed with a Vickers machine gun, it carried 1,000 rounds of ammunition. 'The sides and support portions of the 'Bert' were camouflé, to disguise it against the Verdun landscape. These decorations corresponded exactly to the red clay of the soil and the green of the country – large, irregular placed spots of both colours. Underneath, the 'Bert' was painted sky-blue and bore the French insignia – blue, white and red circles.'[39] On one side of his aircraft in large letters, he painted 'Bert.' On the opposing side, he painted 'Treb.' On the fuselage behind the cockpit, facing skywards, he painted a large letter 'H.' Where he had bullet hole patches, he asked his mechanic Leon to paint dollar signs on them.[40]

Other men adopted logos that personified their backgrounds. James McConnell painted a large footprint, homage to his membership in the Hot Foot Society at the University of Virginia. Clyde Balsley painted a white Lone Star of Texas in honour of his home state on the side of his machine. Rumsey's Nieuport bore the name 'RUM' on the side of it.

Bert was becoming accustomed to the rigours of aerial combat. James McConnell's letter summarising a typical engagement from 1 June 1916, typifies the work that Bert and the men of the escadrille undertook. 'Landed here and the Captain asked me if I could go out at 12.30. Didn't know country at all and saw map for the first time when I climbed in machine. Lovebury [sic] left then I. Just as Hall was starting he looked up and saw a flock of Boches overhead. Lovebury and I must have passed right under them. Capt. T., Cowdin, Prince, Chapman & Hall mounted to attack. Kiffin's machine was on the bum and he couldn't go. They got their height and returned to fight on the 14 Boches who by this time were over town dropping bombs. The Boches used explosive bullets. Cap. T. had a hole blown in his tank and came down.

Prince had the bottom of carlingue blown up and was put out of commission. Cowdin's mitrailleuse went on the bum. Hall and Chapman chased the Boches to the lines but lost them.'[41] Facing more than two-to-one odds, the men of N 124 were obviously not cowards to combat.

Bert's activities on 3 June had him flying in pursuit of a German bomber that had been terrorising the Champagne front. 'I picked him up yesterday just after one of his little bombing parties on the way to Paris. He was several hundred yards higher than me so I had to sit tight while he peppered me with a machine gun. I finally got level with him over Meaux, but of course, as soon as I got ready to fire, he swung off into a cloud bank and I didn't see any more of him until I spotted him winging back over the trench line. I guess I kept him from getting to Paris, but that's not much consolation.'[42]

On 17 June, the escadrille was on patrol near the Meuse River when Victor Chapman saw a formation of German aircraft in the distance. He disregarded the visual commands waved to him by Capitaine Thénault and dived into the midst of the enemy planes. As Kiffin Rockwell put it in a letter to his brother Paul, 'Chapman has been a little too courageous and got me into one of the mess-ups because I couldn't stand back and see him get it alone. He was attacking at the time, without paying much attention. He did the same thing this morning and wouldn't come home when the rest of us did. The result was that he attacked one German, when a Fokker which we think was Boelke [sic] (the papers say he was killed but we don't believe it), got full on Chapman's back, shot his machine to pieces and wounded Chapman in the head. It is just a scratch but a miracle that he wasn't killed. Parts of the commands on Chapman's machine were broken, but Chapman landed by holding them together in his hand.'[43] It was not Oswald Boelcke that claimed the victory that day but was Leutnant Walter Höhndorf who claimed downing Victor Chapman as the fifth of his eventual fourteen victories.[44]

Jimmy McConnell's account matches with that of Rockwell. 'Considering the number of fights that he has been in and the courage with which he attacked it was a miracle that he had not been hit before. His machine was a sieve of patched up bullet holes. The day he was wounded he attacked four machines. Swooping down from behind, one of them, a Fokker, riddled Chapman's plane. One bullet cut deep into his scalp, but Chapman, a master pilot, escaped from the trap, and fired several shots to show that he was safe.'[45] Victor was so anxious to get back into the fight, he showed up at Behonne with a field dressing on his head and asking to go up on the afternoon sortie. Thénault offered him a chance to go to Paris to recover and he refused. The capitaine finally resorted to bribery, offering him a new Nieuport 16 if he stayed out of the air. The ploy worked.

18 June 1916 brought about the first casualty of the escadrille. Clyde Balsley went up on what was to be his first and only combat sortie of the war. Capitaine Thénault led Balsley, Rockwell and Prince on a mission to provide air cover for several artillery réglage aircraft over the German lines. They were flying at 3,500 metres when a large enemy patrol swarmed in on them. The wily Texan angled downwards at a two-seater Aviatik, closing to within fifty metres. He opened fire at a killing range to his dismay, his Lewis gun fired one shot then jammed. Given the gun was mounted high on top of the Nieuport's upper wing, it was difficult if not impossible to clear the jam... not in the heat of battle at least. Balsley tried to get clear of the dogfight but an Aviatik swooped in on his tail, firing at him while another dived in on him from above. He was struck in the hip by an explosive bullet, sending jagged shrapnel into his guts. Years later he described the ordeal:

Around and down I went. It was all over. Soon I should hit the ground as I had seen many friends hit it. That would be all. How strange that I, the I who had seemed undying, should hit the ground like all the rest! I remembered a boy I had picked up when I first started training. I should look like that.

Making a supreme effort, I tried to push my bad leg with my hand, but the controls were so wedged that I could not move them. If I hit here, I should be a German prisoner. Working my right leg desperately with my hands, I felt the kinks come out of the commands at last. Once more the machine was on the level.

Then I heard again the sound of bullets. My gun was still useless, my entire right side was paralysed and I was bleeding like a pig, but at that sound I dived again. This time I kept control of my machine. I was low enough now to see through the mist the trench lines and the snaky curve of the river. I put my plane in more than a vertical dive, shooting back under the Germans, so far that the roll of cartridges fell out, and, falling, hit my arm. I thought I had been struck again. Everything was now falling out.

I looked at my altimeter. Eight hundred feet above the ground. I was going to hit in Germany!

I could see the trenches. I must get home! I went so fast that I could hardly recognise the trenches, and so far that I had left my enemies behind.

I was now growing too faint to go on. I saw a green field, and, making a turn to the left, came up to the wind and dived for the field. Too late I saw that it was filled with barbed wire; I was landing between the front-line trenches and the reserve lines. The barbed wire caught my wheels, and very gently my machine turned completely upside down. I knew that it was going over me. I should bleed to death, after all.

In the field next to me I saw a burst of smoke, then a white spot; then another and another, before I realised what it meant. The Germans were shelling me. They had seen me fall; they were trying to destroy my machine.

When the shelling stopped, someone would come for me. I suffered so little pain that I knew I was not badly wounded. I should be sent to Paris. I wondered who my nurse would be. Then I would come back to the squadron and the next time I would get my German. But it was more of the good times in Paris that I thought than of my job.

The shelling stopped. Tired of waiting, I tried to crawl. I could not move. I got up on my hands and knees to try again, but could no more move than if I had been staked to the ground. Finally, catching the grass, I dragged myself like a dog with a broken back. Inch by inch I made about ten yards; then I could go no farther.

It was now about six o'clock in the morning. The sun, which had driven away the mist, flamed down upon me in the unshaded field. I took the shoe off my right foot; it dripped red. Utterly exhausted by this effort, I could feel only a dumb wonder at the sight. Somehow I could not connect that bleeding foot with myself. I was all right. I must let my mother know this at once.

Then I would go to Paris for those good times.

After I had waited a few minutes longer, four French soldiers came, stooping low; they, too, had kept quiet till the shelling had ceased. Crawling under the barbed wire, they caught hold of me and asked me what was the matter. 'Bullet — in my — hip,' I muttered, choking back with each word a groan at the touch of their hands. The pain of their rough grasp was so severe that now for the first time I wondered, could my wound be worse than I had thought? 'Can you walk?' they asked in French. '*Mais non,*' I said, indignantly.

Two took me by the shoulders, two by the feet. Then, like a beast unleashed, my pain broke from its long stupor. Almost crawling to escape the enemy's eye, the four men dragged me, like a sack of grain, through the long grass, over and under and across the web of barbed wire. The pain had now become such torture that I almost fainted.

I do not know how long that journey lasted. All I do know is that at last we came to the dressing-station behind the trenches.[46]

His Nieuport flipped, throwing him out. Bruised and battered from the crash, bleeding from his hip, Balsley dragged himself away from the wreck. A patrol of French soldiers found and dragged him to an evacuation hospital at Vadelaincourt, near Verdun. Balsley's first and only combat mission had nearly cost him his life. As it was he would walk with a limp the rest of his life. Worse yet, his own severe wounding would cost the Escadrille Américaine its first fatality.[47]

Clyde Balsley was hospitalised with damage to his intestinal tract from the exploding bullet that had gone off on his hip. The nerves to his right leg were damaged as well. Victor Chapman flew up to visit him on 21 June, bringing him is toothbrush. Balsley was struggling with his injuries, made worse by the fact that the physicians not letting him drink water. 'How about oranges?' Victor asked. Sucking on those would be fine according to the doctors. Chapman promised to bring him some oranges on his next visit.

On the morning of 23 June, Victor Chapman had gone on the dawn patrol and managed to damage a strut. Capitaine Thénault led the patrol that included Prince and Lufbery in addition to the late-joining Chapman who had to wait while his mechanic fixed his earlier damage. In his Nieuport, he carried a sack of oranges, chocolate and letters that had come for Balsley. His plan was to fly to the aerodrome near where Clyde was hospitalised but he decided, at the last minute, to continue on the sortie with the rest of the escadrille. The pilots of N 124 on the afternoon patrol encountered five German aircraft. They engaged in a brief dogfight with the enemy and saw Victor Chapman in the mix. They broke off the engagement and returned to Behonne assuming that Victor had disengaged as well, heading off to see Balsley. A nearby French Maurice Farman crew reported seeing one Nieuport tangle with an enemy fighter, only to be pounced upon by three more Germans.

Victor Chapman's natural reckless aggressive combat style did not save him on this encounter. He was seen crashing at Haumont near Samoneux, several kilometres behind the front lines in German territory.[48] While the men of the escadrille had felt that it was Oswald Boelcke that had taken out Victor, indeed that was the story that was released to the press. This helped offset the loss for the Americans, one of their young boys being killed by a top-ranking German ace. It did not soften the blow, however, the Escadrille Américaine had suffered its first fatality. Many sought to make Victor out to be a hero, when in reality he had been wildly reckless and it had cost him his life. While propagandists thrived on creating such myths, the reality was almost as grim as being taken out by Boelcke. Victor was killed by Lieutnant Kurt Wintgens as his nineteenth victory.[49]

Chapman's loss stunned the men of the escadrille. Some, like Kiffin Rockwell, wanted revenge. The day after Chapman's death he wrote: 'I am afraid it is going to rain tomorrow, but if not, Prince and I are going to fly about ten hours and do our best to kill one or two Germans for Victor.' Bert's reaction to the death of Victor was reserved. 'It was here (Bar-le-Duc) that we lost one of our best and bravest men, Victor Chapman. The combat occurred just to the north of Fort Douaumont. Victor was engaged with six or seven German machines and he didn't have a chance. He fought to the last inch and fell, dying, inside the German lines. Just where, I don't know. But some day I hope to find his grave and pay my respects to one of the bravest of the brave.'[50]

The first of the members of the Escadrille to involuntarily leave the unit was Elliot Cowdin on 25 June 1916. Capitaine Thénault officially listed the reason as 'ill health', but this was a ruse to conceal the truth. Cowdin, Bert's old friend from his days in the Legion, did not play well with others. He was known to be a man that curried favours from the commanding officers of the unit. He argued and fought with his comrades in N 124. The men of the unit rallied against him. Cowdin, in response, was known to take unauthorised leaves which made matters worse. The French were known to be lax with foreign volunteers on such matters, but Cowdin was clearly taking advantage of their leniency. Thénault finally had him listed for desertion and he was arrested and brought back to the unit. The choice he was presented was simple: transfer or face the wrath of military justice for desertion. He was sent off to another escadrille.[51] For Bert, it had to be a blow to have someone he knew so well, who had been in aviation in the war from the beginning, to be driven out of the unit. Little did he realise that it was a portent of things to come.

On 30 June, Hall went up with McConnell to provide air support/cover for Norman Prince on a balloon-busting mission. Prince flew a Nieuport equipped with Le Prieur rockets mounted on the vertical struts on the wings. These were essentially giant bottle rockets that could be launched a close range at an observation balloon. Taking out observation balloon was tricky business. These balloons were used to observe enemy troops movements and positions. Filled with hydrogen they were large tempting explosive targets. Their temptation was so great that ground forces on both sides surrounded balloons with anti-aircraft batteries, machine guns and usually had fighters flying in support. Going after a balloon, balloon-busting as it was called, required nerves of steel. Normal bullets tore holes in the gas bag but usually did not set it off. The best threat for such targets were either rockets or explosive bullets. Taking one out with Le Prieur rockets meant that one had to close within fifty metres or so before firing, flying the airplane through a hail of anti-aircraft fire. Providing cover for such a mission meant you too were a target for anti-aircraft fire as well as evading enemy fighters at the same time. Norman took out the balloon with Bert flying in support (though Bert incorrectly recorded the date as 1 August).[52] While Jimmy McConnell spotted the victory, the target was six miles behind enemy lines and there was no ground confirmation possible.

Bert's rough character did not play well with some of the other Americans that were fighting alongside him. James McConnell wrote to Paul Rockwell on 1 July: 'I was greatly surprised at the developments re our boy Hall... Norman predicted that Hall would follow in the footsteps of Cowdin and take 'the cure' but it's hard to say. As we all know his is an awful liar and hot air artist, and every time he sees a fire on the ground he comes rushing back and reports bringing down a Boche but I believe he has the where with all in a pinch. We'll have a long talk all around when you come out, and be damned sure to come out.'[53] It is clear from this message that some of the men of N 124 arranged for Cowdin's departure and were marking Bert Hall for a similar treatment.

In early July, Bert received the Médaille Militaire for his first victory back in May along with Kiffin Rockwell. William Thaw received an accommodation as well. Per Jimmy McConnell, 'Kiffin, Hall and Billy were decorated today. Informal affair which was better than having a lot of swank.'[54] For Bert, it was his first medal in the war. His citation read:

> The Médaille Militaire is conferred upon W. Bert Hall, sergeant of Escadrille N.124 and engaged volunteer for the duration of the war. After having served in the infantry, been twice wounded, transferred to aviation. Has very rapidly become a pilot of the first class and very outstanding gunner. Very intelligent, energetic, and most audacious.
>
> Has fulfilled his demanding missions of great peril and danger over German lines on many occasions. On 22 May 1916 he engaged the enemy in severe combat and destroyed two adversaries within a few hundred metres of our trenches. This nomination carries the Croix de Guerre and one palm leaf.[55]

The men were given leave on 4 July 1915 to celebrate Independence Day. They travelled to Paris and indulged in a party. On Bastille Day, they held a celebration at Bar-le-Duc that was apparently a wild time. The men were joined by Sous-Lieutenant Charles Nungesser, one of France's greatest aces. He had been hospitalised (for the third time in the war) with a broken nose, jaw, a dislocated knee and bullet fragments in his lip. Like so many other aviators, he could not abide simply sitting around the hospital and instead went to visit the men of the all-American escadrille. Per Jimmy McConnell, 'We had a big time on the 14th in honour of France. With the result that Rumsey and Johnson couldn't fly for a while.'[56]

Nungesser was nothing if not flamboyant. He wore his medals proudly, even on his flying suit. He recanted his victories to the men of N 124 and anyone else that would listen. At the time, he was the number two ace behind Georges Guynemer. For a short period of time he was 'attached' to the Escadrille Américaine and scored his tenth victory. If not for the fact that Guynemer scored his eleventh at the same time, Nungesser would have been able to claim that he was France's top ace.

If Chapman's death shook Bert's own courage, it certainly did not show. On 23 July 1916, Bert was heavily engaged with the enemy. Kiffin Rockwell recorded the entire affair for his brother Paul in a letter:

> In the middle of the day Bert and I went out alone. I found an Aviatik and dived on him. Two Fokkers dived on me; Bert dived on the two Fokkers, and two more Fokkers went on him. In that line of battle went down through the air about two thousand metres. I got within ten metres of my Aviatik, shot all of my shots into him, and he began to fall in the clouds, and then I disappeared in the clouds.
>
> I thought that I had gotten the Aviatik, but a post of observation that saw the fight said he readdressed. As for Bert, he shot his shots into one Fokker, then the other two got right on his back. They came d____d close to getting him, plugged a lot of bullets around him in the machine, but he wasn't touched.[57]

In a letter to Alice Weeks, McConnell wrote: 'It was a parade downward, everyone shooting at once. Hall got ten holes in his plane and Kiffin and he got away by hiding in the clouds.'[58] In another letter detailing the battle, Kiffin wrote, 'Hall seemed to be stalking him, then attacked him viciously. He may be a dastardly blowhard, but the man had skill and a killer's instinct...'[59]

The American press, fed by Paul Rockwell, claimed that Rockwell and Hall had been lured into a trap. They employed a new 'Yankee trick', diving into a cloud to break off the engagement. Using the clouds for cover was far from being new or something that the Americans had invented, but to the people back in the US it was an exciting escapade.[60]

Apparently, based on the letters, Bert must have gone up one more time later in the day and secured his second confirmed victory. Per James McConnell's brief description, 'Hall brought down a Boche in their lines. He said he hadn't attacked and was just shooting to bother the German when a lucky ball hit him.'[61] Bert's own account supports this. 'A little later, along in July according to the record in my Aviation Corps book, I brought down my second Boche plane that happened over Fort de Vaux. It wasn't really much of a fight, for I don't think he saw me until it was too late.'[62] It was far from the kind of boastful exploits that Hall is often attributed as taking part in.

Bert's kill was confirmed in August. While difficult to verify, the only German casualty that day was Observer Lieutnant Walter Bräutigam of KG6/Ks 33. The fact that the pilot is not listed as having been killed or taken prisoner, it is probable the machine went down over German lines which fits McConnell's description of the engagement.[63] It was also a victory that exposed some of the interpersonal conflicts within N 124. Kiffin's letters from the period indicate that there were tensions between some of the men and Bert seemed to be bearing the brunt of it.

> Right now I don't care to take a *permission*, as I want to keep up with everything that goes on around her. I want to be changed to a French Escadrille unless certain conditions change here, and several others will follow my example.
>
> I think I have the most hours of flight and the most flights for the month of July on the Verdun front of any Nieuport pilot, but am not sure. I don't think, however, that a full report of my work has gone out of this office, and a number of times my report on a flight has been changed. The machine that Hall brought down X. did his best to prove that it wasn't brought down, and so far Bert hasn't even been proposed for a citation.[64]

Paul Rockwell heavily edited the published letters of his brother after the war, but retained many of the original copies. The mysterious 'X' that was attempting to suppress Bert's victories was, in a reality, Norman Prince.[65] Bert's loyalty and devotion to the men the escadrille, at least when in the air, was unchallenged at the time. As Kiffin Rockwell wrote, 'Hall saved my skin, no doubt about it. When we returned, both our ships were more hole than whole.'[66]

On 27 July, Bert engaged with one enemy plane, nearly downing him. 'On July 27th, I had another one down to three hundred feet, but he escaped as I ran out of ammunition.'[67] The version he told members of the escadrille may have been different. From Kiffin Rockwell's recollection, '...Bert Hall thinks he brought one down also. Yet so far none of them is officially confirmed, so they may report three machines or they may not report any.'[68] On that same day, Lieuenant de Laage de Meux secured his first victory since joining the unit.

What followed that victory was a string of enemy kills by Raoul Lufbery. He earned a drink from the Bottle of Death to avenge his mentor Marc Pourpe on 30 July 1916 when he shot down a two-seater near Forêt d'Etain. The following day he downed another aeroplane over Fort Vaux. On 4 August 1916, he and another future ace, Adjutant Victor Sayaret of N 57, successful scored a victory over another two-seater. Four days after this victory, Lufbery engaged a lone Aviatik south of Douaumont, sending the plane crashing down in flames. In twelve days, Lufbery had scored four victories and put a serious dent in the Bottle of Death.

On 24 August, Bert went up in the afternoon with Dudley Hill on patrol. Bert was engaged in combat but secured no victories. That changed on 24 August when Bert went on patrol with Laurence Rumsey and Dudley Hill.

Bert was credited with downing an enemy northeast of Douaumont at 1900 hours. For Bert, it was destined to be the last time that he would take a drink from the Bottle of Death, though it would not be the last victory he secured in the war.

Sometime near the end of August and the start of September, Bert received a new aircraft, a Nieuport 21. Rather than continue his paint scheme of 'BERT' and 'TREB', Hall picked a design that was more befitting his personality. He had the ground crew paint large dollar signs on the sides of the fuselage.

Flights and dogfights happened almost daily during the summer of 1916. Hall witnessed plenty of strange events while engaging the enemy. 'I once saw a Hun fall fifteen thousand feet from an aeroplane when nothing had happened to the machine. The only thing that I can figure it out is that he was not strapped in. We were chasing him at the time, and I remember the thrill of horror I had when I saw him pitch over to the side. You don't mind it very much if you shoot any enemy down in a fair fight; but to see him fall, through an accident, is not very inspiring.'[69]

In September, Bert was in the air often. On 2 September, he went out on a morning patrol with Paul 'Skipper' Pavelka, Dudley Hill and Didier Masson. Pavelka was a known personality to Bert as they had both served in the Foreign Legion together. The next day, he went up with Masson, Johnson and Rumsey in the afternoon. Bert got into an engagement with the enemy, but was forced to break off the attack when his gun malfunctioned. After two days of rain on 6 September, Bert was in the skies once more with Hill and Pavelka. Kiffin Rockwell went up at the same time and he too had to break off with an enemy aircraft when his gun jammed as Bert's had two days earlier.[70]

Didier Masson was no novice to aviation. He had first flown an early Farman in 1909 and had been a flight instructor in New York prior to the war. For a short time he flew for the Mexican Army. When the war broke out, he returned to his native France and served in the 129th and 36th Infantry regiments before transferring to the air service in 1915.

On 12 September, Capitaine Thénault received a telegram from Lufbery who was supposed to be on leave. 'I am in prison at Chartres.' A railroad employee had been rude to him and had laid hands on him physically, something that Lufbery took as an offence, given he had been recently awarded the Médaille Militaire. His response was to punch the railroad employee in the mouth, breaking six of his teeth. Thénault was able to negotiate his release, but for a short time after his return Lufbery carried the moniker of 'jail bird.'[71]

The escadrille was ordered back to Luxeuil on 14 September 1916. The purpose of this was to have N 124 provide support to Capitaine Maurice Happe's bombers. Happe's Group de Bombardement No. 4 had already become the most infamous bombing unit in the French Air Service. Capitaine

Happe was energetic and a red-bearded man that earned him the nickname 'Le Corsaire Rouge' (The Red Corsair). His unit favoured using slow and obsolete Farman pusher aircraft. While vulnerable to attacks from the rear, the lumbering aircraft could operate for four hours and carry almost a hundred pounds of bombs. Because of their slow speed and vulnerabilities they needed strong fighter support. Happe's bombing raids had been so successful the Germans had a 25,000-mark bounty placed on his head.[72]

The Americans assigned to protect Happe's planes who were flying Nieuport 16s were upgraded to Nieuport 17s during this period. The fighter had an increased wing area and a new fuselage design which combined to make it easier for aviators to manoeuvre. The Nieuport 17 had an additional twenty-square feet of wing surface and a 110-hp motor which gave the aircraft good speed and climbing rate. It could climb to 7,000 feet in less than six minutes. While its ceiling was 18,000 feet, it was still less than contemporary German fighters at the front at the time.

While the personnel and gear were relocated to Luxeuil, the aviators were given three days leave in Paris. The Nieuport 17 had a Vickers machine gun mounted in front of the pilot and synchronised with the propeller. The escadrille picked up a number of replacement pilots during this leave period. Robert Rockwell, a distant cousin of Kiffin and Paul, transferred from the Ambulance Service into the French Air Service and had recently completed his training. Likewise, Willis Haviland joined the unit along with Robert Soubiran and Frederick Prince, Norman's brother.

The most curious addition to the unit came via a newspaper advertisement in the Paris edition of the *New York Herald*. Dudley Hill saw a classified advertisement put in by a Brazilian dentist that caught his eye. The dentist had a four-month-old lion cub for sale. He had initially purchased it for his office to entertain his clients, but some had found the presence of a growling lion disturbing. The men decided that the lion cub would make a perfect mascot for N 124. Hill, Hall, Johnson, Prince, Thaw and Kiffin Rockwell all pooled their money together to get the 500 francs that the dentist was asking.

Having a pet lion forced the aviators to change hotels in Paris. To get him back to Luxeuil, Thaw had planned to simply take him on the train purchasing a 'dog ticket'. Unfortunately, the cub's playfulness and growling upset several female passengers and Thaw was told that his 'African dog' was not allowed to ride with the passengers. Bill had to pay for a wooden cage so he could travel with the luggage.

The daughters of the owner of the Pomme d'Or Hotel where the aviators were lodging developed an instant love of the cub, tying pink ribbons around his neck. For his part the lion developed a taste for the occasional saucer of whiskey, which earned him his name. Along with the three dogs that were considered mascots for the escadrille, Whiskey soon became the most popular. With the American press, the pet lion added a great deal of appeal with the newspaper readers and helped make members of the escadrille stand out even more than before. Within a few weeks, Whiskey was more widely known than some members of N 124. If nothing else, he added to the mystique of the escadrille.

Whiskey proved to be friendly and playful. He rarely scratched or bit anyone other than playing, but his habit of chewing pillows, boots, dress uniforms, hats and other personal gear made him somewhat less lovable. With their new pet also came onlookers.

Hardly a day passed that we didn't have from twenty-five to fifty visitors, mostly poilus in rest camps and the like, curious to inspect the planes and attracted by stories of the Americans and their lion, stories which, before their arrival, few of them credited.

Luf would wait for a good opportunity, then send Whiskey around the corner of the barracks out of sight, while we lined up to see the fun.

His thoughts far away on other and perhaps more amorous matters, an unsuspecting poilu would stroll by the corner where Whiskey lay in hiding. Luf would give the signal. Whiskey with a ferocious roar, would leap out, throw his huge paws over the shoulders of the victim and drag him to the ground by sheer weight.

In most cases the unfortunate soldier would be so petrified with fear at the apparition of this savage best springing out on him so unexpectedly, that his knees would simply collapse under him. He'd go down and lie like a low, stark fear in his eyes, as Whiskey poised over him, apparently ready to tear him to bits.

Then Whiskey would put his head back and open his mouth wide, showing all his yellowed fangs in a silent laugh. At least Luf always said it was a laugh...

Luf would quickly call Whiskey, and he'd come trotting over, purring over his achievement, begging for another victim. Sheepishly the rescued victim would get up, come over and be urged to pet the savage appearing but docile animal, which, if he did at all, would be done most gingerly and suspiciously.[73]

Whiskey was not the only pet in camp and Bert's was one that was most unique.

It's a funny thing about animals. Of course all of us had pets in camp. You'll never find a bunch of decent men anywhere, in that kind of life, that won't have annexed something that goes on four legs. I had a goat for my particular pet and, just like all of the other fellows, I was crazy to take him up in the air with me. I did it once when I wasn't going too high, but when I landed he acted as if he was drunk – reeled around as if he'd been on a regular bat. Dogs will die at six thousand feet altitude, and cats can't go up more than three thousand feet.[74]

On the surface, and to the many visitors, the relationship of the men in the escadrille seemed strong. Any undercurrents of discord were rarely seen. The return of operations at Luxeuil began again on 23 September 1916. For the men of N 124, this was to be devastating day. And for Bert Hall, it was to begin the spiral that led to him leaving the all-American escadrille.

CHAPTER SIX

A Falling Out Among Eagles

Many of the things which I am going to tell about my pals in the Foreign Legion and the Lafayette Escadrille happened after we broke up and got scattered, but no matter. We were together more or less until the Boche got one after another of the bunch. A few of us are still here to get back at him. We were proud of being Americans, and that is why I want to tell the records of these men, the things I saw and know about them.[1]

– Bert Hall, 1918

The loss of Victor Chapman reminded the men of the Escadrille Américaine that they were indeed mortal. But there was always a little hesitancy in what the men wrote or said about Victor and his demise. It was always tempered with his aggressive and reckless nature, a subtle implication that his own actions had contributed or even caused the fate that befell him. The next loss to the men was one that was going to sting deeper and in Hall's case, cause a rift that would pester him throughout his life.

On the evening of 22 September 1916, Kiffin Rockwell told James McConnell and the other men of N 124 that if he were ever brought down he wanted to be buried where he fell.[2] It was a solemn subject to bring up but not uncommon with such comrades in war. These men had been at the front for months and had fought savage battles in two of the Great War's most brutal campaigns, Champagne and Verdun. The loss of Chapman had to have stirred Kiffin's thoughts of his own mortality. Little did he realise how soon his request would be fulfilled.

On 23 September, Kiffin took to the air with Lufbery in a search for Germans to engage in battle over the Vosges. They spotted several Fokkers on patrol over Hartmansweilerkopf, but Lufbery's machine gun jammed. Luf broke off the engagement and headed to the aerodrome of N 49 near Fontaine in hopes of initiating some fast repairs. Kiffin flew along with him but did not land when Lufbery did. In typical style, he set off for the front alone while Luf made quick repairs to his Nieuport's synchronisation gear. Unable to find the flight of Fokkers he had seen earlier, Kiffin spotted a two-seater Albatros far below him. The best course of action for engaging the Albatros would have been to come at him from below and behind, under the firing arc of the pivot-mounted rear machine gun. This would have been the safest and best way to take on the enemy… but it was not Kiffin's style. He reduced his engine power and dove down on the German.

The observer in the Albatros opened up at long range, but Kiffin held his fire as the machine gun tore into his Nieuport. He waited until he was within thirty metres before letting loose with his Vicker's. His shots were far too few. One of the explosive bullets that the Albatros was firing hit him in the base of his throat and upper chest. His death was instant.

Observers who saw the battle watched as Rockwell's Nieuport falter in the air and then tumbled to the ground. On its way down one of its wings tore free only adding to the death spiral. Kiffin's plane crashed into a field of flowers in the rear of the French trenches.[3] He died three days after his twenty-fourth birthday. German artillery zeroed in on the wreckage and targeted it for a barrage to ensure that the aircraft was unrecoverable and to kill Rockwell if he had somehow survived. A handful of brave French infantrymen rushed through the barrage to pull Kiffin's shattered body from the debris. The ground observers quickly telephoned the news to the aerodromes nearby. When he heard the grim news at Fontaine, Lufbery took to the air looking for any German so as to provide payback for his friend's loss. He hovered over the German lines at the Habsheim aerodrome challenging any German to take to the air to fight him, but no one took the bait.[4] Vengeance was going to have to wait for another day.

Kiffin was arguably Bert Hall's second closest friend in the escadrille, his closest being Bill Thaw. The bond of battle that he and Thaw shared from their days in the trenches in the Legion was unshakeable, but Kiffin seemed to understand Bert and Bert respected Kiffin. Thaw and Bert were in Paris at the time and found out about their comrade's death at their hotel at noon when a call was placed to them from Luxeuil. Thaw set out to find Paul Rockwell and '…broke the news to him as gently as he could'. Bill Thaw escorted Paul Rockwell back to Luxeuil while Bert stayed in Paris.[5]

Hall's reaction to the news of the death shows an odd detachment. Rather than mourn the death of his friend, Bert allegedly '…rushed off to the Paris office of the *New York Times* and to other American journalists and peddled the story of his comrade's death to the newspapers.'[6] This was perfectly within Bert's devil-may-care attitude. It is doubtful that he realised that this action would earn him an enemy for life in the form of Kiffin's brother Paul.

The loss of Kiffin Rockwell hit all of the men of the escadrille hard. McConnell wrote, 'No greater blow could have befallen the escadrille. Kiffin was its soul.'[7] Kiffin's death changed Paul Rockwell and his attitude towards Bert Hall. Up until this point, he was all too eager via his role in public information/relations to promote Bert Hall and his exploits. 'Bert Hall is an aggressive fighter, unafraid of combat.'[8] Part of this was natural. Paul was not just Kiffin's brother, but had fought with him in battle when they had been in the Foreign Legion. Paul had been living vicariously through Kiffin since his infirmaries had prevented him from joining the French Air Service. His role in public information had made his promotion of the Escadrille his primary work.

Paul Rockwell wallowed in Kiffin's death. He then lionised his brother with an elaborate funeral. In a war where millions had died in senseless slaughter, the affair that Paul orchestrated for Kiffin seemed strangely out of proportion. Worse yet, he ignored Kiffin's last wishes to be buried where he fell. Fifty English aviators marched in the procession, along with 800 RFC mechanics and support personnel. These were augmented by '...a regiment of French Territorials infantry, a battalion of Colonials, and hundreds of French pilots and mechanics'.[9] Paul brought to bear the entire weight of French and American newspapers who took photos of the parade and funeral bier. Kiffin was not just a dead American aviator, he was turned into a hero. One grave was not enough for the fallen Rockwell. Paul asked that a cross be erected where his brother's plane crashed in addition to his burial site. Paul's personal files are filled with photographs of the site of the plane wreck and letters from aviators that visited the site. He kept them all as a personal shrine to his fallen brother.

Oddly enough Victor Chapman's death was noted by Paul Rockwell but largely downplayed except as a footnote of being the first American aviator to be killed in the escadrille. Some of this was likely to be because Chapman's body was lost behind enemy lines, but that does not account for all of it. It is clear that Paul Rockwell was carefully crafting the role that his brother played in N 124 in the eyes of the world.

A citation signed by General Joffre was read which praised him as '... an American pilot who ceaselessly won the admiration of his chiefs and his comrades by his sang-froid, his courage and his daring'. Kiffin was posthumously promoted to sous-Lieutenant. At the packed gravesite, Capitaine Thénault said: 'When Rockwell was in the air, no German passed ... and he was in the air most of the time ... The best and bravest of us all is no more.'[10] He closed the ceremony by simply stating, 'I could give no higher praise then to tell simply what he had done.'[11] James McConnell's comments revealed his regard for his fallen friend: 'Kiffin was imbued with the spirit of the cause for which he fought and gave his heart and soul to the performance of his duty. He said, 'I pay my part for Lafayette and Rochambeau,' and he gave the fullest measure.'[12] At the end of the ceremony, as if on cue, several aeroplanes circled overhead dropping flowers on the spectators. A teary-eyed Capitaine Thénault told the men under his command, 'The best and bravest of us is no more.'[13]

Bert was absent from the parade and the lavish spectacle that it had been corrupted into. This stung deeply at Paul. 'He did not return to Luxeuil for Kiffin Rockwell's funeral, nor did he ever express any feeling over Rockwell's death.'[14] But was this in Bert's character? He was a person that moved on with almost every aspect of his life. Bert had been in battle for over two years, death was something that he was no stranger to. Having witnessed the carnage and death of trench warfare and the savage brutality of aerial combat, he may not have wanted to take part in such a ceremony. And the fact that Bert was not at the funeral did not mean he was unmoved by Kiffin's untimely demise. It is possible that he was with his wife Suzanne nursing his emotions or was at a bar drowning his sorrows.

Paul's bitterness that Bert never expressed his feelings about Kiffin's death were more of a matter of bruised ego than anything else. Still, it was all that Paul Rockwell needed to begin his lifelong smear campaign around Hall.

Lufbery's quest for vengeance continued on 9 October when he went after a lone Fokker near the German aerodrome at Habsheim where he had all but dared the Germans to come into the air after Rockwell's death. This time he spied a lone single-seat Fokker, diving on it from behind. In ten minutes of twisting and deadly combat, Luf's Nieuport was riddled. His engine was knocked out and he was forced to glide across the lines back to the French side. When he landed he discovered that he had several holes in his fuel tank, one of his interplane struts was blasted and his left aileron was destroyed. Lufbery had been fortunate to survive the encounter: a bullet had grazed his chest and another had ripped open his left flying boot.[15] Revenge was proving to be both a seductive and dangerously mistress.

The entire reason for bringing N 124 back to Luxeuil was to have them work in conjunction with Capitaine Happe's bombers, acting as fighter protection. For the first time in the war, the French were contemplating the use of the rudimentary principles of strategic bombing. The intention was to use Luxeuil as a forward staging base to support the bombers. They would strike at key supply bases in Germany to cripple war production while at the same time major ground offensive operations would be launched. This would stress the German supply reserves and hopefully turn the tide of the war. The Somme campaign was launched on 1 July, but the bombing efforts up until that point had been marginal at best. An attempt to bomb the German fuel storage areas at Mulheim on 30 July had been done with only nine bombers and had not inflicted the necessary damage.

The new target chosen for the campaign was the Mauser arms works at Oberndorf. The target and date were kept secret until the day before the attack. On 11 October, while Thénault was on leave, the Escadrille Américaine received word that the following day they would be escorting Happe's bombers. The raid would consist of over sixty aircraft. Moreover, it would be a joint operation with the British. The plan was to launch a diversionary effort on Lörrach to force the enemy to respond to an attack there while the force would continue on deeper into Germany striking at Oberndorf. The fighters provided by the escadrille and the British would not have enough range to provide cover all of the way in – the flight was over 300 kilometres one way. So while the bombers continued on, the fighters would turn around at Ettenheim on the Rhine River to refuel, with the Americans landing at Corcieux.[16] They would then go up to rendezvous and escort the bombers on their return trip. It was a complicated plan given the lack of radios, the distances involved, the fact that the return would be in the evening and the aircraft were not equipped for night missions. Bert did not go on the raid. He received a new 110-hp Nieuport that day and made a training flight instead of being assigned to the attack force.[17]

It was early afternoon when the massive attack force got underway. The attack force consisted of fifteen Sopwith 1½ Strutters provided by the Royal Navy. These would be followed by sixteen Farman and Breguet bombers. Six British fighters provided additional RFC cover. The remainder of the force consisted of Nieuports assigned by French escadrilles. The Escadrille Américaine would provide four of these fighters. The men chosen for the mission were de Laage, Masson, Prince and Lufbery.

The outbound attack force went fine for the fighters, but after their escorts headed back for home, the bombers faced heavy anti-aircraft fire between Colmar and Neu-Breisach. They had counted on very little enemy fighter activity once they were that far into Germany, but instead the bombers were under almost constant pursuit by fighters. The attack went off as planned. The returning bombers eventually linked up with their escorts… along with numerous German fighters. Complicating matters, the bombers did not return in a single group, but trickled across the front in small groups, having been separated by the long flight and constant attacks by the enemy. The result of this was that rather than simply flying back across the lines with their charges, the escorts had to hang over the front for a prolonged period of time.

As such, crossing the front back into France was no easy affair. At least six German fighters were shot down during this period, including three by the men of the Escadrille Américaine. Norman Prince downed his third fighter, tying him with Bert Hall in terms of confirmed victories. Lufbery engaged with three Fokkers and secured his victory of the raid taking out a Fokker head-on under a hail of bullets.

Flying escort for the raid, Didier Masson pulled off a victory that is the stuff of legends among aviators of the First World War. He had not been watching his fuel gauge and in the excitement of combat his engine died, courtesy of a dry fuel tank. He began to glide towards the French lines, but his opponent, sensing Masson's plight, zoomed in for a kill, riddling Masson's Nieuport. His windscreen was shattered as was the instrument panel in front of him. His fuselage and upper wing were peppered with bullets, but he kept calm and managed to stay in the air. Didier could do little but attempt basic manoeuvres, each one costing him more and more altitude and putting him at risk of landing on the German side of the lines. As Masson's aeroplane slowed, the German miscalculated then overtook him. Masson angled his dying airplane over and fired at burst at the Fokker. The enemy pilot, so confident of a kill a few moments earlier, slumped over dead. His plane crashed in a ball of fire. Masson came so low over the German lines in his glide that infantry opened up on him. His barely crossed the front line, crashing his crippled plane into a shell crater. He scrambled away from wreck site just before enemy artillery zeroed in and destroyed the crippled fighter. Despite the loss of his machine, Didier had managed to shoot down an enemy fighter while gliding![18]

Darkness began to fall and the fighters and aerodromes were not equipped for night operations. Lieutenant de Laage made his way to the nearby aerodrome at Plombieres before it got too dark to land safely. Norman Prince and Raoul Lufbery chose to try to land at Corcieux. Even the skilled Lufbery struggled to land in the darkness with the field surrounded by trees and no lighting to guide the planes in. On his approach, he nearly hit high tension lines strung out at the far end of the field. Without a radio, he had no way to signal his comrade as to what was coming. Prince was not as fortunate. As Lufbery watched in horror, Prince's landing gear snagged a cable. The fighter flipped forwards and over, crashing onto the dark landing field. Worse for Prince, his seat belt snapped and he was thrown out of the Nieuport like a toy doll. Both of Prince's legs were shattered in the crash. He was still conscious when the first men rushed to him. 'Hearing the hum of a motor, and realising a machine was in the air, Prince told them to light gasoline fires on the field. Don't let another fellow come down and break himself up the way I've done.'[19]

Lufbery accompanied him to the hospital. 'I placed him in an ambulance, urging the driver to hurry him to the hospital at Gerardmer. Throughout the trip, Norman did not cease to talk and chat with the good humour that was one of his charming characteristics… He spoke of his desire to be back with the squadron soon. But in the meantime, he began to suffer horribly and at times his face would be distorted with pain. His hand, which I was holding between my own, was wet with sweat. His endurance was remarkable and when the pain became so intense that he grew faint, he sang to keep from losing consciousness.'[20] For a short time, it appeared that Prince would recover, though his flying days were likely to remain as a memory given his injuries. The day after his wreck, a blood clot formed in his brain and he went into a coma. The prognosis was grim. On 14 October, Capitaine's Happe and Thénault came to his bedside and issued the unconscious founder of the escadrille a field promotion to sous Lieutenant and decorating him with the Chevalier of the Legion of Honor.[21] The next day, Prince died. Prince's funeral rivalled that of Kiffin Rockwell, but was somewhat smaller. His caisson was draped in French and American flags and marched at the end of a parade of men from other escadrilles and his own N 124. He was initially interred in the chapel at Luxeuil, though his father would eventually rebury his son no less than five times in hopes of enshrining him as a hero of the Great War. Bert attended the funeral of Prince, indeed he was photographed sorrowfully at the event with the men of the escadrille.

Two days after the death of Prince, the escadrille was relocated to Cachy, north in the Somme sector. Only three of the men of the escadrille had planes that were able to make the flight to Cachy – Masson (with his new replacement), Lufbery and Thénault. The escadrille was told at that time it would be part of the newly-formed Group de Combat 13 that was made up of a number of escadrilles: N 124, N 15, N 88 and N 65. The thought was that small escadrilles could work in unison to achieve, what would be called in future wars, air supremacy. The days of the lone wolf aviator had begun to wane in the summer and fall of 1916. What was starting to emerge was the need for aviators to work together, in unison, as part of combat groups.

Thus far in the war, the men of N 124 had lived in comfortable hotels and billeted in posh homes, chauffeured to the aerodromes when needed. That changed in Cachy. The weather in the north was colder than what they were used to and wet. Their quarters were a leaky portable barracks 'erected in a sea of mud'.[22] 'It was a cluster of similar barns nine miles from the nearest town. A sieve was a water-tight compartment in comparison with that elongated shed. The damp cold penetrated through every crack, chilling one to the bone. There were no blankets and until they were procured, the pilots had to curl up in their flying clothes.'[23] Cachy was in the valley of the Somme river and was plagued with fog, limiting flying time. They were so close to the front that the rumble and roar of artillery was constant. No provision for a mess had been made, forcing the escadrille members to rely on other French escadrilles until Bill Thaw and Didier Masson went to Paris to meet with Dr Gros. They were able to receive cash funds to keep N 124 fed.

It was there in Cachy that Bert Hall's relationship with the Escadrille Américaine came to an end. The reasons behind this are varied. While Bert's performance in the air seemed beyond reproach, it was his activities on the ground that earned the ire of some members of the unit. Most accounts of Bert's irritations came not from the members of the Escadrille, but as part of a life-long smear campaign by Paul Rockwell. Still stung by a perceived slight at Kiffin's funeral, Paul painted a dark picture of Bert. In one interview he said, 'Hall had a mouth like a sewer.'[24] In another, he portrayed Hall as, '... one who'd risk his skin to shoot down a German, then land beside the crash to steal the pilot's watch and wallet'.[25] Certainly there was some truth to that claim. Bert's own father had managed to profit from his military experience. There was no reason for Bert to not think any differently.

It is worth noting that in Paul Rockwell's own words, 'Hall just wasn't the sort of person suited for our American volunteer group.'[26] In Rockwell's role in public information for the war department, he took ownership of crafting the public image of N 124 for publicity and propaganda purposes. He had apparently decided, on his own or with the influence of others like James McConnell, that Bert Hall did not represent his own lofty standards. Rockwell had no official standing in the escadrille – his association was by blood and his own self-determined positioning.

But was Bert the only person attempting to profit from the popularity and notoriety of the escadrille? No. Before Victor Chapman's death, he wrote:

Cowdin and Prince returned from Paris with a press reporter, and a cinema yesterday. Well, we pulled it off this morning despite the rain and the clouds. I never was so be-photo'd or ever hope to be again. In large groups and small ones; singly, talking, and silent, in the air, and on the ground, by 'movies' and in poses. The united Press reporter was fine, beaming all over the thrills of it. 'Hated to sink his individuality but had to promise to give it too *all* papers to get the job.' First time he'd been to the front (Front! Sixty-five kilometres to leeward of it), 'or been on an aviation ground with *so many* machines.' (Many! thirty!), and he smiled with his gold teeth and spectacles, like the matron of a boarding-house. The first part was the most difficult, and everybody had some suggestions to make, more brilliant to the last. And nobody agreed with the movie man, who planted himself firmly in the middle of the field, 500 yards off, and waited for the cage-á-poules to come on. Of course we ran in the M.F.'s – a simulacra bombardment, don't you see. Pleased Captain Happe immensely, *we* to accompany and to protect the big machine! First the Farmans lined up, roared and buzzed , and by ones and twos flitted past the camera man up into the air. Then one at a time we bumped out and rushed by him. I must say that he had ever for we *décollé* just before him, then came round and landed. You will see it all I expect something this summer; for it is to be given to some American cinema company in Paris. I understand that Kiffin and Berty Hall were much peeved to think that some _____ person was going to make heaps of money out of us, and we risked our necks for nothing (None of us liked to manoeuvre so close together with the *plafond* at 300 metres.) 'Think of the honour,' said I. 'Oh no, give me the cash and keep it,' said Bert.[27]

From this alone one can be assured that Bert was attempting to cash in on his role in the escadrille. Bert earned some ill-will from his comrades in arms, that much can be assured. This is supported by a comment made at Bert's promotion to adjudant by one of the members of the escadrille to a reporter who was allegedly told that, '...he should have won a 'the notorious medal of shame for his bad table manners, boozing every day, a penchant for paid ladies, being overly shrewd in card playing and dice rolling, bad checks, and signing others' names to mess chits.'[28] A noted historian of the period who had met members of the escadrille seems to validate this perception of Bert. He claims that Hall was, '...a pathetic rascal whose perversity has been pigeon-holed as an overgrown inferiority complex. It was manifested in his unpopular practices such as kiting checks from squadron buddies, and outright forgery.'[29]

Hall was unabashed about his behaviour, flaunting the regulations at times, which certainly did not settle well with his colleagues. After Victor Chapman's loss, rather than sulk, Bert coped the way he usually did – on leave. On 19 July, Jim McConnell wrote to Paul Rockwell, 'Hall was so long overdue that the Captain wanted to report him as a deserter. He's back with a story about chasing a spy for four days. Prince saved his hide for him.'[30]

To offer perspective, Bert was a person who lived by his own wits most of his life. Many of the younger men in the escadrille came from wealthy families. We will never know for sure what Bert was thinking or how he felt about taking money from them, but it would not be out of character for him to point out that they could afford to lose some money. Supporting this, Historian E. L. van Groder wrote, 'These were men whose ethics and personal conduct were a very far cry from Hall's (self expressed) philosophy of 'grab what you can, when you can and the devil take the hindmost...'[31]

An alleged quote from one of the members of the escadrille paints Bert as audacious in his corruption. 'He's a pathetic rascal with real perversity. He actually enjoys devilling us by kiting checks and outright forgery. He does it right in front of us.'[32] This seems closest to the true character of Bert Hall. He had no need to be covertly devious, Hall was very open about what he was doing.

Even his closest friend, Bill Thaw, spoke about Bert with two perspectives: good and bad. 'He was genial, charming, and probably the biggest liar in the

Legion… always telling us he'd been both a bank robber and lawman in the western frontier.'[33] In his own mind, this was simply how the men lived. 'Aviators in groups on any of the battlefronts have an odd time of it. We play poker, dice, roulette, and if any one wins all the money, as some' one usually does, it doesn't matter greatly. You go around and borrow what you want and nobody keeps any account of it, since we know this thing is going to last a good while and there will be nobody left to worry about debts when it's over.'[34]

Paul Rockwell declared throughout his life that Bert was known to claim victories that he did not earn, but this is a claim that is never substantiated by other members of the escadrille. In fact, Kiffin Rockwell's letters point to the fact that Norman Prince was actively working to block Hall from getting victories (author's note: see the previous chapter). What is clear is that there was a caste system emerging in N 124; those that lived up to the image that Paul Rockwell was crafting of the unit and Bert Hall.

Bert's philosophy was that an aviator *should* claim victories no matter what. That in itself was not wrong – many aviators did it. His own recollection was that such activities were expected and deserved.

> Take Victor Chapman, for instance, as straight and fine chap as ever walked the earth or sailed the sky. I never realised just how fine he was until one day when a French aviator got the credit for a German plane that Victor brought down. That made me mad. Good Lord! When you've fought a Hun and got him, and you can't help feeling pride in it! And when I saw that a mistake was being made, I blurted out: 'You brought down that Hun Victor! Why don't you say so?'
>
> I'll never forget the way he looked at me and smiled. 'What difference does it make who gets the credit?' he said. 'The main thing is that the Hun is down. *That's* what counts.'[35]

In Bert's mind, giving up the credit was simply against his character. In the eyes of the other men, he was attempting to steal credit that was simply not due.

There is also the matter of Bert's alleged use of prostitutes. Rockwell supported this claim in the years after the First World War, often portraying that Bert and Bert alone visited brothels. This claim was substantiated by historians that reached out to Paul Rockwell in his capacity as the 'official historian of the Lafayette Escadrille'. One such piece of correspondence in Rockwell's personal papers led historian Karl Knorr to write, 'Poor Bert Hall. He bedded so many girls that he never learned the names of most. It's a miracle he wasn't a walking venereal epidemic as he serviced prostitutes, mostly…'[36] This was based on one source, Paul Rockwell.[37] Rockwell's desire to smear Hall was something that carried on for years. As Knorr would later say,

'When one considered his nocturnal bottle bouts and wenching excesses, one wonders how he had the time or physical ability to fly in the combat. But the records show he did.'[38] Rockwell's correspondence mentions the 'wenching' and 'Hall's constant drinking.'[39] No other firsthand accounts refer to this, however, further lending weight to Rockwell having an axe to grind.

Bert was a married man, though his faithfulness was always questionable. His wife Suzanne was known to accompany him to Luxeuil.[40] Why he kept this a secret is unknown, but she was in constant contact with him. This opens up several possibilities. One: Bert was visiting Suzanne and the men assumed he was visiting a prostitute, perhaps at his insistence to keep her relationship with him secret. Two: Bert was visiting both his Suzanne and prostitutes. Three: Bert was only a visitor of brothels. What little evidence is available in family history indicates that Suzanne was not a prostitute and had ongoing relations with Bert during 1916, indicating that options one and two were both possible. In all fairness, Bert's abilities to stay in a long-term relationship was still years away.

Paul Rockwell used his influence as Kiffin's brother and creator of the public image of the escadrille to influence authors to downplay or outright disregard Bert's contributions. He used his position to slant history's perspective of Hall. When asked about Bert bragging about being a lawman, it would be Paul Rockwell that countered, 'More likely Bert was wanted full time by the law.'[41]

Noted historian Phillip Flammer, who wrote *The Vivid Air*, considered by many to be the most authoritative history of the Lafayette Escadrille, came to conclusions about Bert that were sourced from correspondence that Rockwell provided. He portrays that Bert was disliked in the escadrille from the start. Yet oddly enough, almost every account written by the members of the unit do not portray Bert as disliked. There are exceptions of course, namely James McConnell. Edwin Parsons, who joined the escadrille after Bert's departure, wrote chapters on almost all of the original members of the unit. In the case of Hall, he mentions him, but does not write a chapter about Bert. Parsons and Paul Rockwell corresponded heavily about his work, and, per Rockwell's comments, Bert did not deserve mention. Even Thénault's history of the escadrille published years later only mentions Hall five times. Either he had the respect of the men he flew with or they avoided the wrath of Paul Rockwell by simply downplaying his contributions.

The surviving Rockwell would add to his accusations to cast dispersions on Bert Hall's character. While he would often reference the fact that Bert tried to sell the newspapers an account of Kiffin's death, the *New York Times* Paris branch and no other tabloid ran articles which quoted Bert on Kiffin's demise. Furthermore, Paul would later claim that Hall was selling an 'eyewitness' account of his brother's death rather than attending his funeral; yet none of the published accounts portray Bert as being present when Kiffin died.[42] Paul Rockwell's accusations serve few purposes other than to paint Hall as a liar who was despised by the other members of the unit.

The surviving Rockwell brother often claimed that Bert was a braggart. This seems in character, yet there are odd contradictions that poke holes in Rockwell's accusations. In Bert's only real autobiography, *'En l'air!'*, he discusses other probable victories which would have brought his kill count to upwards of eight or nine. But if Bert was the kind of character that sought out the press to extol his victories, why is there no newspaper accounts of his confirmed 23 August victory? Would Bert not have told the papers even an exaggerated version of that victory? Oddly enough, the claim of braggart (at this point in his life) seems thin at best. McConnell always tried to balance his descriptions of Bert as a 'liar and hot air artist' while at the same time stating '...but I believe he has the where with all in a pinch'.[43] The truth most likely lies between those two perceptions and both may very well be correct.

Regardless of the validity of Bert's indiscretions, one thing is sure, the surviving members of the escadrille were through with his antics. The precedent for this was the 'voluntary' transfer of Elliot Cowdin who did not get along with members of the unit and was put in a situation where he faced jail or transfer. Jim McConnell referred to the conspiracy against Cowdin as 'the cure' that was a far cry from the lofty standards that the wealthy young men alleged they were defending.[44]

This was not the case with Bert. Some historians such as Phillip Flammer have claimed that he was asked to leave the unit. Others have indicated that he was forced out. At least one has claimed that Thénault asked him to transfer. In later years in his own personal papers, Paul Rockwell revealed the true story: 'Bert Hall was <u>not</u> asked to transfer to a French escadrille by the officer commanding that Escadrille. The pilots of the Escadrille Lafayette made things unpleasant for Hall, because of his absolute lack of honour, honesty, and common decency – he often cheated at cards, passed bad checks on them – that he got out of the Escadrille. The pilots of the French Escadrille to which he changed soon tired of being cheated and robbed, and Hall asked to go to Russia.'[45] Even with his dislike of Bert, this is probably the most balanced account of what happened. Hall was not confronted openly, but treated like an errant fraternity pledge that was blackballed by his colleagues.

Rockwell added, 'Because they had been in the Foreign Legion with him, Kiffin Rockwell and William Thaw always stood up for Bert Hall against the other members of the Escadrille Lafayette, but they had no respect for his character. Hall <u>did</u> some good work in the early days of the Escadrille, and was decorated with the Médaille Militaire and the Croix de Guerre. After Victor Chapman was killed, he flew as seldom as possible, and in July, 1916, he actually had his teeth pulled out one by one, in order to report sick day after day.'[46] Even in his post-war book on American volunteers in France, Paul begrudgingly pays Hall a compliment, 'Bert Hall also did good work in the early days of the Escadrille...'[47]

Paul's claim about Bert's teeth seems farfetched and has no documented support beyond Rockwell's accusation hinting at Bert's cowardice. What *is* known is that Bert's front teeth were removed in 1916. In a 1918 interview, Bert's version of events is that the loss of his teeth was the result of combat: 'Lieutenant Hall has been wounded three times, once in the mouth, resulting in the loss of most of his teeth, in and arm and in the leg.'[48] Bert never showed scars on his cheeks from being shot in the mouth and the angles necessary to take out the front teeth without such a wound are improbable at best. Also, such an injury most assuredly would have been documented by someone in N 124.

But does Rockwell's claim hold water? There were plenty of other ways to feign illness rather than resort to something as physically painful as having teeth pulled. With all of his years on the road, it is likely that Bert had never seen a dentist before and that having his teeth pulled could very well have been for legitimate reasons. Paul Rockwell has most likely assumed that it was an act of cowardice. If Hall was avoiding combat, it is only somewhat demonstrated in the records, but certainly not to the extent that Rockwell claims. Bert only flew ten flights in July for 18.7 hours in the air, one of the lowest in the unit for that month. But after that, he flew for 22.5 hours in August (there were six pilots that flew less than him that month) and 5.5 hours in September, near the middle for the escadrille members at the time.[49]

Rockwell's testimony, while slanted, does have a basis in logic. The original member of N 124 were being killed or off the roster as casualties. The influx of new pilots might have tipped the scales against Bert. Where older members who had been there from the beginning might have been more forgiving of him, the new members were not. While Kiffin and Thaw had always been accepting of his less than reputable practices, the loss of Kiffin meant that even his long-time friend Thaw could not sway the members of the unit to support his old comrade.

Bert applied for a transfer on 29 October 1916. He received word that he was accepted in another Nieuport escadrille, N 103. On 1 November, he departed for his new assignment. Former Legionnaire Emil Marshall, a member of the escadrille's ground staff, wrote in his diary that as Bert left the unit, he shook his fist at the other pilots and shouted, 'You'll hear from me yet!'[50] He would later comment, 'We were not sure whether Hall meant his last remark as a threat of vengeance or whether he meant he was going to show us all up with a brilliant war record.'[51]

As it was, his words rang with prophetic quality...

CHAPTER SEVEN

Romania and Russia

Before I finally left for America I had, all told, three years of genuine sport. I don't know how much longer the war will last and my only idea is that I will have to work when it is over. I hate to think of it. Perhaps some kind philanthropist will put us on pension. I hope so, as work would be an awful shock after so much pleasure and so many good times.[1]

– Bert Hall

Bert transferred to N 103 under command of Capitaine Jean d'Harcourt. The transfer was relatively easy for Bert. When he had flown in M 38, he had flown with d'Harcourt who had been a lieutenant at the time. While Bert is often painted as a bit of a rogue, Capitaine d'Harcourt knew Bert and must have realised what he was getting with Hall joining his unit.

Escadrille N 103 was stationed at Cachy along with the Escadrille Américaine – so he did not move far. The escadrille was flying Nieuport 17s, so for Bert this was an easy transition. The insignia for the Escadrille was two-fold. One, a bright red star that was what was used at the time Bert Hall flew with the unit. The other was a stork (cigogne) emblazoned on the side of the fuselage. The escadrille had been in service since 1914 and was stationed all over the Western Front, flying in support of the key campaigns of the war. This was a battle-hardened group.

Paul Rockwell's dispersions aside, Bert Hall was quick to prove that he was not a coward. He was put on the flight line and flew missions almost daily. According to French records, he secured a victory on the afternoon of 6 November near Buire, though Hall remembered it being near Raucourt.[2] The corresponding German records do not record the victory but, if verified, it was Hall's fourth victory. There is a possibility that this victory was not confirmed but simply recorded. Per James McConnell in a letter to Paul Rockwell: 'Yes, Bert Hall is at our field. There are 8 escadrilles de chasse here. He's in N 103 and claiming up a Fokker.'³ Not only does this validate the claim but it also showed that Bert was still cordial with his former escadrille. If he harboured ill-will, he certainly did not show it.

He received his fifth victory on 26 November for which he received a citation that detailed his exploits:

CITATION
November 26, 1916
BERT HALL, Adjutant Pilot in Escadrille N. 103
Clever, energetic, and courageous pilot, full of spirit. Daily attacking enemy planes at very short distance. On November 26, 1916, shot down a German plane at two hundred metres from our trenches. The following day, after a combat held quite near, returned with his machine hit by several shots, also a shot in his helmet.⁴ (three additional citations)

Technically speaking, this would have been Hall's fifth victory entitling him to use the title of 'ace.' Regardless if it was justified, Bert adopted the title for the rest of his life. Bert apparently did not enjoy the companionship of the men of N 103 or simply desired a change. Perhaps the close call of a bullet grazing his leather helmet reminded him of his mortality.

On 19 December 1916, he requested a transfer from the escadrille to a less stressful posting. The option presented to him was to transfer to the French Mission to Romania. He went to Paris on leave for a week when he was promoted to sous lieutenant.⁵ While in Paris, Bert made his first acquaintance with John Jacob Niles. Niles was a ferry pilot with the American Air Service on leave from his training duties. He and Hall hit it off well, most likely over drinks. It was a relationship that would both benefit and twist historians' view of Hall in years to come.⁶ Bert departed for Romania on Christmas Day, leaving behind the Western Front for the political and military chaos of the Eastern Front.

Before he departed for the Eastern Front, he learned that his former unit had undergone a change of name. The German ambassador to the United States complained about the name of the Escadrille Américaine. The very name seemed to call into question the matter of American neutrality, yet again. Relations between America and Germany were already frigid thanks to Germany's sinking of the *Lusitania* and the matter only seemed to rekindle memories of Thaw, Cowdin and Prince's trip to the US a year earlier. The State Department felt that matters with the Germans were bad enough to not add this to the long list of complaints. German ambassador Bernstoff was infuriated at not just the name of the unit, but that the American aviators were painting their aircraft with new insignia for the escadrille – the head of a Sioux Indian in full war bonnet – an overt American icon.[7]

On 16 November 1916, the French minister of war proclaimed, 'Hereafter, when squadrons are not designated by their number... the N.124 will be called the Escadrille de Volontaires (Volunteers).'[8] Dr Gros in his role in the Franco-American Committee felt that such a designation did not fully capture the essence of the spirit of the men that were flying and dying for France. He suggested another name, one that would help with the recruitment of men in the US and still generate some of the mystique that was being created by the public relations machine that Paul Rockwell was leading.

For their part, the men flying in the escadrille had no idea that they were once more the centre of a political sparring match. The French minster of war liked Dr Gros' idea and adopted it. 'The Minister of War announced that in order to satisfy a demand emanating from the United States, he had decided that the Escadrille des 'VOLONTAIRES' shall hence forth be designed the Escadrille 'LAFAYETTE.'[9] The name also was adopted by the Franco-American Flying Corps that became known as the Lafayette Flying Corps. Lafayette stirred both Frenchmen and Americans who remembered the commitment and support that Lafayette had given the American colonies during the revolution.

It was made official to the men of N 124 on 6 December 1916, they were now the Lafayette Escadrille. As Capitaine Thénault put it in his memoirs: 'Henceforth we shall never be known by any other name.'[10] References to the old Escadrille Américaine faded into obscurity. Many books written only refer to the Lafayette Escadrille title since it had become so engrained in the hearts and minds of Americans by the end of the war.

Romania was one of the backwaters of the Great War thanks to its political back peddling and changing sides. At the start of the war Romania was technically allied with the Austro-Hungarian Empire which it had traditional and royal ties to. That was not to say that relations between the two countries governments was good – they were not. Transylvania, a province of Romania, was occupied at the start of the war by the empire that only soured their paper-thin alliance to begin with. Also, the treaty only required Romania to come to the Empire's defence if it were attacked. That was not the case in the Great War, the Austro-Hungarians had initiated the conflict.

The Austro-Hungarians initially did poorly against the Russians and the Romanians, waiting until 1916 to see what side was prevailing, to declare war on their former allies. This lack of insight put Romania in a nasty situation. The Russians held the Romanians in open contempt for being opportunists and the Austro-Hungarians sent their armies through Romania to get at the Russians. Their fall/early winter counteroffensive in late 1916 sent several Romanian armies into retreat, mangled and bloody. While the other governments had years to master the new style of warfare and adapt, even marginally, Romania faced a meat-grinder that it was ill-prepared to fight.

In December, the Romanian capital of Bucharest fell, but proud Romania still clung to life. The Allies were saddled with the tiny country and letting her fall simply did not make political or military sense. Russia had already suffered significant losses and defeats at the hands of the Germans on the Eastern Front. If Romania dropped out of the war it would potentially overtax the faltering Russians.[11]

The survival of Romania was not a matter of honour, it was a necessity. The allies did not fear losing the small country, their ultimate fear was that Russia would drop out of the war. If that were to happen, Germany would be able to shift hundreds of thousands of men to the Western Front and possibly alter the fate of the war for France and England. As such, Romania had to be kept in the war. In early December, France and Britain sent a massive wave of material and personnel to re-equip and retrain the battered remains of the Romanian military. They sent over 150,000 rifles, 2,000 machine guns, over a million grenades, hundreds of artillery pieces and hundreds of aircraft. The French mission, which arrived while Hall was still flying for N 103, had 1,600 experienced troops to train the Romanians on their new arms.

The aircraft that were sent to the Romanian Air Service received 322 fighters from the Allies. The French sent Nieuports, models 11, 12, 17, 19, 21, 23 and 28 with the majority of these being airplanes that had been obsolete and retired for service. A number of Farman bombing and reconnaissance airplanes, French and British Sopwith 1½ Strutters, Caudron G.4s, and Breguet-Michelin bombing airplanes rounded out the inventory. Over the course of one month, Romania had gone from having forty-four airplanes and less than a hundred pilots to being nearly five times that size. Having the planes was one thing, having trained pilots was another.

The Romanians were grateful for the assistance. When the leader of the French military mission, General Henri Mathias Berthelot, arrived in December, he was met by I.I.C. Br`tianu – Romania's Prime Minister with the greeting: ' Welcome, General! I salute you, if I may be allowed, as the Chief of the Romanian Armed Forces General Staff.'[12] General Berthelot was regarded from that point forward as the father of the modern Romanian army.

Bert Hall arrived a month after the official French mission landed in Romania. His name does not appear on the official roles of the French mission, most likely because of his late arrival. The French military's public relations machine played up the fact that Bert was in Romania, issuing press releases that made their way into newspapers in the US. In arriving on the Eastern Front, he became noted as the first American aviator to be posted on that front of the war.[13] Hall's formal assignment was to help

instruct at a French-run school of observation for the Romanian aviators.
He was posted to this school with sous-Lieutenants Bonneton, Bretonniere,
Lafon, Nielson and Pistor. They trained the Romanians with ten Farman
40s, fifteen flying the older model Nieuport 10 and ten piloting the large
Caudron G4.[14]

Bert's impression of Romania was grim at best.

> Thousands of Rumanians are dead and tens of thousands are dying from
> typhus and other epidemics brought on by famine.... More than 300,000
> persons are crowded into Jassy, a city designed to accommodate about
> 60,000. There is little or no food. Doctors and nurses are scarce and
> thousands are dying.[15]
>
> Doctors went through the wards where the wounded lay three to a bed,
> prodding the men with long goads. If the wounded men grunted he was kept
> for further treatment: if no grunt was forthcoming he was buried. It was all
> they could do, poor devils. They had nothing to treat them with. If they had,
> there would not have been enough surgeons to do it.[16]

His words rang true to the plight of those suffering on the Eastern Front.

> From one end of the Eastern Front to the other was chaos, everything and
> everybody. The French officers who had been sent over were doing what they
> could to bring about order, and in spots things were cleaned up, put in shape
> and organised to some extent. It made me want to laugh and weep at the
> same time. My work took me from a point about one hundred miles south
> of Riga at the north to the very end of the Romanian line on the Black Sea at
> the south. I had a chance to see what was going on everywhere, and I mixed
> with the officers and men of both armies, the Russian and Romanian.[17]
>
> I couldn't get a meal and it seemed almost sacrilegious in the midst of all
> this horror to hunt for cigarettes. There were none anyhow. But that was
> nothing. There was no soap, no sugar, coffee, tea nor clothing. To eat you
> must only get corn meal cooked in a sort of mush and served cold. We had
> some beans but no other vegetables, meat sometimes twice a week. Not a
> bath house was open in the city. The cold was intense. There was no wood
> or coal for heat and the temperature was about twenty-five degrees below
> zero.[18]

The Romanian mission was not limited to Romania, they were also there
to help France's other ally, Russia. The French aviators visited their Russian
colleagues and Bert did go with them on at least one of these visits.

In the Russian aviation things couldn't have been worse. I found that the men would fly only when they felt like it. They almost never passed over behind the German lines. The average Russian aviator aims to fly six hours per monthly. His pay is two hundred roubles and after his six hours he takes a good long reset. Then I started in to really do some flying they thought I was a patriot and a fool. In fact, they didn't make any bones about telling me so. They let the German machines do what they pleased; they flew around our lines and were never molested by the Russians.

Socially the Russian aviator is certainly a good fellow. They can all play a good game of poker and can put away a lot of drinks. I think they have the Germans beat in these branches. But as fighters they are nil. No patriotism, no enthusiasm, and not too much courage. About all they did in the aviation corps was drink champagne, play poker and '66', a German game. The men always say, 'to-morrow.' They are never in a hurry and they don't worry. The Russian has no idea of what war means in the air. They are well equipped, having all of the latest types of fighting machines. But the Russians are not air fighters.[19]

Bert claimed that he demonstrated to the Russians how to fight by taking a fighter up and engaging a German airplane on or about 20 January 1917 near Menelkov (a village that disappears off Russian maps in the 1920s or 30s.)

I saw him come over in our lines at about 1,500 feet altitude and I went after him. I suppose that he thought I was a Russian as he did not pay any attention to me. I proceeded to shoot him down. When I returned I was very much surprised to find that my comrades did not approve of what I had done. They said: 'We have been here a long time and the Germans have never bothered us. Now they will get mad and come and drop bombs on us and may kill some of us.[20]

His conclusion about the Russians was simple: 'They are not patriotic and care nothing for Russia.'[21] Bert's victory is mentioned in some documentation on the history of the French mission, but from the descriptions it appears they may have relied on his erroneous biography, *One Man's War*, as their source. By their own admission, '...the records of the aviation activities of the French mission have not been documented'.[22]

The Russians were so appreciative that the Frenchmen were awarded the Cross of St George. Such awards to foreign war heroes was common with allies as a gesture of goodwill. Bert would claim that he received his award from Czar Nicholas personally, '...only four days later he lost his job', referring to the revolution that swept Russia in 1917.[23] If Hall's recollection is accurate, this would have placed him getting the medal on 19 March 1917. Unfortunately, there are no supporting documents to verify that the Czar did present the medal to him personally other than the fact that Hall had the medal. Hall claims that it was a reward for his bravery and victory for his kill while flying for Russia. In reality, he was not the only member of French aviation to receive the medal, so most likely he was not singled out.

Once back in Romania, it is likely his time was spent attempting to pass on his experience to the Romanian aviators. Bert's emphasis was training on target shooting with a machine gun from a plane.[24] Bert claimed that he shot down an aeroplane near Galatz on the Danube River on or about 20 February 1917.[25] As with his previous victory claim on the Eastern Front, the documentation and verification of the victory is questionable. One thing is certain, Hall was not just on the ground in Romania and Russia, he was also in the skies. As part of the French mission, he received the St Stanislaus medal.

Things dramatically changed for Bert on 6 Apri 1917 when the US declared war on Germany. The US entry into the war was long in coming. America had been profiting from three years of fighting, selling arms and munitions to the British and French. The sinking of the steamship *Lusitania* in 1915 took the lives of 120 Americans and had been the first push for the country to enter the war. On 24 March 1916, the cross-channel ferry *Sussex* was torpedoed after the German U-boat incorrectly identified it as a minelayer, taking another twenty-five American lives. The neutral US pressed diplomatically to have the Germans halt their unrestricted submarine warfare which put its citizens at risk. President Wilson, attempting to appease both the isolationists and the hawks who desired war, threatened to sever diplomatic relations with Germany if they did not halt the indiscriminate sinking of ships on the high seas. Not wanting the US to enter the war on the side of the French and British, Germany reluctantly agreed.

By early 1917, however, Germany's fortunes of war changed and they announced they would once more start sinking any ships attempting to deliver any cargo to Britain or France. America still did not declare war, though relations between Germany and the US were at a point where they were beyond repair. On top of the unrestricted submarine warfare, the Germans had been waging a covert war of sabotage against the US. A bomb had been set off by a German sympathiser in the US capital in 1915. There had been blatant sabotage at the munitions factory in Kingsland, New Jersey, which had destroyed the plant and another explosion of munitions at Black Tom, New Jersey, had shattered windows in Manhattan and damaged the Statute of Liberty. Despite this, Americans were still reluctant to join the Allies against Germany. The bloodbath of the war, the sheer numbers of dead on the Western Front alone were staggering. In 1917, there seemed to be no end in sight.

What tipped the US into entering the war was British naval intelligence staff that had been intercepting and deciphering diplomatic and military messages from Germany. In one, dubbed the Zimmerman Telegram, Germany reached out to Mexico to propose an alliance. If America were to side with the Allies, Mexico would attack and could take parts of the southwest US as a reward. The Mexicans were in no shape militarily to even consider the proposal. When the British leaked the decoded telegram to President Woodrow Wilson, there was no course of action left to the US. America declared war on German on 6 April 1917.

When Bert heard that news that the US had finally entered the war, he immediately asked for a thirty-day leave of absence. The purpose of that leave was to return to the United States, visit his father and to enlist in the US Army Air Service. His request was granted. Bert had hoped to travel back to the US via Sweden and then France and England, then home; however, the Swedes had barred him from travel via that route. Now that the US had declared war, Bert had issues because he was carrying a French Consulate passport but was an American.[26] For Hall, this left only one logical route – to cross Russia, then the Pacific to reach the US.

Bert faced several problems when he arrived in Petrograd in April. The largest issue was that Russia was descending into civil war. The communist revolution in Russia that spring was a series of revolts and riots starting in Petrograd in March, just prior to Hall's arrival. Strikes and demonstrations ruled the day as the Russians shook off the yoke of royal rule to attempt to rule themselves. The Czar sent in the army only to have the green troops he had sent revolt in outright mutiny themselves. By mid-March, it had become clear that the Czar could no longer hold onto power. Czar Nicholas abdicated his throne only to be taken prisoner along with the royal family by the provisional government. The acting government had very little control over its people and Petrograd was a hotbed of revolutionary protests and ideas.

A friend of mine, a lady living at the Hotel du Nord, had an experience which is typical of the condition of the city (Petrograd) at the time. The Hotel du Nord is just in front of the Nicholas station. She was awakened one morning by firing in the street and the station. She looked out to see what was the trouble, just in time to get the end of her nose shot off by a passing bullet. That is a good example of Russian marksmanship. When they are shooting at you, you are safe. But if they are shooting at something else, you had better hide.

You can guess what went on in a city of 3,000,000 population during a time like that, with no law or order. All the convicts were liberated, but some of them went back to the prison for protection. The people were taking everything they could get their hands on; most all the stores were closed. IT was very difficult to get anything to eat and rubles were like pennies. Everyone was arrested about twice daily. But, with a few rubles, you were safe.[27]

Bert's second problem was money. Since leaving the escadrille his pay was no longer augmented with Vanderbilt money. He had been forced to live on a typical French sous-Lieutenant's pay, a step down from what he had been experiencing. Getting back to the US was going to take funds, so he turned to the most logical place, the American embassy in Petrograd. David Francis of the State Department sent on a letter explaining Hall's intentions and his need for money.

April 17, 1917
The Honorable Secretary of State, Washington D.C.

Sir:

I have the honour to write you concerning Lieut. Bert Hall, an American citizen who is returning to the United States for the purpose of tendering his services to Col. Geo. A. Squires, Chief of the aviation Section. Lieut. Hall was in the United States Army during the Spanish War. At the beginning of the European War he tended his services to France as an aviator; they were accepted and since August 1914 he has been in continuous service in France and Roumania. He brings to me a letter from Captain H. E. Yates, military attaché of the American Legation in Roumanian who states that Lieut. H. has received the Medaille Militaire and has achieved distinction by bringing down five Germans.

Lieut. H. is hastening to American where he is informed, and I am advised, that the services of aviators are greatly needed. As Lieut. H. has not sufficient means to pay his transportation and subsistence to the United States via Vladivostok and the Pacific, I have advanced to him $248.34 for which I enclose receipt in duplicate. Will you kindly collect this from the War Department and credit to the Contingent Fund of this Embassy? In the event that War Department is unwilling to make this advance, Lieut. H. as you will observe from this receipt agrees to reimburse the Department from his personal means. I think however, there will be no objection on the part of the War Department to defraying Lieut. Hall's expenses to the extent named. Liet H. had sufficient funds to pay his return via the Atlantic but thinks that

he is more likely to get to America via the other route.
I have the honor to be, sir, your Obedient Servant,
David R. Francis[28]

How Bert came across Captain Halsey Yates to secure a letter
is unknown, but he did indeed exist which reduces the odds of
Hall having forged the letter. It is worth noting that Bert had also
created a fictitious prior military experience. In the receipt that was
forwarded, Bert gave exacting details of his imaginary service. 'I am
an American citizen, having served in Company K., 6th Missouri,
Spanish-American War and from August 22, 1914 to December 24th
1916 as a volunteer in the French Aviation Corps and was sent to the
Roumanian [sic] Front as a French Mission on December 25, 1916,
and I am returning to the United States to enter the service of the
United States Government, it having declared war on Germany.'[29]
Bert's service in the 6th Missouri was completely fictitious, verified by
a check of the Missouri State Archives and the US National Archives.
But it is so detailed that few people would doubt its veracity. One of
the trademarks of Hall's lies...

His own account of the trip back to America lacks the glamour and
excitement of a Bert Hall exaggeration. He never references going to
the US embassy to get an advance of funds. 'When I came to try and
get away from Petrograd my real troubles began. The railroads were
disorganised completely, absolutely no system. It took seven days to
go seven hundred miles on a passenger train, and three months to get
a goods trail from Vladivostok to Petrograd.'[30]

From the port of Vladivostok he caught a ship to Yokohama, Japan.
On 10 May 1917, he took the steamship *Koren Maru* to California
and San Francisco.[31] By the end of May, Bert was back on US soil
for the first time since 1912. He had been at war since August 1914,
possessing more modern combat experience than most of the officers
in the US Army. In terms of aviation, he had more expertise than
any officer in the American Air Service. At the time, he was one of
a handful of people in the US that had ever flown an aeroplane in
battle. He had a great deal to offer the fledgling Army Air Service, if
they were willing to take him on.

CHAPTER EIGHT

Crafting a Myth

It is quite possible that you can do some business with this because the title is rather good and because it shows an American hero of the original Lafayette Escadrille. You can safely make considerable fuss about Miss Day as one of the coming favourites of the screen, billing her as the star of the big musical success 'Going Up,' because I believe that most of your fans will like her work.

Don't promise anything very specific about the production or plot, because it is painfully mechanical and artificial melodrama: There are no big scenes to rave about, but you may talk a little about the escape of Lieutenant Hall from the German lines in a German aeroplane although this action as pictured was quite tame because the Germans were perfectly willing that Hall should escape since he was carrying with him into France, a spy. I believe that Americans will be more than willing to turn out to see one of our aviator heroes and certainly Mr. Hall is one of the heroes of the war...[1]

– Marketing information, *A Romance of the Air*

Bert arrived in a United States that was hungry for war heroes. While the war had been raging across the globe for years, America was now preparing for war. Despite all of the ominous warnings, the nation was ill-prepared for the fight. Her army was relatively small. Her air force existed more on paper and in the hopes and dreams of the officers that were in the service. On 6 April 1917, when the US declared war, not a single aviation unit had been trained for war. The Aviation Section of the Signal Corps, where the Air Service was all but buried, only had two operational flying fields and fifty-five trainers (airplanes). General John J. Pershing said, '...51 were obsolete and the other four were obsolescent'[2] Worse yet, there was no pipeline of combat-ready aircraft forthcoming. In Europe, aircraft technology was evolving by the month and the US was far behind the times. While America had worked hard at selling arms and munitions to supply the war, it was woefully unequipped for battle.

In terms of personnel the situation was just as grim. In the US Army, only twenty-six officers were considered fully trained in early 1917. The whole of the Aviation Section consisted of 131 officers and 1,087 enlisted men.[3] The officers knew it would take thousands of trained and skilled aviators to have a functioning Air Service, but in April 1916, there were only a handful. One of the biggest hopes that the US lay with two groups that they had spurned: the Lafayette Flying Corps and the Lafayette Escadrille. Here were battle-seasoned American aviators with more combat experience than almost anyone in the United States at the time... which included Bert Hall.

The terms and conditions of Bert's thirty days leave was that he was going to go home and enlist in the US Army Air Service. On 26 May 1917, Hall landed back in the US announcing '...patriotism for his native land inspired him to return to American and join Uncle Sam's air forces.'[4] While there are no official records of Bert attempting to take a physical, an article that ran in newspapers late in 1917 indicated that he had taken the Army physical and had been rejected. The same article also said that William Thaw and Raoul Lufbery also failed their physicals for the Air Service.[5] In the case of Thaw, that was the truth. Despite the fact that many of the Americans flying for France had extensive combat experience, they did not meet the Army standards for pilots. This was regardless of the fact that in the case of Thaw and Lufbery, they were still in the air almost every day engaging the enemy. The fact that the article specifically references Bert Hall, its source was likely the Army and indicates that Bert at least tried to enlist in the Air Service.

Hall remained in California for some time, allegedly writing articles and his autobiography. Bert did maintain a diary of his travels and chances are he used this period of time to develop his draft of *En l'air!*, his only true autobiography. How he earned money is unknown, but Bert did some benefit work in Los Angeles in June for the Red Cross. He also did a few paid speaking events in San Francisco in July.[6] When he appeared he wore his black uniform, replete with his medals from France, Romania and Russia. To those that saw him, he was a hero. He spoke of exotic lands and people in wartime. Since America was just entering the war, Bert was a novelty. His tales of the latest technology (aeroplanes) and of landing spies behind enemy lines and shooting at the Boche struck a patriotic chord with the people that attended.[7] Hall was most likely befriended by local citizens, getting free room and board on his name and self-perpetuating reputation alone, a common happening for celebrity speakers.

While the details are unknown, it was noted that Bert did incur some debts while in California. As Bert did in his life, he moved on, working his way across the country doing public speaking as he headed towards Missouri and home. Apparently, the individuals that had loaned Bert money reached out to the French Consulate since Bert was wearing the uniform of the French Air Service at the time he incurred the debts.[8] The French government was outraged at this set of circumstances. A check of their records, which took some time during the war, showed that Bert Hall was absent from active duty and was long overdue on his thirty-day leave. They refused to settle the bill and made their disdain known in California. As far as the French government was concerned, Bert Hall was not a hero but a deserter.[9] Bert's interpretation was likely to have been very different. He had tried to join the Air Service, and as of yet, had not visited his father. The fact that his thirty days was up was most likely viewed as a mere technicality in his mind.

The accusation of being a deserter apparently did not shake Bert in the least: he continued his speaking engagements. Hall did not shy away from any venue, speaking at churches and universities alike. He had no qualms on speaking about political issues as well. 'The allies are better off without the help of Russia, for the people are ignorant anti unpatriotic, and the officers are mostly pro-German.' He also did not pull any punches with his own country with statements like, 'The people of the United States talk too much and don't act quickly enough.'[10] When Bert did speak, he played up his injuries, real or imaginary. In one audience, he spoke to 3,000 attendees, playing up to them like a master showman. 'He spoke in a low tone, explaining to his audience before he started, that this would be necessary for the reason that he had part of his jaw shot away and lost a portion of his teeth in serving as a soldier to bring democracy to the world at large.'[11]

What no one realised at the time was that each time Bert spoke, he was refining and honing the story of his life. He was testing the stories that he would include in his upcoming book, seeing which ones would play well and which ones garnered the most interest. As one reviews the newspaper articles of these events, small details emerge and some disappear as Bert tried out the material he was planning on putting in his book.

In early September 1917, Bert finally returned to Higginsville, Missouri, to spend time with his father. 'Mr. Hall is the son of George Hall of this place and spent his boyhood days on a farm in Higginsville. He has acquired a great reputation as an aviator and is constantly gaining public notoriety. He visited his father at this place a few weeks ago, and his former acquaintances and friends were eager to talk with him and have him relate his many and thrilling experiences since being engaged in the great world war.'[12]

While at home, he spoke in Kansas City at the City Club to an audience of over 200 about his exploits. 'There are two million Germans over there waiting to be killed. Somebody has to kill them to end this war. Sure, I'm going back and do my share of it.'[13] Hardly the words one would expect from a deserter. Hall went on to talk in an almost cavalier tone about the combat he had witnessed: 'It's the greatest sport in the world, this combat in the clouds, with a man's life at stake. The fighting aviator enjoys all the pleasures of a keen athletic contest with the added spice of danger. Sailing so high that his is invisible to earth, lord of all he surveys until he runs into an enemy, he fights, like the original caveman, for the supremacy of his domain. I was not afraid. It was both work and play.'[14]

Bert was still legally married in France and his wife, Suzanne, was deeply concerned about her husband. She contacted the French authorities who reached out to the Secretary of State Robert Lansing in hopes of finding her wayward husband. The French Ambassador to the US, Jean Jules Jusserand, took up her cause:

Embassy of the French Republic
Washington, September 16, 1917

Mr. Secretary of State,
    I have received from Mrs. Bert Hall, of French birth, now residing in France, wife of Lieut. Bert Hall, an American aviator, a letter which she asks me a favour, if possible information about her husband.
    Lieut. Bert Hall, aviator pilot of the aviation department at Washington, enlisted in France, she writes, for the time of the war. For five years he was a member of the Lafayette squad, then went to Romania as a mission. From that country he announced his departure for America; his last letter written in May was dated from Honolulu. Since then Mrs. Bert Hall has not heard from her husband.
    I shall be thankful if your Excellence, if you would kindly go forth and probe quarter Mrs. Hall's inquiry in order that suitable matters be taken for her, the information that she requires.
    Jusserand[15]

For all intents and purposes, Bert had abandoned Suzanne back in France and had moved on with his life. It is clear that they were not divorced at the time either. It was a pattern that he often followed. It would not be the last time that he encountered her, however. The State Department reached out to the War Department who did not have a record of Bert Hall serving in the military. From that point on, the matter seems to have been lost in a bureaucratic shuffle. Oddly enough, Bert was appearing in newspapers at the time across the country and would have been relatively easy to track down, if any real effort had been made.

By the end of October, Bert had returned to California where he spent some time as an instructor at a flight school in San Diego.[16] Little is known of his time in this job or where the airfield/school in question was, but chances are Bert was brought in more as a guest lecturer than an instructor.

Hall augmented his income for the period on the lecture circuit. Bert found that some audiences were not receptive to a war hero. With the war, the US was instituting a federal income tax for the first time. While fighting the war against Germany was widely supported, paying for it via a tax was not. During his speech at a packed theatre in Omaha, Nebraska, on 2 December 1917, a local heckler began to complain loudly about the income tax. When Hall's lecture finished he encountered the man in the lobby. 'It's a hell of a country,' he sneered. 'Right you are,' Hall responded. 'A hell of a country that permits a selfish hound like you to remain out of jail.' Allegedly, the man made a move to punch Bert. Hall responded with a blow of his own, blackening the eye of the heckler in the process.[17]

Bert was accompanied by a woman that he claimed was his wife who had come with him from California. Chances are this woman was simply his latest acquaintance, but with Hall it was difficult to say for sure given his growing collection of wives. A local family had invited him and his companion to visit them during the Thanksgiving holiday and Hall had simply extended that visit.

In January 1918, as the American Army was still attempting to gird its loins for battle in Europe, Bert was voicing concerns about America's involvement in the war in Philadelphia. 'All of this talk of peace talks is 'bunk,' and all of this talk of France being played out is 'bunk'.' He also offered an unpopular view as to potential American involvement in the war. 'But this war is going to last four or five more years and America will have to put four to five million men in the field before this is over.'[18] For an America who had been on the sidelines of war for years, his words were deeply sobering and ominous.

Bert went to Washington DC and met with the employees of the income tax division of the Treasury Department, thanking them for a flag they had sewn to present to the Lafayette Escadrille. 'I'm going back to France in April. I wouldn't miss a summer's flying in France for a million. It's the greatest sport on earth.'[19]

Bert was doing something that seemed almost out of character for him – he was going back to Paris. Bert was a man that always seemed to be moving on, turning another chapter and disregarding where he had been before. For him to go back to Paris while the war was still raging was both honourable and oddly out of character for him. Shortly after his talk in Philadelphia, Bert boarded the steamship, *Rochambeau* to return to his second country, France. On his passport application, his reason for going to Paris was to rejoin N 103, the last squadron that he served in.[20] There is no documentation of Hall ever having smooth matters over with the French government or war department regarding his technical desertion. If anything, the matter was still left open. In addition, there is no record of him having met with his wife Suzanne, though he certainly must have been compelled to do so since she no longer launched any formal requests to find her straying husband.

Bert's activities in France in 1918 are not fully known. Historian Dennis Gordon was able to verify that on 12 April 1918, he married a vaudeville actress named Della Byers.[21] A check of the Paris records does not reveal a marriage certificate there. It is highly probable that he met Miss Byers in Paris and they were married in the United States upon his return. There is no record showing him having divorced Suzanne so either the records are yet unfound or Bert's marriage was an act of bigamy. It was most likely the latter. Surely, if the French authorities wanted to bring him up on charges they could have done so easily while he was there, but no action appears to have been taken. It is most probable that he returned by July before the end of the war. It is known that by early February, Hall was back in New York with his wife, still lecturing about his war experiences. At the same time, if he had smoothed things over with the French Government, they were not showing signs of his past being forgiven.

They contacted the District Intelligence Officer in El Paso, Texas, of the Bureau of Investigation (the precursor to the FBI) in March 1918 to lodge a complaint about Bert: 'The French Military Attaché has just informed me that Mr. Bert Hall, who served at one time in France with the Flying Corps, has given a lecture before the National Geographic Society in Washington on February 15th dressed in the French uniform. The Military Attaché states that Mr. Hall has no longer has the right to wear this uniform, since he does not now belong to the French Army. He further states: 'As Mr. Bert Hall abused last year the use of the French uniform to incur some debts in California, and I want to avoid, as much as possible, the repetition of a similar occurrence, I would be very grateful to you if you could take steps to prevent any future appearance of Mr. Bert Hall in the French uniform.'[22]

Investigator Gus Jones responded as best he could. 'We have, of course, no law by which we can proceed against an officer of a foreign service wearing the uniform of that service in this country, but it is requested that if Mr. Hall appears in your vicinity, posing as an officer of the French service, that you take steps to notify the people whom he is associated, of his proper status'[23] It is unknown if Hall ever was aware of the complaint, but if he was, it certainly did not stop him from donning the uniform of the French Air Service. The press, especially the social columns in California, thrived on the news. While Bert appealed to the common man, in the wealthy social circles he earned nothing but animosity. 'There was much excitement in the smart set when the story that Captain Bert Hall of the French aviation corps had no right to his uniform flashed across the front pages of the newspapers. All the doubting Thomases from Blingum to the Pacific Union Club rose on their hind legs and barked: 'I told you so!'[24] Bert had been snubbed by wealthy families before, but at least their sons were at war at his side.

Della Hall became pregnant by Bert shortly after they were married. They returned to the US settling in New York. During this period he finished his autobiography *En l'air!* The book came out at a time when the war was winding down. Bert's attempt to cash in on his war experience by writing was common. A number of aviators had done the same thing and Hall was simply following the pack. The US involvement in the war was measured in a matter of months, though losses were staggering, even in the wake of Germany's eventual defeat. The war was still a hot topic for people, though its popularity was waning as the final casualty reports came in. Despite this, *En l'air!* was heralded as a bestseller in the autumn of 1918. Critics would cite that the stories in the book were more engaging than the literary prose.

En l'air! was written in the style of the time, that is to say that it was a book that was listed as non-fiction but was a blur of facts and made-up tales. Bert, like many authors of the era, expanded (lied) about certain events to make them more incredible. Some of his aerial combats cannot be even remotely verified with official or non-official accounts and are highly suspect. Perhaps the most outrageous story in the book is one that came from his time in Romania, crafted by Hall's fertile imagination where he describes leading a bombing raid against the Bulgarian palace at Sophia while the Kaiser was in residence. The only recorded raid on Sophia during the period that Hall was there is one where propaganda leaflets were dropped on the yard of the royal palace.[25] If Hall had bombed the palace, it most certainly would have been big news.

In terms of his writing style, Bert learned a lot working on *En l'air!* In an article in *The American Magazine*, he summed up his efforts.

I want to own up to two things right at the start, before I get my motor going. One is that I'm not a 'literary cuss'. The other is that, in spite of that fact, I have written a book. I mention this because I want to refer to a chapter in that book, which I called, 'My Pals'. In it I told something about the fellows who were my friends in the Foreign Legion and the Lafayette Escadrille. But I've found that writing a book is like building a house. When you're through, the point that hits you the hardest is the thing you left out. Of course, I told some things which seem pretty fine to me, about those pals of mine, but I didn't really tell the finest thing of all.

After three years of fighting in the air in the biggest and most lasting memory I have of it all is the splendid loyalty and devotion those men showed each other. A man could be square and true in almost any old place: in sport, or business, or anything. But it is in war, believe me! That you find out definitely whether there are any yellow streaks in what you have fondly supposed was your true blue character.[26]

These were remarkably kind words given how his departure from the escadrille took place.

Bert does not write in any detail about his departure from the Lafayette Escadrille in the book, glossing over the matter entirely. Moreover, his final chapter of the book only has glowing words for those airmen he served with, with a paragraph or two about each of them. The only omission is Lufbery who Hall does not write about. While most of the Legionnaires and aviators get words of praise, his description of James McConnell, one of the men who rallied against him, only offers kind words about his writing skills. His kindest words are for Bill Thaw who he says, 'Bill is my best friend, for I know what is in him.'[27] He even has kind words for Paul Rockwell describing him as a '...good old southern boy' and ending with 'I hope Paul is as good a husband as he was a soldier.'[28] One must wonder if he included those as a gentle poke at Rockwell or if he was oblivious to Paul's disdain for him. If there was any bitterness about the men of the escadrille, Bert certainly did not express it in writing.

Hall embellished his work, but this was done by other authors of higher acclaim during the period and was an accepted practice at the time. Beyond his claims of additional victories that evaded official records, *En l'air!* remains as the most accurate account of Bert's time in the French Air Service and the Lafayette Escadrille. Of course, his old unit was nothing like what it was when he had been prodded out. The American Air Service was ill-prepared to absorb the men of the Lafayette Escadrille and the Lafayette Flying Corps into their ranks. Their physical tests, as already stated, had disqualified some of their best potential pilots – Thaw and Lufbery. Once those matters had been straightened out, there was the issue of ranks. The American Air Service was attempting to bring in seasoned combat veterans at ranks equal to those of raw recruits. When they realised that they were infuriating the very men that they needed, General Billy Mitchell brought in Frederick Zinn, Hall's old friend from the Legion and the Lafayette Flying Corps, to straighten the matter out. But some of the damage was already done.

James McConnell, one of the harshest critics of Bert Hall, perished on 16 March 1917. He had been in a dogfight with Edmond Genet, taking on two German two-seaters. Genet became separated from McConnell who did not survive the battle. His body had been found stripped by the German infantry that had found his remains.

The Lafayette Escadrille had been equipped with Spad aircraft, becoming SPA 124. When it transferred into the American Air Service it came as a whole, becoming the 103rd Aero Squadron... though the French maintained Escadrille 124 in its own ranks.

Lufbery did not remain with the unit, instead he went on to train the 94th Aero Squadron. On 19 May 1918, Lufbery was the leading American ace in the war when he tangled with a German Rumpler aircraft flow by Gftr Otto Kirschbaum and Lieutnant Kurt Scheibe. Accounts vary as what happened. The popular account is that Lufbery's plane was on fire and he jumped to save himself, though other accounts say that he was thrown from his airplane. The effects were the same: Luf was impaled on a picket fence in Maron, France.[29] Not long after Lufbery's death, Hall commented on his fear of fire. 'An aviator's only fear is fire. Burning is a terrible death, and planes burn easily and rapidly. The tracer bullets which tear flaming through an aviator's gas tank are the most awful enemy. Aviators do nothing about dangers in the air. They only think about their narrow escapes after they are over; but fear has no place in an aviator's makeup, for if he entertains any fears he ceases at once to be an aviator.'[30]

Of the original American members of the Lafayette Escadrille, William Thaw, Elliot Cowdin, Kiffin Rockwell, Norman Prince, Victor Chapman and James R. McConnell and Bert Hall, only Cowdin, Thaw and Bert survived the war. Each passing month ended the life of another aviator or two that Hall knew and flew with, consumed in the never-ending flames of the Great War. For Bert, this had to be a sobering reminder of his time at the front.

Even from his early days in the escadrille, Bert had made no qualms about wanting to profit from his war experience. His book was only the first step in that programme. Hall had seen the motion picture crews filming the men of N 124 during the war and knew that film was a medium that had a large draw. As his book ran up the sales charts, he unleashed the next phase of his self-promotion – a venture into the world of silent movies.

The success of *En l'air!* was both financial and publicity-wise, and gave Bert the notoriety that he sought. He proved himself the master of self-marketing when he approached producer Carl E. Carlton about doing a movie based on the book. Silent movies were exciting entertainment, despite their obvious limitations. The only problem was that *En l'air!* did not lend itself to being a good movie: it lacked any elements of a plot and moviegoers wanted to have a story that they could follow. Bert's book does not mention females either, something that was considered a necessity for a box office draw.

Carl Carlton needed aircraft for the production of the film, so he made overtures to both the French and American governments. 'Our present picture, *En l'air!* is approved by the United States war officials as well as the high French war commission.'[31] Clearly, if the French government still had any open issues with Bert, this was their opportunity to speak up. Instead they offered an endorsement. Perhaps the propaganda value outweighed Hall's past indiscretions. So *En l'air!* was changed into a romantic love story. Bert drafted the script and recast his war stories in his autobiography into a romance. He penned himself as the lead character and acted in that role in the movie. The plot of the film was:

> Lieutenant Hall, detailed to an important flight, is wounded in a fight with a German aviator and is forced to descend. He finds the German dead, and exchanges uniforms with him. He is found in hospital by Edith Day, a young American girl, and his own playfellow, who is who is held in Germany by the Archduke of Moravia and his sister, the Countess, because of the value of the news she receives from America. She causes his removal to the castle, and they plan an escape in an airplane. The Countess pretends a hatred of Germany and persuades them to take her with them in their flight. Once within the French lines, she establishes a liaison with a German spy who is impersonating an American correspondent and plans that suspicion will be directed against Bert, who, is condemned to death, but he is saved through the timely arrival of the real correspondent, who reveals the trickery.[32]

For a silent movie, it was overly complicated, heavy with text, making it a slow-paced film to watch. The story deviated so far from Bert's book, it was re-titled *A Romance of the Air*. Other actors in the movie included Herbert Standing who played Bert's friend Major William Thaw. The lead female was Edith Day, a twenty-three-year-old actress from Minneapolis who had appeared on Broadway as the lead in *Going-Up*. She was a contract actress for Carlton Studios, having appeared in one other movie, *A Grain of Dust*. She had been an actress since her teens appearing on the New York stages in productions of *Pom-Pom*, *Follow-Me*, and *The Six Little Widows*.[33] Carlton held her in high regard and hoped that she would be the next big thing in films.

The filming of the movie was to take place in Ithaca, New York. Before the age where Hollywood became the film capital of the world, Ithaca was one of the prime locations for movies of the silent era to be filmed at. The man that put Ithaca on the map as far as movie production was concerned was Theodore Wharton. He was a producer from Chicago and arrived in Ithaca in October of 1912 visiting relatives in the vicinity. Cornell University served as the backdrop for several of his films and can be seen in the background of Bert Hall's first production. Along with his brother, Leopold, they established a film studio at the southern tip of Cayuga Lake.

Between 1914 and 1918, the Wharton Brothers brought in most of the darlings of the silent movie era who used their studios and sets for filming. Lionel Barrymore, Oliver Hardy and Pearl White all appeared in films made in Ithaca. Some of the films that came out of the Wharton studios included the serial series, *The Mysteries of Myra*, *Beatrice Fairfax*, *The Exploits of Elaine* and *Patria*.[34] In early 1918, the Wharton Brother fell on hard times when their elaborate twenty-episode serial, *The Eagle's Eye*, bombed at the box office. This series starred King Baggot, a widely known silent movie actor. The serial was an adaptation of uncovered 'true' espionage schemes used by German spies in America in the early stages of the First World War.[35] When the serial was released, it came out as America's interest in the war was waning. Combined with the Spanish influenza outbreak that kept people from attending movies, the once prosperous Wharton Studios floundered and eventually closed their doors.

They rented out the facilities and the local personnel that had worked for them when anyone wanted to film there. Since Ithaca had a large functioning airport near the studio and Thomas Brothers Aeroplane Company and airfield outside of town, it was a natural place to pick for the filming of *A Romance of the Air*. 'The several dare-devil airplane stunts will also interest picture goes, as they are re-enactments of the kind the hero used as a Lieutenant in the Lafayette Escadrille while fighting in France.'[36] For viewers of the film, it would present their first chance to see Bert Hall in the air.

The film's distribution was to be different than what is done now. Rather than release on a large number of screens nationwide, during the silent era, movies were produced in small numbers, sometimes only a handful of copies. Bert's film debut was one that planned to leverage his popularity and former standing in the Lafayette Escadrille and as a way to generate box office sales. Per Frank Hall (no relation), the President of the Independent Sales Corporation who handled the distribution: 'There will be no releases made, however, in any one territory, of this adventurous love story of cloud-land, until after Lieutenant Hall has made a personal appearance of several weeks at one of the large theatres In that particular territory. This plan of releasing a picture while the star is arousing public interest by appearing in person and talking informally to his audiences is new, and exhibitors will recognise the value such publicity will mean to their box office.'[37] *A Romance of the Air* was shown only where Bert Hall appeared to talk about his war exploits.

The movie meant that Bert had to be on the road almost constantly, starting in November 1918 when the film was released in New York. For him this was

Bert Hall, early 1916. (*Library of Congress*)

Above: A photo used to promote Bert Hall's autobiography. (*From* The American Magazine, *1918*)

Below: Line-up of aircraft of N124 at Luxeuil. (*Charles Woolley Collection*)

Above: A confident and serious Bert Hall during the early months of the N124. (*Willis Haviland Collection*)

Right: Paul Rockwell stands alongside James McConnell's Nieuport with the Hot Foot Society insignia. (*Willis Haviland Collection*)

Left: Bert from the opening moments of the movie, *Romance in the Air.* (*Library of Congress*)

Below: Kiffin Rockwell. (*Willis Haviland Collection*)

Right: Raoul Lufbery with Whiskey. (*Willis Haviland Collection*)

Below: The sombre gathering of N124 at the funeral of Norman Prince. Seated (*left to right*) Bert Hall, Lieutenant de Laage, Capitaine Thénault, Bill Thaw, Father Armonier, Johnson. Standing (*left to right*) Rumsey, Pavelka, Marshall, Masson, Hill, and Robert Rockwell. (*Willis Haviland Collection*)

Left: Bert Hall and Lawrence Rumsey share some wine – most likely at the Bastille Day celebration, 1916. (*Charles Woolley Collection*)

Below: The Escadrille Américaine. (*Left to right*) Kiffin Rockwell, Capitiaine Thénault, (obscured from view – Bill Thaw), Norman Prince, Lieutenant de Laage, Elliott Cowdin, Bert Hall, James McConnell, and Victor Chapman. (*Library of Congress*)

Right: William Thaw, Bert's closest friend in N 124, taken after his wounding. (*Museum of the United States Air Force, Archives, William Thaw Holdings*)

Below: Bert stands in front of his Nieuport. Note the reverse spelling of his name 'Treb' on the aircraft. (*Charles Woolley Collection*)

Above: A photo of the Escadrille Américaine. (*Left to right*) Lieutenant de Laage, Johnson, Rumsey, McConnell, Thaw, Lufbery, Kiffin Rockwell, Didier Masson, Norman Prince, and standing apart from his comrades – Bert Hall. (*Washington and Lee University, Paul Rockwell Collection*)

Below: Kiffin Rockwell prepares to take-off in Bert Hall's Nieuport. (*Washington and Lee University, Paul Rockwell Collection*)

Above: The Americans parading through the streets of Paris to enlist in the Foreign Legion. (*Washington and Lee University, Paul Rockwell Collection*)

Right: Bert Hall confers with Kiffin Rockwell who is flying his aircraft. The film error exists on the original. (*Washington and Lee University, Paul Rockwell Collection*)

Left: Bert Hall during the happier times in N124. (*Washington and Lee University, Paul Rockwell Collection*)

Below: The members of the Escadrille Américaine. (*Washington and Lee University, Paul Rockwell Collection*)

Right: Capitaine Thénault poses in front of Bert's Nieuport. (*Charles Woolley Collection*)

Below: Bert stands with an unknown Chinese officer and Robert Short, a fellow American aviator in China. (*Author's Personal Collection*)

Above: Bert plays cards with Chouteau Johnson and Kiffin Rockwell on the wing of a Nieuport. (*Washington and Lee University, Paul Rockwell Collection*)

Left: Bert Hall in later life, just prior to his death. (*Author's Personal Collection*)

Above: Bert stands in front of a Romanian-painted Nieuport with his mechanic. (*From* En l'air!)

Below: Didier Masson and Bert Hall. (*From* En l'air!)

Bert Hall flying over the front lines, returning from a patrol. (*From* En l'air!)

Above: Bert Hall with Mrs Edith Ogilvie, the first woman to fly – and Robert Ripley. (*Author's Personal Collection*)

Below: Bert Hall and Edith Day in *A Romance of the Air.* (*Library of Congress*)

Above: Bert Hall facing a firing squad in *A Romance of the Air*. (*Library of Congress*)

Below: Bert Hall's Sturdy Toy Company's products. (*Author's Personal Collection*)

no burden at all, but for his pregnant wife Della, it had to be disheartening. Even worse, as a vaudeville actress, she would have been the logical choice to play the lead role in the film. However, in her pregnant condition it was possibly another burden for their marriage.

The film debuted to a large crowd on 11 November 1918, strangely enough the day of the Armistice that ended the Great War. While the rest of the world was rejoicing an end of the conflict that consumed so many lives, Hall was using the war as the means of supporting himself.

Although the movie was not compelling, what seemed to bring people in was Bert Hall himself. Bert appeared several times an evening in New York for screenings, standing on stage both before and after the film to lecture and take questions. For film audiences, it blurred the lines between fiction and reality, almost as if Hall were endorsing the film as a docudrama of what really happened in the war. With Bert standing on stage in full uniform, wearing his medals and regalia, the film was well received. *The New York Tribune* said of the film, 'This picture is interesting mainly because one knows that much of what happens on the screen is true. It is a story of spies and miraculous escapes, and even if Dulcinea did say it, 'Truth is stranger than fiction'.'[38]

In Boston, the film was a huge hit. 'As for 'A Romance of the Air', this picture at its initial showing at the Rivoll Theatre played to the biggest receipts of any feature picture shown there for three months,' said Carl Carlton of the film.[39] In the same interview he said that war movies were beginning to lose their draw. While he was hopeful that thousands of American soldiers coming home would welcome a good war movie as long as it was personal and had a strong plot, he acknowledged that Americans were getting tired of war.

While some critics panned the movie's plot as lacking romance, one could not argue with the income it generated. 'Boston critics unanimously acclaim 'A Romance of the Air' the most thrilling serial production, devoting as much as three columns to interviews and criticisms. Thaw and myself guests of honour at a special banquet for Allied Aviators and Radio Operators at Boston City Club Thursday night,' Bert wired Frank Hall.[40] For Bert, this is the first time that he and his best friend got together since Hall's departure from France. There is no recorded comments from Bill Thaw about seeing himself portrayed in the film.

While in Boston, Bert offered nothing but glowing words for the former members of N 124, especially Thaw and Prince who were considered local New England boys. 'Norman Prince was rightly named. He was a Prince every inch of him, and a hard worker. He had influence and managed to raise the funds to equip the organisation and we became the Lafayette Escadrille.'[41]

For Bert's part, he was on the road constantly. While the speaking engagements drove up sales of his autobiography, they had to have been exhausting for him. He went to a total of twenty-eight cities on the east coast with the movie. Unlike today, movies remained in release much longer, often for a year.

In the middle of his movie tour, Hall took a jaunt to France for several months. Once more he met John Jacob Niles at the American Aviation General Headquarters at the end of January 1919.[42] Several days later they met for dinner at the Ratt-Jazz, a restaurant near the Hotel Richelieu. They both swapped stories of wars and women. Niles was a musician who was compiling some of the songs associated with the war while serving as a replacement/ferry pilot for the American Air Service. He had to have been impressed with Bert's flamboyant style and colourful language. The two met again the next evening at Harry's New York Bar and had dinner at L'Aubergue du Clou. It was then that Bert agreed to share with Niles his diary with the thought that Niles might be able to take Bert's abbreviated entries and beef them up, turning them into something more digestible in book format. It was a verbal agreement only at this time, but the two agreed to stay in contact. He had been working on his own autobiography at the time, but may not have had a publisher yet and was hoping to leverage Niles to secure one. There was no indication that he ever told Niles that he was already working on his life story, so the depth of Hall's thinking is not fully know. Yet he did openly admit to sharing his diary with Niles in later years.[43]

While her husband was in France, Della gave birth to Weston Bert Hall in New York City on 26 February 1919. What Della could not have known was that while she was alone raising their infant, Bert was back in Paris apparently tracking down his French wife, Suzanne. While details are scarce about whatever excuse Bert gave for abandoning her for two years, it is apparent they reconciled. By the time that Bert left France, Suzanne was pregnant with his child. Hall returned to Della's waiting arms. For a short time they settled in Connecticut, but it was only a respite for Bert's tours. He set out on tour with *A Romance of the Air* again and left Della behind with his infant son, never to return.

Hall was not lonely for long. Less than one month after abandoning Della, he married Helen Marie Jordan who became the fifth (known) Mrs Bert Hall.[44] She was a short woman with grey eyes and dark brown hair. Bert was still married to Suzanne in France and to Della, but that did not matter. Bert married Helen in Shaker Heights, Cuyahoga County, Ohio. On his marriage licence he indicated that he had been previously married but was divorced, which was true. Bert's taste for younger women had not faded in the least, Helen was a mere eighteen years old when he married her, though she lied about her age listing it as twenty. Strangely enough, Bert listed his birthplace on the marriage application as Greene, Kentucky. She was from Kansas City,

Missouri, and would prove to be one of the longest relationships he would ever have with a wife. They settled in Kansas City.

Meanwhile, back in France, Bert's wife Suzanne gave birth to their daughter, Nadine Hall.[45] Bert may not have even been aware at the time that Suzanne had given birth, given his constant changing of address. For Bert, there was never looking backwards, he was always looking forwards. The ever-fertile Hall had a good reason to marry Helen: she was already pregnant by a month at the time of their marriage that may account for why Helen lied about her age and why they were not married in her hometown of Kansas City. On 29 October 1919, Weston Bert Hall Jr was born to Helen and Bert. This was the second child to bear that name, born in the same year, but by different wives and the third of his children born in 1919 by three different wives. Keeping track of Bert's marriages and children, even for Bert, must have proven to be a challenge.

Bert enjoyed a special treat on 9 June 1919 when he went returned to California. He took *A Romance of the Air* with him to show in San Francisco. In doing so, he took a flight from the marina up to Oakland, California, flying the plane himself. With him was Major John Yost, the chief of recruiting for the US Army Air Service who was clearly leveraging the presence of Hall to generate potential recruits. Once in Oakland, Colonel William Thaw arrived to spend several days with Bert. Hall did speeches at the Oakland Chamber of Commerce where both Bill Thaw and Colonel 'Hap' Arnold attended. Bert gave away over 1,000 tickets to *A Romance of the Air* to generate publicity for the film.[46]

The next day Bert received the laurels and accolades from the mayor of San Francisco. 'San Francisco feels honoured in having Lieutenant Bert Hall as a visitor and his presence here recalls to our minds the magnificent service of the men who throughout the entire war made up the daring personnel of the Lafayette Escadrille, the original American organisation which rallied to the cause of France. Please accept my most cordial greeting and every good wish. Very sincerely, Ralph McLeran, Acting Mayor.'[47] While the warm greeting from the mayor was nice, for Bert the true treat was to spend five days with his old friend Bill Thaw. Bert arrived for the Fourth of July in his hometown of Higginsville, Missouri, with his father. He managed to arrange for *A Romance of the Air* to be shown at the Rex Theater for three days where he performed his usual introductions. Even in the town of his birth, facts were beginning to blur with reality. 'Lieut. Hall was wounded and shot down behind German lines, changed clothes with his dead adversary, and escaped in a stolen German airplane.'[48] In this instance, the scenes were from the movie, not real life. In Bert Hall's life, there was very little difference. The image that he was building was one that was larger than real life. He was learning that he could craft stories that were outright lies and that the public was more than willing to accept it as gospel.

Given how he lived his life, moving from one opportunity to the next, he was more like a 1919 version of the Kardashians. Whatever the truth was, it did not matter. Bert was in a constant state of reinventing himself in the public eye. Not only that, but Hall had mastered the use of the newest communication medium, the silver screen to help mould that story. While in Kansas City, Bert's occupation was listed as 'a producer of movie pictures.'[49] Hall, for at least a short time, saw the movies as his opportunity to cash in even further on his fame.

CHAPTER NINE

The Roaring Twenties

When Hall was introduced, she raised her lorgnette and stared at him for a full half-minute, then asked loftily *which* family of Halls he was related to. When Bert replied that he didn't know, she sniffed audibly.

After several verbal jabs, she commented that polo was the hobby of most of the men present. 'And yours?' she inquired, looking down her patrician nose. 'What might your hobby be, Captain Hall?'

'Sexual intercourse,' Hall said casually, silencing the land for the rest of the evening. The incident is noteworthy because it is an example of Hall's ability to take care of himself in any situation. He was as devastating in matching wits with a supercilious dowager as with a blood-letting enemy. Hall was like a character from the pages of a Richard Harding Davis yard with a generous seasoning of Dumas thrown in. Dashing, flamboyant, an awesome fighter and volcanic lover, he was a type that has disappeared from the world scene.[1]

Bert and Helen moved to California to be in the new burgeoning heart of the movie industry by the end of 1920. He was making a living by performing public appearances to talk about his time at the war by playing bridge tournaments. Ever the master card player, Bert was considered an outstanding bridge player and made some money via this avenue, but such income was thin and far removed. Bert had money from the sale of his book and the revenue that he made from *A Romance of the Air*, but the movie was out of distribution and the sales of Hall's book were beginning to wane.

Even his personal appearances were beginning to drop off. The First World War was already moving into the hazy memories of Americans and his 'hero' status simply did not have the glamour associated with it any longer. If Bert was going to survive, he needed steady work. In California, he found employment in the movie industry, specifically with 20th Century Fox. Starting in 1921, he worked for the studio as a writer, actor and aviation consultant. His movie credits do not list any action outside of his own productions, but he clearly was on the payroll and was getting a relatively steady pay check as a contract employee.[2] As a contract employee, Hall worked from movie to movie with occasional downtime between productions.

In 1921, wife number four, Della Byers, had managed to track Hall down – most likely through his father in Missouri. She filed for divorce while he was living with his new wife. Meanwhile, in Paris, wife number three, Suzanne, was raising his daughter. Bigamy was obviously not a concern for Hall. Despite working at a movie studio, Bert was preparing to launch out on his own motion picture venture. He formed Lieutenant Bert Hall Pictures Corporation, bankrolling his first film on his own, *The Border Scouts*. Bert cast himself in the role of Mel Taylor, writing the script for the film and directing it. It was the story of a boy scout that becomes an aviator. The hero, Tex Clarke (played by Tom Hammond), convinces a number of scouts to join him at his uncle's ranch in Texas that is being threatened by Mexican raiders that have crossed the border. The boys concoct a scheme and capture the leader of the bandits, proving themselves as heroes.

The Border Scouts was a gamble on the part of Hall who was still a relative newcomer to the film industry. War movies were being produced, but westerns were on the rise. Bert's cast consisted of unknown actors who were no more than extras and failed to star in another film. Part of the draw of successful silent movies was to have actors/actresses that were well known – Bert did not have any. He cast only one female for the film, Kathryn Bohart, and she was a virtual unknown to film audiences. Moviegoers liked good mixes to the casts and having only one female was another mark against the film. While Bert was able to demonstrate his ability to pull together a film, he lacked the businesses sense in terms of marketing and distribution. The film only showed in a handful of cinemas and when it did appear was often listed as the second film being shown. What made Hall's first movie a success was the fact he personally appeared with the movie and was integral to the draw. *The Border Scouts* did not lend itself to this. It was a western in an age where new westerns were released every week. The movie fizzled badly, costing Hall his investment. Even to this day there are no known copies of the film in existence.[3]

Despite the losses he incurred with *The Border Scouts*, Hall was determined to continue in the movie business. In 1922, he applied for a passport to go to Japan. His occupation was 'head of a film concern.'[4] His application was stalled for a day when it was discovered that his citizenship was no longer valid. All of this tied back to the war when Cowdin, Thaw and Prince had come to the US on their Christmas visit that had drawn attention to their status as Americans fighting for France. Apparently in a fit of bureaucratic

efficiency, someone had flagged the names of the members of the Lafayette
Flying Corps and Lafayette Escadrille and had their citizenships revoked.

With a taxicab waiting outside of the Federal Building to rush him to
the *Taiyuo Maru*, whose funnels were already waving he black fumes of
departure, Weston Bert Hall, well-known aviator, was transformed by Judge
William P. Hunt in the United States District Court yesterday noon from a
French citizen to an American citizen again. He had just repatriated in time
to sail to Japan as a citizen of the United States.

When the Great War broke out, Hall immediately enlisted in the aviation
corps of the French Army. To enlist he was obliged to swear allegiance to
France and thus automatically lost his United States citizenship. Under a
special provision of Congress, an American who thus lost his citizenship
may be repatriated. Hall made application for repatriation some time ago
and yesterday, because of a sudden business engagement in Japan required
his presence there, he obtained the decree.[5]

He spent time in Yokohama, Japan, apparently with an eye to filming a movie
there. He wrote to his father George in Higginsville that there was '...a large
interest in his concern and he was doing nicely'.[6] On 28 January 1923, Bert
returned to the US at Seattle onboard the *SS President Grant*. Details of the
film deal that Hall was brokering have been lost since they never materialised.
What is known is that he convinced his wife Helen to join him and, two
months later, his father. For the elder George Hall, such a journey must have
been both tiring and exhausting.

They remained in Japan with side trips to China until the autumn, returning
in November 1923. Whatever his filming interests were, they did not result
in a production. Bert returned to California with Helen and his father where
he continued to work with 20th Century Fox as a contract consultant. For a
few years, Bert seemed to settle down to an almost normal life. He stopped his
public speaking engagements as interest in the First World War waned even
further. Helen gave birth to two sons, Norman Rockwell Hall in 1926 and
Donald Jordan Hall. Bert memorialised Norman Prince and Kiffin Rockwell,
both with the naming of his son, something that had to have driven Paul
Rockwell into fits. He had a steady income and remained (to the best of
anyone's knowledge) loyal to his wife Helen, setting a record for stability in
married life.

However, Bert had lived his life seeking adventure and a nine-to-five job,
even with a movie studio, was not how he had existed for years. Bert surprised
the world again on 8 June 1927 when he announced that he would be flying
across the Pacific from San Francisco to Tokyo. 'The San Francisco-Tokyo hop

would be the first of a proposed 18,000-mile air flight touching at Tokyo, Singapore, Suez, Paris and across the Atlantic to New York.'[7] His plans called for him to make the flight in September and Hall announced that he was leaving for Seattle to arrange for a special kind of monoplane to make the flight.

To understand the context of Bert's daring and boastful announcement, Charles Lindbergh had made his solo flight across the Atlantic only a few days before. Lindbergh had flown the *Spirit of St. Louis* on 20 May 1927 landing the next day in Paris. Several men had failed in their attempts to fly across the ocean, including First World War fighter ace Charles Nungesser who disappeared with his navigator a few days before Lindbergh's epic crossing. In making the flight he had won the Orteig Prize, a cash award of $25,000 and had become a global hero overnight. Aviation suddenly was front page news again and men were announcing endurance flights, races or other gimmicks to win over public attention and garner a few moments of fame. Now, only a few days later, Bert was planning his own trip across a larger ocean: the Pacific.

Given the atmosphere and sudden renewed excitement about flying, Hall's leap back into aviation on such a grand stage was not seen as outrageous. Also, this was not the first time that Bert had courted the idea of an aviation race or long-distance flying. In June 1916, Bert had proposed going after the Pulitzer Trophy while flying for N 124. He had floated the idea to the French to loan him a Nieuport fighter to take back to the United States to compete for the trophy. 'My route would be direct through Chicago, Omaha, Denver, Salt Lake City and Reno to San Francisco. A Nieuport can climb so well that I will not be afraid of the high altitudes in crossing the Rockies.'[8] While Bert felt he was more than up to the task, the French were not so willing to give him the leave or the much-needed aeroplane for the race. Hall remained in the escadrille.

He began to plan his trip, but it was clear as September came and went that there were delays into the spring of 1928. Bert learned that, like the Orteig Prize, there was money to be made in crossing the Pacific. The Seattle Chapter of the National Aeronautic Association and the Imperial Japanese Aviation Society offered prizes of $27,500 for the Pacific flight.[9] If he could pull it off, he stood to make more money that Lindbergh had done on his flight. His flight route changed with a start in Seattle (or Portland, depending on the accounts), then flying non-stop to Tokyo. 'If he is successful in that he will continue across Russia to London, and then across the Atlantic. He intends to fly alone in a specially constructed monoplane.'[10] Bert anticipated that the flight would take forty-seven hours, strenuous work for a forty-three-year-old aviator that had logged little flying time since the end of the war. On the day

Bert made his announcement, Lieutenant George Pond and Captain Charles Kingsford-Smith announced they were planning a globe-hopping flight to break the world's endurance record in flight.[11]

The plane that Bert planned on using was Guiseppe Bellanca-designed monoplane being built in a Long Island factory. The hope was that he would be making the flight sometime after 15 April 1928 when his plane would have flight tests completed. Suddenly and without announcement, Hall cancelled his plans. Captain Charles Kingsford-Smith with C. T. P. Ulm, H. Lyon and J. Warner successfully made the first flight across the Pacific, arriving in Oakland, California, on 9 June 1928 flying a Fokker F.VIIb-3m. While not a solo flight, it was enough for them to secure the prize money offered as well as the requisite fame. Aviation records were being broken monthly as a result of Lindbergh's flight and it had to have been clear to Bert that his window of opportunity was fading to set such a record.

Interest in the Lafayette Escadrille was rekindled in the summer of 1928 around the world. For several years, citizens of France and America had been raising funds to build a memorial to commemorate the Americans that flew for France in the war. Originally, it had been envisioned as a memorial to the Lafayette Escadrille though the idea morphed over time to include members of the Lafayette Flying Corps. The decision did not sit well with some of the survivors of the Escadrille who felt that the memorial should only be dedicated to them and their sacrifices. Since the memorial site included an arch patterned after the Arc de Triomphe and a tomb for housing those men that had died both in the war and after, the matter was hotly contested by both the survivors of the Escadrille and the Flying Corps which battled over who should be honoured at the memorial. In one reunion gathering (which Bert Hall was excluded), it was Lafayette Flying Corps pilot Austen Crehore who swung the argument. 'We have brought you our dead. Don't exclude them. We all fought for the same cause.'[12]

The board of the association for the memorial included dignitaries such as Ferdinand Foch and Ambassador Myron Herrick. The board had Dr Gros as a vice president and Paul Rockwell as secretary, along with family members like Charles Prince and Capitaine Thénault, the former commander of the escadrille. For Paul Rockwell, this was not just a memorial to the men that flew for France, it was a shrine that was worthy of his fallen brother.[13] Since the war he had been the keeper of the proverbial flame in terms of the history of the Lafayette Escadrille. Rockwell had formed The Trench and Air Association for the American veterans who fought in the Foreign Legion or flew for France. Paul had made himself the living lynchpin to the 'official history' of the Lafayette Escadrille. Finally, the time had come to eradicate Bert Hall from that history.

After much debate, it was decided that the memorial would house the remains of those men that flew for France in the First World War, regardless of when or where they died. Thirty-eight men eventually served in the Escadrille (both French and as part of the American Air Service) and some were still alive. Of the original members of the unit, only Bill Thaw, Bert Hall and Elliot Cowdin were still alive and the American newspapers at the time assumed that they would be playing a key part in the dedication ceremonies on 4 July 1928 – if not Cowdin, at least Hall and Thaw.[14] The story of the memorial's dedication was carried on many newspapers so it would have been difficult for Bert to not be aware of the event. Paul Rockwell, however, had other plans.

In messages sent between Rockwell and Dr Gros, Cowdin was the first casualty of Rockwell's re-crafting of the escadrille's history. The excuse was that Cowdin had been a deserter that had led to his transfer – so he did not belong on the role of honour for the memorial. There was no objection from Gros. It was Dr Gros who initially raised the question whether Bert Hall should then be included. Paul Rockwell seized upon this, citing that he believed that Hall was also a deserter and that disqualified him from being included on the memorial. These decisions were not taken up by the entire board, but were handled in backroom notes passed between Rockwell and Gros.[15] Despite the fact that the charter for the memorial foundation did not provide for distinctions as to the service the aviators provided, their actions were unilateral and aimed at creating a polished image of the escadrille at the expense of men that served it. Rockwell's notes on the matter stressed that Hall had no place in such a memorial of honour.

Their efforts were not limited to Cowdin and Hall. Harold Wright of the Lafayette Flying Corps was excluded as well as Eugene Bullard, the First American black aviator. Wright was a liar of the first degree and a deserter, so it made sense to erase him from the list of those to be honoured. Such was not the case with Eugene Bullard. Dr Gros was an outright racist in his thinking about Bullard whose military record was exemplary. Southern-raised Rockwell was more than willing to endorse his exclusion as well.[16] He did not veto Gros' efforts, instead his primary focus (per the existing documentation) was to make sure that Bert Hall was not included. With Gros compliance to his efforts, Paul could always feign plausible deniability if pressed on the issue. These two men arbitrarily determined who was to be a part of the escadrille's history. The men that served with Hall were quick to point out that he did serve with distinction, with four confirmed kills while flying for France. Unfortunately, by the time their objections were noted the stone had been carved and the memorial dedicated.[17]

Ambassador Herrick gave an impassioned speech at the dedication.

The people of the United States owe a very special debt to these Americans in the Escadrille Lafayette and their comrades of the Foreign Legion. During three years, terrible long years when the sting of criticism cut into every American soul, they were showing their countrymen could fight if only allowed the opportunity.

Without the boys of the Lafayette Escadrille we might still have entered the war, but the trumpet call they sounded was answered by millions of passionate voices urging to action the authorities of the government. It is therefore, a most fitting thing that these first defenders of our country's precious name should be singled out for special love and reverence.[18]

Bert was never invited to the ceremony. His name was not listed on the memorial programme as one of the aviators that flew with the unit, nor was he listed as a member of the Lafayette Flying Corps. After ten years, Paul Rockwell had successfully erased Bert Hall out of the history of his brother's unit, extracting the revenge for Bert not telling him how sad he was that Kiffin had died.

Over the years there have been accounts that Bert was invited to the ceremonies but did not attend. It has been said that three of his wives showed up instead, hitting each other with their purses to fight over the seat for 'Mrs Bert Hall'. This account is pure fiction, most likely spread by Paul Rockwell or someone else as a joke. Bert was never invited to the ceremony at all, so there would not have been a chair for him or his wife. It is probable that his French wife Suzanne did show, in a hope of seeing her husband and father of their child Nadine. Her arrival and possible asking of questions about where Bert was could have contributed to this myth.

As the dust settled from being black-balled from the memorial's dedication, Bert, as always, was looking ahead. In this instance he was looking at China as the next big potential prospect. Stories were beginning to circulate about former war aviators finding work in China. The vast country was in the middle of a civil war and the need for men with combat experience, especially those that knew about aerial combat, was high. Bert applied for a passport to go to China on 25 September 1928. He listed his emergency contact as Roy Seely (friend) as opposed to his wife Helen.[19] It was clear that Bert was planning on leaving Helen behind for this trip. According to one published account several years later, Bert left Helen a note when he left stating, 'See you Thursday.'[20] He simply had not bothered to say *which* Thursday. Hall abandoned his fifth wife and their three children to head out to China to attempt to strike a new fortune in a role that would make him an icon, that of a soldier of fortune.

Over the years Hall corresponded with John Jacob Niles about publishing short stories that Bert had been drafting. There was no mention by either man of the material Bert had left Niles in the form of his diary. In February 1928, Bert had sent Niles a short story, 'Setsu the Eurasian', in hopes that Niles could leverage his literary contacts to help sell it. Their agreement called for a split of the profits from the story: 66⅔ per cent to Bert with the remainder going to Niles. Niles did not have any luck pushing Bert's work of fiction, but it seemed to have rekindled his possession of the notes that Bert had provided him. Niles apparently believed that he could turn Bert's diary into a book that was worthy of publishing, despite that *En l'air!* was released in 1918 and had been a bestseller.

For his part, Niles had taken extreme literary licence with their agreement and was not working with Bert at all, but working solo. Using Bert's notes and diary, he began to pull together a series of three short stories under the title of 'Wings, Gasoline, and Gunpowder, the Story of Lieut. Bert Hall.' Niles positioned the series, with Bert's apparent blessing, with *Collier's Magazine*. The arrangement that he negotiated was to sell the stories at $800.00 each. 'If Lieut. Hall undertakes the flight across the Pacific, and is successful, we shall increase the number of articles used to seven, and be paid for at the same rate.'[21] While Bert's dreams of flying across the Pacific fizzled, *Collier's Magazine* picked up the stories as written by Niles.

Niles took those stories and apparently used them to pitch the idea of a new Bert Hall autobiography. Bert had not seen copies of the stories nor had input to them. Niles, per his own initiative was able to sell the book, titled *One Man's War*. Part of Niles' marketing was that Bert was in China and that his adventures there would spawn another possible follow-up book. In writing *One Man's War*, it is clear that he did not take advantage of the material that Bert had written in *En l'air!* Per Niles, he had worked with Hall collaboratively on the project, but that was a lie. Niles claimed that research had been done in Cleveland, Chicago, New York and Paris to verify the material in the book, but that does not seem to be the case at all. Even using basic resources available at the time, he should have been at least able to produce a fictional work that jived with real life. To promote the book, Niles released to newspapers a postcard sent by Bert from Moscow, 'Hello Jack, on my way to China, Bert'. Per the message, Bert was in China, living as General Chan.'[22] The article ran in newspapers nationwide, sparking new life into the image of Bert Hall and spurring on sales of *One Man's War*.

There were several fundamental issues with the book. First, Bert Hall had nothing to do with its writing other than providing some of the scant source material years before. Second was that Niles had fictionalised the book dramatically, making it more of a work of fiction than an autobiography. To the first issue that Bert was unaware of the book, Hall responded by attempting to secure money. He and Niles did not have a contract for *One Man's War* and he had issues with the book. In a 28 September 1929 letter to Niles, Hall wrote: 'What the H--- has taken place over there? I received a letter from Holt in June stated they expected big sale on book, etc., etc., and if I needed funds to draw on them, which I did, to the extent of G\$1,000.00 and the drafts were not honoured. I wired them and they said all monies had been paid to you. Jack I should have approved this contract and should have been consulted as to the title, price, etc... The title is lousy; the price is too high for the big sale and there are several errors. What has been done on the serial rights, etc. I want a copy of the contract. I understand it is running in the Atlanta paper at present or recently. Now write me and give me all of the details.'[23] Hall went on to say, '...send me a copy of the manuscript'. Combined with these comments regarding the errors he claims are in the book, indicates that Bert had never seen the manuscript before its publication. Some historians have referred to the book as being ghost-written, but the reality is that is Niles wrote *One Man's War* without any input from Bert.

Niles had published the book without Hall's consent or input... which was bad. Bert made matters worse attempting to draw funds from the Henry Holt and Company publishing corporation. In their response to Niles, they sent the following: 'I am enclosing a copy of the most recent communication from our friend Bert Hall. He continues to mention a letter from us dated June 3, 1929, of which we have no record whatever, and which I do not believe was ever written. I have asked him to send us a photostat as soon as possible. So far as I can make out, Hall has probably gotten money from one of the banks in Shanghai and is trying, through these letters, to justify himself.' They closed the letter with a warning to Niles, 'It will be a good plan to get together all the evidence you have of your arrangement with Hall in case any legal action is taken. I do not believe this is likely but if Hall has stung a bank something of this kind may occur.'[24] In essence, Niles had sold Bert's fictionalised life story to *Collier's Magazine* and to Henry Holt and had collected the money. Bert's response had been to forge a letter from Holt and borrow the money from a bank in Shanghai, essentially stinging Henry Holt. This was a question of who was attempting to steal from whom and the answers rest with *both* Hall and Niles.

Rather than admit that he was resorting to his old habits of stealing, Hall hired a law firm to review Henry Holt and Company and attempt to sort out just how much money he was owed. The matter was even more complicated because the publisher found itself in a difficult situation. They had published the 'autobiography' of Hall but the man they were working through, Niles, did not have permission to have the book published. Bert did not let the situation ruin his relationship with Niles in the least. He was sending him telegrams and letters from China letting him know how things were going and prodding for sales figures on the book.

Most men would have been upset at the thought that someone else had written and sold their autobiography, and had not validated it for the facts. Bert Hall was not a normal man. Rather than scream outrage at the misrepresentation of his life story, Hall simply embraced *One Man's War* as fact. Some of this was Bert's personality, he was constantly reinventing himself in the public eye. A larger part of this was greed. Bert was being paid in China, but he hoped that the income from *One Man's War* would be similar to the bestselling dollars of *En l'air!* ten years earlier. The collapse of the stock market at the time may have put pressure on Bert to allow *One Man's War* to remain in print unchallenged. From the public perspective, they accepted (as have some historians) *One Man's War* as Bert's work without question. Those historians who see the numerous errors and inconsistencies between it and *En l'air!* use this to refute Bert in general. This is not fair given the new facts presented here. The published endorsement of the book by Elliott White Springs, a respected First World War aviator and writer on his own accord, only seemed to add credibility to the book as non-fiction in the minds of the readers.

The truth be told is that Niles was a far better writer than Hall. His prose was flowing and he offered incredible details that only seemed to add more weight to this written account of Bert's life. The reviews for *One Man's War* were very positive. *The Philadelphia Public Ledger* wrote: 'It will be surprising if 'One Man's War' does not speedily become a bestseller. The vivid fighting experiences of an American aviator who served under French colours from the beginning of the World War, the frank personal impressions of some of the great and near-great in Europe and numerous episodes featuring beautiful women make this book as racy a yarn as any 'thriller' that ever kept a reader up at unlawful hours.' *The New York Evening Post* review commented, 'Most vernacular diaries, when served up in print, have the stale flavour of warmed-over victuals; but Hall's courses come hot and hotter from the range. He has the born talker's capacity to take you with him, make you see through his eyes, yearn over what tugs at his entrails, laugh at what tickles his funny-bone.'[25] The only thing that none of them knew or would ever know is that the story was not that of Bert Hall but the fertile imagination of John Niles.

What hurt *One Man's War* was that the global economy was free-falling into a depression and books were seen as a luxury item that many people suddenly could ill-afford. The book became a victim of the crashing economy as did most titles in publication in 1929. From a historical perspective, *One Man's War* has to be viewed for what it is, a well-written fictional account of Bert's life. An entire book could be written refuting the book line and verse, but there were some key elements that bordered on the ridiculous. Perhaps the most glaring error is that Niles has Hall's character referencing that he was a

'Kentucky hillbilly'. While Hall was fond of planting false leads as to where he was from and even in *En l'air!* referred to Bowling Green, Kentucky, openly. He did not position himself as a 'hillbilly' though. In *A Romance of the Air*, Bert refers to himself as a 'Kentucky gentleman', the image he was hoping to convey. It is obvious that in his 'research' for the book, Niles was a misled by Hall's varying accounts as was everyone else.

The Niles version of Hall's life is littered with British lingo and references to British pilots. This comes from the fact that Niles' aviation ties were to British aviation as opposed to Hall's which was based on training with the French. Niles littered the manuscript with very precise details which made the content somehow appear more accurate. Bert used the same techniques, such as his claim to have served in the Spanish American War. While Bert used the same method to frame his fabrications, the extensive use of British references, which Hall would not have had much exposure to in the war, points to Niles' lies. The Niles account of Bert's early aviation career is in direct contraction to *En l'air!* In the new account, Bert was America's first fighter pilot, using an aeroplane in battle before the First World War during the fighting in the Balkan Wars starting in 1912!

In the book, Hall began flying aeroplanes for the Turks in their fighting against the Bulgarians. When offered a chance to fly for payment in gold by the Bulgarians, Hall switched sides. The Bulgarians betrayed him and attempted to arrest him to avoid him escaping with their gold, but Bert managed to give them the slip. The story may be flowing and entertaining, but it was pure fiction.[26] Even if it were true, how could it be reconciled with the account, substantiated by others, that Bert had never flown an aeroplane until he had joined the French Air Service? The answer is that it cannot. It also validates that Niles 'research' did not include reading or using Bert's previously written accounts.

Throughout *One Man's War*, Hall has constant interactions with the German spy Mata Hari. According to Bert's accounts, he knew right away that she was a spy – yet oddly enough, he does not report her to the authorities. Niles portrays Hall as a womaniser willing to risk the lives of his comrades to fulfil his carnal desires. While the first part of that sentence is valid, the second is not. In his departure from Russia, he helps a rich woman smuggle out thirty-eight million dollars worth of jewels on his trip out of Russia. This was not mentioned at all in *En l'air!* and is even further refuted by the fact that Bert was so short on funds that he had to go to the American Embassy to borrow money necessary to return to the United States.

Perhaps the only piece of the book that can be considered as a glimpse into Hall's life during the war is Niles' story of Bert's beloved Suzette, most likely based on the character of Hall's wife Suzanne. Just how accurate this account is unknown, though it is substantiated somewhat by the family verbal history.[27] From Niles' version:

> My sweetheart, named Suzette, was extremely pretty; in fact several officers of high rank tried to take her away from me. Alas! She occupied a rather humble position in the social scale – she was only a washerwoman, a blancchisseuse. But how that girl could wash!
>
> With the single exception of shelter, which was supplied by the army, and cigarettes, supplied by ourselves whenever we could buy them, we possessed everything life could offer. Suzette had, however, several distressingly bad habits. First of all, she spent most of her time (when she should have been washing like a good girl) praying and mooning over the fact I might be bumped off. And then as she was going about collecting soiled linen or delivering clean linen, she used to stop at the Flying Field, wooden shoes and all – stop and ask the sentries and mechanics all kinds of silly questions about the triumphs of her petit poilu. I cured her of these first two habits, but to the day of her death, she never gave up her desire to load me down with lucky trinkets, crosses and baubles.[28]

Most certainly this account may have been based on Bert's wife Suzanne; however, in Niles' account, Suzanne is killed by a German bomb, driving Bert into a search for fictitious revenge.

Hall's diary and other material had been lifted by Niles and pushed as true-life fact to the public. There were no cries from people who questioned the authenticity of the book, except Paul Rockwell. In his Ashville, North Carolina, home, he typed his own rebuttal of Bert's book – two pages of venom and frustration – just so he could see it as the written word. In infuriated him that in *One Man's War*, Bert was claiming to have flown in Turkey.

> Bert Hall first learned to fly in 1915; his tale of having flown first for Turkey, and then for Bulgaria, in 1913, is news to all the men that knew him during the World War. He was driving a Paris taxi-cab in August 1914, and his claim (page 23) that he was one of the organisers of the American Volunteer Corps is false. He did not know Jimmie Bach, Bill Thaw, Phelizot, or any of the other American volunteers until after he enlisted with them.[29]

For Paul Rockwell, self-righteous keeper of the history of the Lafayette Escadrille, Hall's book was a slap in the face. Oddly enough, Hall managed to pay back Rockwell for his slight at the dedication of the Lafayette Escadrille Memorial without having any part in it. For two rambling pages, citing page numbers and quotes, Rockwell fumed. He claimed that Niles must have written much of the material using James Norman Hall's *Lafayette Flying Corps* volumes as primary source material, not realising just how close to the truth he was. From Bert's perspective, he simply embraced the book as the new and revised story of his life. If the book stated that he learned to fly in Turkey, then that became part of the Hall myth. Some of this was the need for any cash that the book might be generating, but another part of this was that Bert felt that the story was indeed good. Seducing the spy Mata Hari? Of course! Smuggling jewels out of Russia? Absolutely! And what Bert learned was that the public did not question the stories in the book, and oddly enough none of the other men that were alive who knew him seemed to speak out publicly to rebuttal his account.

Another aspect of Bert embracing the fiction of *One Man's War* was that he was in China at the far end of the civilised world in 1929. It was just the kind of place for a crafty and imaginative man like Bert Hall was destined to make a mark in.

CHAPTER TEN

General Hui-Chang

They call him Gen. Chan in China and he is the chief of the air forces of the Nationalist army – or was chief. His name is not Chan at all and he is not Chinese. He is Lieut. Bert Hall, veteran of the Lafayette Escadrille, chum of Guynemer and Lufbery, and aviation's first great soldier of fortune.[1]

In the 1920s and 30s, China was not an industrial superpower and resembled the American Wild West. It had been spared the horrors of the Great War, mostly because it had no central government and was similar to the Balkans than the superpower it is today. The massive country was divided into eighteen provinces, each one ruled by a warlord. Each warlord ruled his domain as if it were his own nation. They fielded their own armies, had their own taxation systems, and, in some cases, their own currency. Until the late 1920s, there was no Chinese army, just eighteen armies, some little more than armed militias. There was no standard weapons, no common training. The warlords squabbled among each other for tracts of land and petty power dreams. The warlords squabbling dissolved in many cases into small civil wars. These were predominant in China before the 1920s. That changed dramatically with the rise of two forces. The first was the influx of communists into China from Russia. The second was the rise to power of Chiang Kai-shek and the drive to create a single Nationalist Chinese government. The Russians saw a great opportunity in China to expand their revolution and pressured the Chinese communists to launch a military campaign, the Northern Expedition of 1924, in an attempt to defeat the warlords in the north and bring them under a single communist government – one with the strings being pulled ultimately by Russia.

General Kai-shek had his own ambitions for unifying China which did not include the communists. His Nationalist Army struck with a vengeance, eventually occupying Shanghai in 1927 and brutally killing thousands of communists. His government, the Nanjing government, squashed the centralised Chinese communist authorities with such brutality that they were forced into smaller revolts and protests, rebuilding their power base with the simple peasants in the fields and farms. The communists managed to rally and by 1927 had established themselves with military bases only a few hundred miles from Nanjing. China had changed from the civil wars of petty warlords to a larger civil war between the Nationalist and Communist forces for control of the entire country.

With the end of the First World War in 1918, the Allied victors proclaimed that they did not want to sell arms to China. But all had massive stockpiles of weapons and many governments were cash starved. While none formally broke their agreement to sell arms, they found loopholes. Rather than governments selling arms directly, they were often done through shady foreign brokers and dealers. China's warlords, the Communists, and the Nationalists, were all ripe markets and there was a steady influx for over a decade of modern weapons pouring into the backwaters of China.

The weapon most desired by both sides in the civil war was the latest technological innovation in warfare, the aeroplane. In 1929, the Nationalist government announced publicly that its view was that an air force was considered essential to the defence of the country. But what China had was a hodgepodge of hardware at best. The Aviation Department consisted of five squadrons of five to nine airplanes each. Most of the planes were First World War surplus with a sprinkling of newer models. The US Army Air Service's assessment of the Chinese Air Force was not optimistic: 'The Air Force of the Chinese is small. The equipment is not uniform and the aircraft are old types with the exception of a few recently acquired. The military efficiency is poor. These forces could easily be destroyed by one pursuit squadron.'[2]

With the onset of the Great Depression, economic pressures mounted on governments to sell aircraft to China. The US Government's State Department maintained that the embargo of the sale of military aircraft to China remained in place. The Commerce and War Department's, however, both advocated that the US arm and equip the Nationalist Chinese forces. More loopholes were discovered by creative aircraft manufacturers during this period. If the sales of armed fighters and bombers were not allowed, what if unarmed fighters and bombers could be sold instead? The fact that the Chinese armed the aircraft seemed a mere technicality.[3] Arms were not the only items to make their way into China – men also trickled in. Combat veterans from almost every nation came to China in search of employment. Purchasing new arms did not ensure victories for the warlords: their men needed training on the new technologies in order to avoid the bloodbaths that had dominated the Great War. Who better to train them then veterans with experience with those weapons?

The mention of Americans flying for China conjures up images of Claire Chennault and his growling tiger P-40s from the Second World War. In reality, there were a number of Americans that had already found their way to China to engage as soldiers of fortune, paid mercenaries for the various factions. One of the first to arrive was Floyd Shumaker, a native of Fullerton, Nebraska. When the First World War broke out, he had been in Shanghai working as an electrical contractor. Shumaker had enlisted in the British Army in Hong Kong, but when the US finally declared war in April of 1917, he returned to the US where he enlisted in the US Army Air Service. Shumaker eventually rose to rank of Major. When he left the service in 1919, he became the vice president of the Aviation Corporation of America as their Chinese representative. Shumaker's role was simple – he was a front man, a go-between for the Douglas Aircraft Corporation to sell aircraft to the Chinese Nationalists.

Shumaker made a name for himself in the Chinese War Department by putting together his own consultant's view of how the Chinese Air Force should be structured, staffed, trained and organised. While the Nanjing government was impressed with his proposal, it was really just a veiled effort on his part to sell them seventy-two Douglas observation aircraft which could be armed as both fighters and bombers.[4]

Shumaker caused his own diplomatic rift on 14 July 1930 when he piloted an aeroplane on a bombing mission against the communists. He had attempted to bomb the railway bridge at Chengzhou over the Yellow River. Shumaker did not deny his involvement, his justification being that the Chinese lacked trained pilots and he was available. It is just as equally as likely that Shumaker thought his participation might help him sell more equipment. The State Department informed him that he would be risking his citizenship if he continued such activities since America was a neutral player in the Chinese civil wars. The same warning was passed onto Hall to dissuade him from taking similar actions. Robert Short of Washington State arrived later, but would go on to incredible distinction for his service to China. He had been in the US Army Air Service but quit just after his flight training. In the US, he had flown mail and some commercial flights. He had accepted a job offer in Shanghai and ended up being an active and engaged aviator for the Chinese Air Force, providing training and more than willing to climb into the cockpit and fight if needed.[5]

Other American figures in China included Allen 'Pat' Patterson, a stunt pilot for films which included the popular Howard Hughes production of *Hell's Angels*. He and a friend, Carl Knamacher, the owner of a failing Hudson car dealership in Shanghai, found there was no problem becoming authorised aircraft sales representatives for United Aircraft, Boeing, Lockheed, Curtis

Wright and Douglas Aircraft.[6] The American companies, facing the hardships of the Great Depression were willing to let anyone who wanted to attempt to sell their products. Into this mix of down-and-out businessmen, renegades, idealists, adventurers and mercenaries came Bert Hall. Bert proffered his services at first to the local warlord in Nanking. Bert began calling himself 'General Chan', but it was the ever-crafty John Jacob Niles that gave him the full title: 'General Chang Hui-chang'. Whether this was done on Niles part to help trump-up sales of *One Man's War* or whether it was Bert's idea, no one can be sure.[7]

The issue around the name that he had chosen was that General Chang Hui-chang was Bert's employer in Nanking. The net result of utilising the same name in his sparse press releases and interviews with reporters was that they often confused the two men. Any actions or exploits by the real General Chang Hui-chang would be attributed to Hall and vice versa. It was the 1920s-1930s version of identity theft. And if it was Bert's idea, it was a masterstroke of public relations. General Chang Hui-chang was a graduate of the American Aviation School in the 1920s and earned a national reputation by building a duplicate of Charles Lindbergh's *Spirit of St. Louis*, taking it on a tour of Chinese cities. He was dubbed 'The Chinese Lindbergh' for his efforts, performing his own identity theft. The real General Hui-chang was renowned for his role in co-ordinating the air campaign in the war between Canton and Kwangsi provinces. It was the first campaign in China in which bombers were used. By 1929, when Bert arrived and offered his services as a military advisor, General Hui-chang was the Director of the Bureau of Aviation in the Ministry of Military Administration.[8]

If the real general had an issue with Bert using his name, he did not say so publically. Reporter Ernie Pyle who would go onto fame in the First World War as a correspondent, finally exposed Bert's name-borrowing ruse in 1930, but the American public paid no attention or did not care.[9] Bert embraced the new identity as openly as any parts of his falsified life story from *One Man's War*.

In 1929, General Hui-chang entered into negotiations with the Nationalist Government to arrange for him and his tiny air force of seven aircraft and pilots to defect to the Nationalist side.[10] Their doing so made worldwide news and in many circles Bert was the recipient of the credit for the defection. While he was no doubt involved with the defection, it is doubtful that he personally orchestrated the effort. Bert's role as advisor to the General evolved overnight to him being named as an advisor to the Nationalist government under General Chiang Kai-shek.

In late 1929, Bert became embroiled in a dispute over the sales of aircraft. Earl Baskey of the Gale Company (owned by L. E. Gale) was the sole agent for China for selling their Chance-Vought Corporation manufactured Corsair aircraft. The Chinese were excited about purchasing these aeroplanes. Gale submitted his bid. At the same time, Bert, in his capacity as advisor to the Nationalist government, submitted his own that was substantially lower. Hall had created his own corporation, the National Import Company, to sell aircraft to China. Bert claimed to have his permit to sell the aircraft, not from the US, but from France. Regardless of the origins of his bid, it brought his activities into the glaring eyes of the US State Department.

Per a message from the American Consulate, Walter Adams to the Secretary of State about the Mayor of Nanking's request for a direct price from Chance-Vought:

> The Mayor is in possession for some five or six hundred thousand dollars contributed mainly by overseas Chinese for the purpose of improving the military aviation equipment of the National Government. The military aviation department is I understand, in possession of substantially an equivalent sum to be expended on the same purpose. A number of American and European aeroplane manufacturers have been competing keenly for the plane orders made possible by these funds.
>
> Mr. L. E. Gale (American) who is, I understand, the sole agent in China for the Vought Corsair planes, succeeded in interesting the military aviation authorities in these planes and made quotations to the Mayor and to the military aviation authorities. His offer was being favourably considered when a Mr. Bert Hall, of doubtful nationality, representing French aviation interests, gave the aviation authorities quotations upon Vought Corsair planes that were considerably lower than the quotations made by Mr. Gale. It is my understanding that Mr. Hall was not in a position to delivery Vought Corsair planes at any price.
>
> The effect of his quotations was, however, to raise a suspicion in the minds of the military aviation authorities that the prices quoted by Mr. Gale were unreasonably high. This suspicion led the Mayor to desire direct dealings with the Chance Vought Corporation and to request that I obtain direct quotations for him.[11]

While the State Department wrangled with the issue, Earl Baskey of Gale's company managed to secure the contract to sell twelve Corsairs to Nanking. These originally were requested as observation aircraft, but the Chinese asked that they be fitted with bomb racks and armed with machine guns. The State Department was not just made at Bert, but at Gale since this action would have been in violation of a 1923 law regarding the sales of armed aircraft to China.

Little could Hall or anyone have realised that his submission of a bid would stir such a political storm. With regards to his bid there are several potential reasons for it. One, Hall may have been a legitimate sales representative for Chance Vought out of France and that the company got cold feet and denied his involvement once he soured Gale's sale at a higher price. Two, Bert could have been executing a scam on the Chinese to take their money and not deliver aircraft. Three, the Chinese may have secretly asked him to submit a false bid in an effort to drive down the price of the aircraft. All three scenarios were possible.

The result of all these shady dealings in China is that the State Department suddenly began to place the sales of aircraft to China under much greater scrutiny and drove a change in US policy. The American economy was bleeding profusely from the Great Depression and the opportunity to increase jobs and bring money into the country was far greater than the fear of an armed China. At the behest of President Harding, on 13 January 1930, the War Department issued permission to ship military equipment, including aircraft, to China. Within the next year, Britain sold a number of its surplus and new armed aircraft as did Germany. Bert Hall had indirectly influenced foreign policy both back home and aboard.

The US interest in China and her air force was heightened at this time. While China was now able to purchase aeroplanes, qualified aviators were in short supply. China's Finance Minister, T. V. Soong, requested to send Chinese students to America to learn to fly. At the same time, the Commerce and State Departments, sensing potential dollars, wanted to learn all that they could about China's needs and subsequently sell them American hardware and planes. In April 1930, the Commerce Department sent a delegation to China to explore Chinese aviation. They met with Minster Soong and, to their chagrin, Bert Hall in his capacity as an aviation consultant.[12]

As a consequence of these meetings, the US government sent the Jouett Mission to China later that year. Headed by Colonel John Jouett, this relatively covert operation was to help China lay the foundation for a modern and effective air force through the establishment of a world-class training school. The changes that Colonel Jouett recommended and implemented were sweeping. Soon China was producing graduating classes of fifty student pilots every three months. He proposed to the Nanjing government that they have two bombardment squadrons, one observation squadron and one pursuit squadrons. Obsolete aircraft were to be retired or used for non-military purposes. Many of Colonel Jouett's recommendations were adopted.

During the heydays of the civil war in summer of 1930, Hall and Shumaker both took an active role in military operations for the Nationalist Chinese military. Shumaker worked on the front lines, operating out of an aerodrome directing (and possibly leading) bombing missions. There is little evidence that Bert saw combat, but he was in command of the Nationalist airbase in Hangzhou. Both men informed the US military attaché that they were involved in military operations as the Nanjing government was experiencing great difficulty in obtaining sufficient pilots to carry on operations in an effective manner.[13] As a Chinese newspaper account stated: 'Shortly after the founding of the Canton Government it is known that Mr. Hall was in Canton. He was reported to have been active in helping to organise the Canton Air Service, under the leadership of General Chang Wai-chang, its chief.'[14] Bert was everywhere at once or so it seemed.

For Hall, this was a different kind of military experience and one he threw himself into. Bert had never led men into battle as a commander nor had he directed operations at a strategic level. From the surviving records, it is assumed that Bert had control of no more than six aircraft and during this summer period when he was in direct command of the aerodrome, he suffered no losses. He had flown as part of a squadron but had never been placed in command of a unit in fighting. His record in China demonstrated that he had the skills to fulfil this role. If he was a general in title only, Bert certainly stepped up and filled that character with zeal. The result of the fighting in 1930 was that General Chang Kai-shek was able to consolidate his hold and bring several provinces under his leadership. This was usually referred to as 'bandit suppression'.[15]

Bert knew how to position himself with western journalists too, which only added to his public appeal. The *New York Times* listed him as a modern-day D'Artagnan, putting him in the same league with Colonel Thomas E. Lawrence, Lawrence of Arabia. 'Flying soldiers of fortune, such as General Chan, are naturally of recent appearance in the field (of adventurers). The most outstanding aviator soldier of fortune is unquestionably this Bert Hall, as he is still known in Higginsville, Mo., where his father lives. Hall became an air soldier of fortune when aviation was in its infancy.'[16] The fact that Bert claimed to have been from Bowling Green, Kentucky, Higginsville, Missouri and Texas all helped him get noticed as a 'local boy' around the country. The articles often blurred in a mix of truth and bits from *One Man's War*, which was being accepted as the true story of his life.

Back home, Helen had moved with their three sons back to Kansas City. Bert's final message to her, 'See you Thursday,' had not prepared her for this kind of desertion. While Bert was likely compensated for his activities in China, there is not any evidence that the money was flowing back to his current wife. On the 1930 census, Helen was working as a secretary. For her marital status, she listed 'widow.'[17] This may have been a mistake on the part of the census taker or simply wishful thinking on Helen's.

1931 was sad and frustrating for Bert. His father George Hall died on 25 March at the age of eighty-four. The wily old soldier died in the Confederate Home where he was one of the few surviving soldiers. His death was covered in several newspapers around the world due to his son's fame, but it is doubtful that Bert learned of his father's demise until days if not weeks later.[18] Most certainly he was not home for the funeral.

Floyd Shumaker and Bert had become close friends and business colleagues while working together in China. Shumaker was a licensed agent of the Douglas Aircraft Corporation among his other titles and duties, and was brokering a large deal with Julian I. S. Laing, an associate minister of aviation in the Nanjing government. The deal involved purchasing five aircraft and Shumaker wanted to leverage Hall's influence to help sway Laing and other officials into the deal. Allegedly, Bert was made a co-agent on the deal, entitling him to a commission as well – he even had a cablegram from Douglas Aircraft to support the claim. Together, the two men were able to broker the contract. Floyd was working closely with his brother Eugene back in Denver, Colorado, to help him arrange the details of the transaction and to purchase/manufacture additional hardware for the planes.[19]

Laing arranged to provide the men with $101,866.51 to purchase the aeroplanes for the benefit of General Chang Hsueh-liang (aka Julian I. S. Laing). Rather than transfer the funds to a Douglas account, Laing handed the money over to the men. Putting that kind of money in the hands of a man like Bert Hall was a gamble, even on a good day. Both he and Shumaker boarded the SS *'Empress of Asia'* in Hong Kong heading for Victoria, Canada, arriving 17 August 1931. Their departure must not have been expected on the part of the Chinese who grew wary of the two men departing with their money. Laing contacted the State Department regarding a possible course of action and by the time the two men docked, a civil lawsuit had been filed in San Francisco alleging that the two men had fled with the funds. By the time the two men arrived back in Los Angeles they were greeted with the Sheriff's Department. The men were found with an express parcel with $78,000. 'The truth of the matter is that the money was not turned over to me by either the Canton or the Nationalist factions, although it was meant to be used on behalf of the Canton or communist movement. I planned on purchasing the planes all right. And I had already entered into agreements with several persons. This legal move is merely an attempt to get the money back so a certain person can use it for personal purposes,' Bert claimed from jail.[20]

Both men were arraigned and bail was set at $25,000. Shumaker made his bail the next day. It took Hall another day. Meanwhile, the Department of Justice announced on the same day that they were opening an investigation of their own to see if the aeroplane sale violated any laws regarding the old embargo of arms to China.[21] Hall's legal troubles, at least for a few days, seemed to be compounding. Ten days later, Shumaker's brother, Eugene, was added to the list of people indicted and he was arrested in Denver for his alleged role in the scam.[22] Some of the money the Chinese provided had been sent to Eugene Shumaker in his role as treasurer of the Eversman Manufacturing Company who was engaged in manufacturing some of the military components of the airplanes.[23]

Bert's troubles only seemed to continue to plague him. While out on bail, word of his arrest was front page news around the world. Apparently four years earlier, Bert had passed a bad cheque in Trenton, Missouri, to the sum of fifty dollars. When the Missouri law enforcement were made aware of Hall's arrest, they contacted his attorney, who in turn contacted the Los Angeles Sheriff's Department. The charge filed against him was forgery. When he read about the charges being filed, Bert turned himself into the Sheriff's Department and once more was put in jail. He was only locked up for a few hours and released on a $200 bond, but it was yet another humiliation for Hall.[24] Two weeks later, the charge was dropped – as it turned out, it had been a mistake all along. The old charge against Bert had been resolved four years earlier. The man filing the charges had simply forgotten that Hall had made good of the fifty dollars.[25]

The start of 1932 offered Bert a chance to start life anew and as he had done so many times before: it was to be with a new potential Mrs Hall. While at the Hotel Muchleback in Kansas City, he was captivated by Elizabeth Chapline. She was an actress and eighteen years his junior, but youth was never a barrier for Bert nor was being married.[26] Bert returned to Los Angeles and a short time later Elizabeth joined him. She had been in town to visit her mother and the two became constant companions. By now, Helen had written off Bert and was contemplating divorce. While Helen had been his longest companion and had been mother to three of his children, Bert was doing what he did best – moving forwards – this time with a twenty-nine year old.

The charges levelled against Bert and the Shumaker brothers were resolved in October 1931 with the return of the $78,000 the men had with them on the trip to China. General Chang Hsueh-liang was apparently embarrassed by the press that the case had drawn and his attorney feared that it would portray him as having been foolish. As it also happened, the aircraft in question, minus their armaments, showed up in China – clearly invalidating the law suit.[27] While pundits point to this lawsuit as validation that Bert Hall was a thief, the arrival of the aeroplanes which were the heart of the suit exonerated Hall and the Shumaker brothers. What had happened to the $23,866.51 that was unaccounted for remains something of a mystery, though there is no doubt that Bert had access to the cash as did Floyd Shumaker.

Out of China came word about the death of American Robert Short who Bert knew from his time there. Short was attached to a pursuit squadron flying an American-built Boeing fighter in February 1932, openly violating America's neutrality by flying combat missions for the Chinese. He fought a battle on 20 February 1932 and managed to damage two Japanese planes. A few days later, six Japanese fighters pounced on him, sending Short to his death. He was buried as a hero of China. While his death helped further cement the support between the two nations, it was a grim reminder of just how dangerous life was for mercenary airmen.

If the legal actions against him or the loss of a comrade had bothered Bert, it did not show. By February 1932, Hall was talking about going back to China once more. More importantly, he announced that he had dropped using his nomine de guerre of General Chang Hui-chang, at least for the time being, perhaps realising that the confusion over his name was not helping him in his business affairs with the Chinese. 'I'm going back to China though. I was once an air officer in the Chinese army. But when I get there I'm going to proceed to Europe to get into a war that'll be a dandy while it lasts. I can make more money in the approaching European war than I can in China, but don't ask me anymore questions. I can't disclose the names of the countries I think will be involved.'[28] Interestingly, Hall was predicting a large-scale war in Europe seven years before it happened. In an interview a few days later, Hall went on to claim that T. V. Soong had contacted him and asked him to return to China 'immediately'. 'I have no official connections with the Chinese Government – yet. But Soong will return soon to his former position, and then, who can tell?'[29]

While Hall contemplated his return to China, other family issues were surfacing, this time in France. Suzanne Hall, his French wife was raising Bert's daughter Nadine and another child, Albert. According to the news accounts they were still considered married and Suzanne had not heard from Bert since either 1922 or 1923.[30] Suzanne was destitute by 1932 and had fallen ill and was hospitalised. Nadine was on the verge of being kicked out of school because her mother could no longer afford to have her attend there.

While Bert was courting Elizabeth and preparing to return to China, his French wife was making appeals in newspapers worldwide for aide. An unlikely source stepped in to help her in the form of Dr Edmond Gros, the man that had helped exclude Bert Hall from the Lafayette Escadrille Memorial along with Paul Rockwell. His motivation was likely to ensure that the image of the Escadrille was not tainted by Hall's abandonment of his French family, rather than guilt over his own actions against Hall in 1928.

Gros wrote a letter to the *New York Herald* that was published in several American newspapers.

In connection with the appeal for funds, which appeared in the Sunday edition of the Herald, in favour of the little Nadine Hall, the abandoned child of former Lafayette flier, Bert Hall, I may say that I have in my possession a certain number of copies of the 'Lafayette Flying Corps History', published by Houghton Mifflin & Co. These war books are remarkably interesting as they contain letters written during service at the front, and as such give a true picture of the French war aviation.

There are two volumes, which were sold at $4 (100 francs) apiece, and I am willing to dispose of at the price of 150 francs for the two volumes. This sum will go towards the upkeep of 12 year old Nadine.

We are told that a sum of 1500 francs will complete the cost of a year's support. This is a good opportunity to perform a generous act and at the same time procure a very valuable war publication profusely illustrated. These books may be obtained at my office, 23 avenue Foch, or at the American Hospital of Paris, Neuilly. Signed: Doctor Edmond L. Gros.[31]

Gros' appeal may not have sold his copies of the *Lafayette Flying Corps* but it did generate some of the much needed funds. Mrs James Corrigan contributed 500 francs to Nadine. A mysterious donor sent another 700 francs to the Woman's Auxiliary of the Paris branch of the American Legion.[32] Several American Legion Posts in the United States sent donations as well. It was apparently enough to stave off Suzanne and Nadine's financial problems for a short period of time.[33] It was not enough. A year later Suzanne attempted suicide by slashing her wrists.[34] Ironically, the one wife Bert had could not bear to part with him was the one he most publicly abandoned and ignored.

Bert did not look backwards in his life, his eyes were always forwards. Unfortunately, Suzanne and Nadine were simply behind him. And despite the legal wrangling with the Chinese, he certainly did not bear any grudges. He was returning to China and was going to take the latest love of his life with him.

CHAPTER ELEVEN

One Man's Swindle

Headline: 'Bert Hall Held As A Gun Runner'[1]

He says he's here because there isn't enough honesty in the fighting business.[2]

Bert and Elizabeth's actions in China were followed closely by the US State Department. Their interest in Hall no doubt heightened by the earlier Douglas aeroplane sales that had gone awry and forced the State Department to get involved to reconcile. It is doubtful that Bert was aware of the diplomatic and political firestorm he had unleashed – politics was not his concern. He wanted to get back to China and broker another deal to make up for his losses during his last visit. With Japan invading China at the time, he had no way of knowing just how long the Chinese government could hold out against the invaders. Returning to China, Bert was hedging his bets that there would still be a China capable of resisting the Japanese long enough for him to make a profit.

Bert and Elizabeth arrived in China in March 1932 onboard the SS *President Hoover* travelling to Japan and from there to the mainland.[3] For a short time, they lived on whatever money Bert had saved from his previous ventures there. Reporter William Gilman encountered Bert and Beth at the Victoria Club in Shanghai shortly after their arrival and his account is the best describing Bert's activities on this trip to China.

> I dropped in at the little Victoria Club in Shanghai, noted for poker fortunes that are made and lost there. Sitting at a table by himself was a thin lipped man, included to stoutness, partially bald and gray. He was sipping lemonade. Our friend introduced him as Bert Hall.
>
> So this was the redoubtable Bert! He is known as the man who will 'try

anything once'. If that is so, he must have once drunk liquor, and the tale must be an interesting one. For he is known now never to touch alcohol.

He appeared somewhat paunchy, but when he began speaking in a little brittle voice that one could see that here was a driver. One could also see the remnants of a man who built himself a reputation as a Don Giovanni. Now he was correspondent for a string of California newspapers, he said. About his other business, he was more reticent, making veiled references to $40,000 owed him and double-crossing. He did not go out of his way to talk about his experiences, but he was no lily when they were brought up.

...Not all of this was the boasting of a man whiling away a sticky hot Shanghai summer afternoon. Hall has his medals. They may come cheap but are not given away. At that time the romantic lieutenant had been back in China only a few months. He had come from San Francisco, where he had successfully liquidated a nearly disastrous episode in his career. The entire affair is clouded with mystery. Hall had been commissioned by military authorities of Canton to buy airplanes. He had been given money. When he arrived in the United States, however, Canton requested Federal authorities here to hold him, charging him with making away with $100,000. Then, somehow, he was released after a large sum of money on his person had been impounded. What happened is known only to the diplomats. Hall says he was freed because he was innocent. Some say the Chinese, at the last moment, refused to go through with prosecution of a man who has really been their friend. Then too, it is likely that his release was secured by Nanking, already at variance then with the Canton faction.

I met him several times again last winter in Nanking during the Jehol War. He was flittering in and out of Government Ministries and running back and forth from the north. He spoke of big deals and was negotiation with Gov. Han Fu-chu of Shantung province. His wife was with him, a beautiful red-haired woman. The two grew up together in Higginsville, according to Hall. They played bridge adeptly and more than paid their hotel bill with earnings. At poker, too, they know how to handle their aces.[4]

It seemed that in Elizabeth, Bert had found the kind of partner he needed in China. Not just someone to bed him, but someone who worked with him in his business – be it with the Chinese governments or at the bridge or poker tables.

Bert returned to Shanghai and by August and September of 1933 was working hard to secure another contract with the Chinese government. This time he was attempting to sell arms as opposed to aeroplanes. He secured the services of a local translator by the name of Liu Yi Te to work with him in ensuring that he got the language of the deal correct. At the same time, he was considering opening a gambling club in Shanghai, specifically targeting the Chinese military. Bert and Elizabeth had met with a local landlord to discuss the possibility of renting a building for Hall's casino.[5]

During 1933, Elizabeth wrote to her mother regarding Bert's business dealings. On 29 April 1933, she penned, 'Really the way conditions are between Bert and me is most amazing. It hardly seems believable that after having been together better than a year, I know absolutely nothing about his finances that is not from him. I guess a great deal, but his is so proud that I don't want to embarrass him by probing too closely. I can't go into detail, but it's something big. He has been so good to me that I adore him and always shall. My love for Bert has intensified everything to an alarming extent.'[6]

The target of Hall's negotiations was the Chief of Ordnance, General Ho Chu-kuo. Bert claimed to be able to purchase a quantity of First World War German arms, which the general expressed an interest in procuring. Hall claimed that he was purchasing the arms from a German in Shanghai by the name of Biulfield. Hall was seemingly desperate, reaching out to the American Consulate to get them to attempt to assist in the deal. From the US State Department's perspective, the last thing they wanted to do was get involved in an arms deal, and one of the last people they wanted to do business with was Bert Hall. It was the general opinion of the Consulate's office was that Hall's previous legal wrangling over the Douglas aircraft sale may have been justified. Bert's going to the Consulate for help did not add the perception of legitimacy to his bargaining, it only brought him under more US Government scrutiny.[7]

After weeks of going back and forth, Hall was able to arrange two contracts with the Chinese authorities. The first was a contract with General Yu Hsueh-chung, Chairman of the Hopei Provincial Government. Under the terms of this agreement, Hall was to provide 1,000 Mauser rifles model 98-24, each equipped with a new bayonet, sling and barrel accompanied with a certificate guaranteeing operation at eighty dollars per rifle. He was to provide ammunition for the rifles at ninety-five dollars per thousand rounds. The entire arrangement when fulfilled was capped at $108,500, a fairly substantial deal that would have rearmed the army in the Hopei Province. General Yu Hsueh-chung provided no funds but expected delivery by the end of the year. No money changed hands with this first agreement. Hall's second contract was the one destined to cause him the most grief. This was to provide General Ho with 100 long-barrel Mauser pistols with 5,000 rounds of new ammunition, 15,000 rounds of older-brand Mauser ammo and ten, eight-shot Browning #2 pistols and 5,000 rounds of ammo. General Ho signed this deal on 12 August 1933 and Bert was provided with a cheque for $9775.[8]

Elizabeth hinted about his business dealings in letters to her mother. On 27 June 1933, she wrote to her mother: 'Bert has been doing some very good business, and is held up now by his inability to get a huchao-a, a government permit for the landing of goods from foreign countries. Money is in the back awaiting delivery. Would be quite a nice profit. One thing I know is that Bert won't throw away and give away as he has always done when he gets his hands on some money again. At least I don't think he will.'[9]

Bert and Elizabeth had the money from General Ho in their hands, the problem was there was no German arms broker named Biulfield. The entire transaction was a scam. Hall was selling arms that did not exist from a man that did not exist. With no supply of war surplus guns, Bert was running out of options quickly. With his interpreter Liu Yi Te in tow, Bert ended up at the China and South Sea Bank Ltd. with the cheque. His desire was to sell the cheque to the bank. By doing this, the bank would hold the cheque and when they cashed it, they would be left holding the proverbial bag with the general. Negotiations were not easy since the transaction was so abnormal, requiring Bert to get the American Express Company to endorse the sale of the cheque. He walked out of the bank with the cash in his pocket on 8 September.[10]

Hall's next stop with Liu Yi Te was the Consulate where he applied for a passport to travel to Japan. Bert told the Japanese Consulate General that he planned on departing on 9 October. He claimed that he was going to Dairen and Mukden where he had been invited to consult on aviation matters with the Manchukuo authorities. Bert confided to the Consulate General that a secretary of General Huang Fu had come to see him and said that:

> ...negotiations were taking place between General Huang and high Japanese officials for settlement of the Sino-Japanese troubles in North China. He stated further that the secretary intimated that he was in close contact with these negotiations and would be in a position to divulge information concerning them and would furnish such information to Mr. Hall, or through him to the American authorities if he could be reimbursed for his trouble Mr. Hall stated that he told his caller that he would ascertain whether any of the American authorities would be interested and I told Mr. Hall that, so far as this office was concerned, no funds were available for the purchase of information and that even if such funds were available the information would not be purchased.[11]

Even with the money from the arms sale in hand, Bert was attempting to swindle the US State Department out of additional money, just as he had done in Russia in 1918. Liu Yi Te sensed something was wrong – he had watched his employer take money from the government, pocket it, and was now planning on leaving the country. Moreover, Liu Yi Te had been with Hall almost constantly and the latest information that was being presented seemed to be the stuff of fiction. Even more incredible, Hall was planning to travel to Japan, a nation that had only recently invaded China. Every aspect of Bert's activities did not look credible. His interpreter telephoned General Tung Pac-sheng who, in turn, reached out to the US Embassy. Bert Hall's activities, already seen as somewhat suspect, were now officially suspicious.

General Ho was contacted and immediately brought in Liu Yi Te. Liu was taken to 'Shihchiachueng' to face General Ho and his interrogators. Liu first had to convince the general that he was not part of Hall's plotting. This was done under the threat of being shot by the general's staff officers. Once this was done, Liu Yi Te told them everything that he knew about Bert's movements and activities.[12] General Ho called the US Embassy as well, only adding fuel to the fire that was burning on Bert's tail.

Bert and Beth boarded the *Choko Maru* bound for Kobe, Japan, on 9 October, oblivious that the game was up. At some point, the possession of cash was transferred to Elizabeth. Meanwhile, the US Consulate contacted the American Prosecutor and issued a warrant for Hall's arrest. Only Bert was named in the warrant as there was no reason to suspect Elizabeth of wrong-doing since she had not been present during the alleged shady dealings. When the ship arrived at port, Elizabeth was met by both a US Marshal and Japanese authorities. When the ship turned around and sailed back, Bert was in cuffs and under escort.

Elizabeth, on the other hand, was not detained. Bert claimed that she was his wife and steadfastly maintained that she knew nothing of the affair. She only stayed in Japan long enough to catch a ship to Honolulu, then on to the west coast. Whether this was the plan all along or circumstance for Bert, it is hard to say. One thing is for sure, Elizabeth made off with all of the money Bert had absconded from the Chinese.

Bert was interred in the Consular Jail at Tientsin Hall. A smart man would have kept his mouth shut, but Hall had always managed to talk his way out of trouble throughout his life. This time it only seemed to make matters worse. He insisted that the funds from the cheque he had sold had been turned over to the mysterious Biulfield. The Consulate had made checks of Germans in the city and there simply was no one who had ever heard of Biulfield. Hall went on to bring up that he was one of the survivors of the Lafayette

Escadrille, hoping to appeal to their patriotism. No one was impressed with his credentials, especially after the Douglas aircraft deal. Bert told them that he was planning on writing a book on his Chinese adventurers, but doubted that the Chinese would allow him to publish the book, presumably because of the inside information he was privy to. The State Department officials, led by F. P. Lockhart, the American Consul General, did not buy into the concept that Bert had any inside information on anything other than his theft of the money.

'He also ventured a statement to one of the Special Officers that during the 'tension' between America and Japan some months ago, incident to the 'Manchukuo' controversy, he was asked by 'certain high Chinese officials' to find some vagabond American who would be willing to blow up the American Embassy at Tokyo for a fee of $500,000. This allegation may or may not be true but Hall's lack of probity makes the statement somewhat doubtful.'[13] Hall claimed that he had paperwork on him that would have verified his story, but Japanese officials had taken it from him when he had arrived. This account was refuted by the marshal that had been present when Bert was taken into custody. Hall was clearly grasping at straws, weaving lie on top of lie in a desperate hope that someone would release him. There was no one in China that could post bail for him and Elizabeth had no intention of returning to her lover.

Oddly enough, no one wanted Bert to go to prison. General Ho had insisted that if Bert would simply return the money, the criminal charges filed by him would be dropped. Ho simply wanted to save face and not look like someone so easily duped by the likes of Bert Hall. Even the State Department was willing to offer him freedom, as long as the Chinese government was made whole. But that was impossible.

Bert secured legal counsel but could not produce a single witness to support his wild story. Pleading innocent and considering the number of witnesses that the Consulate's Prosecutor was prepared to call, Bert's case was going to be equivalent to legal slaughter. Bert's only hope was to plead guilty and explain himself to the judge and hope that his sliver tongue could get him out of the predicament that he found himself in. It was a disaster. He went to court on 1 November 1933. The judge, Milton D. Purdy, did not have any tolerance for Bert and his tall stories. Bert recanted many of his other versions of the story, hoping this would win the favour of the court. He told them that Elizabeth was not his wife. He tried to speak openly and honestly, but by that point his words carried little or no value.

You must understand that you can't deceive courts of justice,' admonished Judge Purdy after a final questioning of the defendant. 'I don't believe a word of what you have said about another person being implicated in this deal. I don't believe that your papers were taken by the Japanese authorities. You planned to steal this money from General Ho. You lived around with this woman for eighteen months, living by your wits. Then you planned to get money this way.

A case of a man breaking into a house is regarded a little more seriously, since life is endangered. But this is just as bad. You gave the money you had taken to this woman and sent her to America, hoping that your record in the service would get you off in court. If she had any regard for you, she would not have left you in this predicament. If your story were true, she would have come back immediately to Tientsin since she is the one witness that could give substance to your story of the gun-runner.

Mr. Hall, it is a great deal better for you to understand that there is one place, a court of justice, where you can't get away with this talk. You have said that you never lie under oath but lie freely to people like this general, to get money from them. The only redeeming feature of your case is that you have pleaded guilty, thus saving the Government expense. Nothing else calls for clemency.[14]

Bert tried in vain to set matters straight. 'I am very sorry that I said she was my wife, but she is very dear to me and I did it to protect her. She is not my wife and she is not the mother of my children; she takes care of them for me. I gave her the G.$1,240 and gave her the rest of the money to a Chinese, Mr. Young, named in this case. I am sorry but I had given my word of honour not to mention his name. He said he would lose his head if I did.' 'I have no confidence in your story,' Judge Purdy replied. 'You have lied to everyone.' 'I have never lied under oath,' was Hall's only rebuttal.[15] His words feel on deaf ears. Bert was sentenced to two-and-a-half years at the federal penitentiary at McNeil Island in Washington State.

On 14 November, he disembarked the *SS President Grant* in Seattle in handcuffs. According to a fellow pilot and friend who knew Bert well:

While he was at McNeil Island, he went up to the warden and said, 'I'm Bert Hall,' and the warden says, 'Yes, I've read some of your books.' Bert says, 'I'm supposed to come in here,' and the fellow says, 'Yes, I've heard about it, but we haven't received any papers on it, incidentally, do you play bridge?'

Bert said, 'Oh yes, I'm an excellent bridge player.'

The warden said, 'Well, my wife and I are, we've got another person but we need a good foursome, and when you do come in, we'll make you chief of our fire department.'

It was all set. So Bert lived up there in a hotel outside of the prison and six months later his paper arrived. Then he went over with the paper. By this time, he'd become such friends with the warden, he didn't even live in the prison, he lived outside.[16]

This story is impossible to ascertain for accuracy with the destruction of Hall's prison records, but certainly smacks of a classic Bert Hall fabrication. While in prison, Bert did grant one interview. The reporter, Cleveland Williams, found a man contrite and a little bitter over the turn of events that landed him in prison.

It's all in the game. I can take it on the chin and still smile. The circumstances surrounding my incarceration were that I had a contract with the North China clique of generals, and they did not pay up. They needed arms and ammunition and came to me to purchase them for them. I was trusted by the Chinese General with a sum of money to purchase arms and retained this money for my own personal use.[17]

My claim for $34,000 due me on a contract with the governor of Hopei province, had been placed in the hands of the consul-general at Tientsin. He finally informed me that he could render me no assistance. Consequently I applied my own methods of collecting...

If the American authorities feel that is a crime under the circumstances, all right. But now that I am here, I regret very much that I was not able to collect the entire sum due me, as Chinese generals obtain their money from the poor people by force. I do not feel as though taking money that is owed you is a crime, even though you use trickery to obtain it. There is a still a balance of $24,000 which I may be able to collect in the future.

Bert's logic is clear, though the fact was that that the two contracts were unrelated and unconnected. In his mind, he was simply taking what was due to him... even if he was taking the funds from another party.

Fighting is a business you know, and should carry the obligation of paying honest debts, like any other business. Whenever I can make more money at some other business, I'll quit the one I have known the best so far.

...my work in China recently,' said the blue-clad Hall, sitting in the warden's office, 'was part flying and part organisation work. And so here I am, with a good war started in China right now. It's not so bad, though. Warden Finch R. Archer is a fine man. I have been doing clerical work in the captain's office, and there is plenty of time to tinker with engines – I like that.

He stared out across the blue waters that surrounded McNeil Island to where the grey prison boat chugged at the dock. 'I have a wife and three fine sons at a military academy in Los Angeles – I would much rather be with them.' 'General Chan' reached into a pocket and found a snapshot. 'I sent them each a real gun,' he smiled, 'and told them whatever they did not to point them at each other. Look at what they sent me!' The photo showed three handsome youngsters in wild-west costume, pointing the self-same revolvers at each other.

A fighting man, an organiser, learns a lot about what is civilised and what isn't. There is a lot of tearing down and building up to be done in this world before it will become civilized. Hall doesn't care for reports that a soldier of fortune is necessarily a wild-eyed adventurer. 'There's too much exaggeration about my business,' he said. 'So when I finish here I'll look out for my family, attend to the books and go back to work,' his place of business, he explained, will be wherever there is a 'satisfactory' war going on.[18]

Elizabeth moved into a boarding house in Seattle to be close to visit Bert, presumably still in possession of the cash that had landed him in jail. Bert's circle of friends began contracting the year that he went to prison. In January 1933, Elliot Cowdin died of flu in Palm Beach, Florida. After being forced to take 'the cure' and being driven out of N 124, Cowdin had drifted to four French escadrilles with a less-than-stellar performance. When America joined the war, Cowdin had been commissioned as a major in the US Army Air Service, though he did not see combat. After the war, he survived on his family money, playing polo occasionally. While Cowdin was a member of the Escadrille Américaine, his time there was limited.

That left Bert's closest and only surviving friend from his time in N 124, Bill Thaw, as the only other original member of the escadrille. While Bert was in prison, Thaw passed away. The years had not been kind to Thaw. As one of America's most seasoned and experienced combat pilots, Thaw suffered from his wounds experienced in the war. Thaw had gone on to command the US 103rd Aero Pursuit Squadron, the American Lafayette Escadrille, then eventually went on to command the Third US Pursuit Group. The man was a legend, both with the French and with the Americans that served under him. Thaw had aged considerably as a result of the war. When he died on 22 April 1934, Bert was in prison, unable to go to his friend's side or attend his funeral services. Thaw suffered from Bright's disease and developed a fever and drifted into a coma. He emerged for only a short time, thanking his wife and doctor that had tried to save his life.

At the age of forty, Thaw joined his other comrades, having 'gone west' as aviators' deaths were often referred to. As the newspaper reported, 'One of Thaw's most prized possessions, locked in his insurance office safe, was an empty bottle which one time contained 90-year-old American bourbon, a memento of his war days.'[19] The infamous bottle of death was the iconic symbol of the Lafayette Escadrille. Its empty state was a tribute to the success of the Americans and the vital victories they had scored.

Thaw's passing left only Bert Hall as the only surviving member of the original members of the escadrille. It was a mantle that Hall would wear for another fourteen years, much to the irritation of Paul Rockwell. For his part, no one other than Rockwell could have been more happy that Hall had landed himself in a prison cell. He wrote in the Trench and Air Association that the law had finally caught up with Bert Hall. An admission of guilt and federal imprisonment gave weight to Rockwell's long one-sided bitterness with Bert. After he sent out the newsletter, a number of members of the association replied seeming to validate his own happiness over Hall's problems. 'I want to thank you for the news you send me of the 'boys' of the Legion. I am always glad to keep track of them and know how they are getting along. I didn't hear anything about Bert Hall but if he is in jail, I would not be surprised (and neither he.)'[20]

About the only friend that he still embraced from the Foreign Legion and Lafayette Flying Corps days was Frederick Zinn. Zinn seemed to understand Bert as a person. He failed to take him too seriously, but also refused to abandon him once he went to jail. The two corresponded with each other and maintained a friendship. It was made even more challenging in that Zinn was close friends with Paul Rockwell too.

The final insult that Bert endured came from the form of his wife, Helen. In 1935, while he was in prison, she filed for divorce. Helen had stayed with him a long time, most likely because it was impossible to track him down long enough to serve him with divorce papers. The grounds was abandonment and to that charge there was little Bert could argue in his defence. The press had covered his travels and arrest in China with another woman, so denial was impossible. Helen had not only been abandoned but dumped for a younger woman and the entire matter was front page news, adding to the humiliation. Helen won her case on 6 June 1935. Bert agreed to pay seventy-five dollars a month towards to the support of his sons beginning three months after his release from McNeil Island. Bert conceded that if he won a lawsuit to attempt to recoup his royalties he felt he was due from the Douglas airplane debacle, then a portion of that would be paid to Helen.[21]

After spending time in a federal prison, having been publically painted as not only a womaniser but a swindler and having lost his wife and closest friend, most men would have been despondent. Not Bert. He was the master of reinventing himself. He was paroled on 11 November 1935, Armistice Day, commemorating the end of the First World War. He was forty-eight years old, weighed 170 pounds and stood 5 foot 8¾ inches tall.[22] Hall was without a job. Rather than succumb to his demons, Bert looked to the future and embraced his freedom with vigour.

CHAPTER TWELVE

A New World War

Ripley: 'Everyone knows that the Lafayette Escadrille was the most famous flying unit in the world, Bert, and I understand that you are now the only member of the original group who is still alive.'
Hall: 'Yes – the greatest bunch of fellows ever gathered together, and now they've all gone west except me.'[1]

For a short period, Bert and Elizabeth lived in Washington State for a few months after his release. He tried to work the lecture circuit again to make money, but the crowds no longer lined up to see him. Some of this was due to the First World War was a rapidly fading memory. The rest was the damage that had been done to Bert's reputation thanks to his imprisonment. Even his marketing himself as a 'Chinese Mandarin' only drew small crowds.

Bert returned to California where he once more secured a job with 20th Century Fox. His official position was 'technical advisor' and 'writer'. He liked to spread the story that he was working on a screenplay about his life, but if that was the case, the script never saw the light of day. He was a consultant on the Shirley Temple movie *Stowaway* that dealt with the child actress going to Shanghai.

According to one account:

He came here with the specific intention of doing a little writing for the movies, but after only a few months he is beginning to find the screen colony pretty dull. Indeed he recently interrupted a job of story writing to fly east on some mysterious mission probably involving airplanes and a lot of sudden death for somebody.

Mr. Hall is 52 and looks it. He has a husky physique but thinning grey hair and pale brown eyes set deeply in a weather-beaten face. But tuck him into a fast fighting ship and he's gone with the wind. Unless Hollywood gets more

exciting soon his family is likely to wake up some morning and find a note
on his pillow: "Please call studio and tell 'em I won't be in today. Got a little
war on down in Parazuela.—Love, Bert." When that happens pretty Mrs.
Hall will sigh one of her stoical sighs, kiss her three strapping sons, pack her
summer clothes and catch the next plane for the rebel capital. Upon arrival
she will not be in the least surprised when she is met by six gold-braided and
obsequious aides of the revolutionary leader and addressed as the wife of the
valeroso commandante of the air force. It usually happens like that.

Said her husband: 'Of course I really intend staying here until next summer,
when I'm supposed to do a little job over in Europe. Sorry I can't tell you
about that just now. But there's always a chance of something popping any
minute. I know of a couple of first-class revolutions that are just itching to
be started.[2]

Hall clearly struggled to fit into the Hollywood scene. 'People at some of the
studios want me to sign a contract, and they just can't understand why I refuse
to be tied down. Right away they start talking about money. They seem to
think there isn't any important money anywhere else on earth. I try to tell
'em that I can make more money at my regular business in a month than
Hollywood would pay me for a year of drudgery. Yeah, I said 'drudgery'.'[3]
Bert was simply not a person cut out for working a nine-to-five job.

Warner Brothers was considering a movie on the Lafayette Escadrille and
Bert was knocking on their doors to become an advisor to the film as the
only surviving original member of the unit. RKO was talking to him about
some technical advising on an aviation epic. Three of Bert's friends were
William Wellman, Reginald Denny and Leroy Prinz, all highly connected in
Hollywood.[4]

Hall did not endear himself much to the Hollywood community.

As you may have guessed, he does not entertain the highest respect for
Hollywood and its methods. 'Gamblers!' snorted the man who has lost
several fortunes on the turn of a card, or a sword.

They talk about taking chances. Why, they won't even take the initiative!
The movie companies all sit around waiting for somebody to start something
new. Then somebody gets desperate and makes, say, an aviation picture.
Immediately the whole caboodle begin making aviation pictures until they're
a drug on the market.[5]

Despite his divorce, Bert tried to maintain some sort of relationship with his
sons. It had to have been difficult given the amount of time he was not around
during their youth.

When my boys get to the age of 18 they're going out on their own.' Hall intends to give each of his three sons, as they successively reach that age, $200 in cash and a ticket to any country in the world they want. From that time on, he said, they must make their own way. His boys are Bert, Jr., 16, Donald, 15, and Norman, 12.

There's another war coming,' Hall said, 'and when it does, I'll be in it. Naturally, I couldn't look after my boys, and besides I'd rather see them look after themselves. Schools are all right. But the big world is better as an educator.[6]

Bert's son Donald remembered his father in only general terms from this period. 'Dad's always dashing off to the wars.'[7] Donald was attending the Southland Military Academy at the time. Hall's son Norman remembered his father during this period somewhat fondly.

He had a film exchange business in San Francisco for a while and then he was in the studios. He was at 20th Century Fox as a writer and a technical advisor, working on several films. One was a Shirley Temple film, *The Stowaway*, which I saw on TV just a few weeks again and he had an on-screen credit as a technical advisor in that one. I went to the studios with him sometimes and I met Shirley Temple. I even did a screen test myself! There was an actor named Michael Whalen who was up and coming at the time and he was due to make a movie in which they needed a ten year old boy with freckles. Dad got me a screen test for it, and they told me I didn't do too bad, although nothing came of it. I don't think they ever made the film.[8]

He always had a scheme going. He left my mother when I was quite young but he used to come around. One time he showed up with his new girlfriend and that went down well! Another time I remember a really heated argument because he had left the family Packard parked downtown and had come home with an orange checker cab he had won from its driver in a poker game.

He knew everybody. He was the greatest guy to go shopping with because we had a lot of Chinese and Japanese grocers around L.A. then and he could always get the best produce because he could speak to them in their own languages....In 1934 he took me to the National Air Races and Ernst Udet was there. They knew each other so I got to meet him.[9]

Newspaper reports painted Bert's lifestyle in a mix of phrases when he allowed interviews.

Here the peripatetic musketeer-aviator has been grinding out stories for the films. His last novel, he admitted was sought after by one producer who said he would be happy to start filming the script early next year. 'By that time,' snorted Hall, 'I might be dead.'

[...] Hall sniffed contemptuously as he thought of his former school mates who are now substantial Los Angeles businessmen. 'Look at 'em,' he exclaimed. 'All shot to pieces. It's this fast American life that gets them. Me – I'm getting out of here!' Plumper and balder than when he was here four years ago attempting to finance a deal in airplanes for China's revolutionaries, Hall lives comparatively quietly in a huge apartment suite, half furnished, but decorated with a corner of what-not containing most of his war medals.[10]

Bert and Elizabeth finally tied the knot on 25 June 1937 in Las Vegas. The sixth Mrs Hall was nineteen years his junior but clearly devoted to Hall and his lifestyle.

Time had not healed Bert's belief that the Chinese had cheated him years earlier. Despite the fact he and Elizabeth had appropriated the near $10,000 which had landed him to jail, Bert felt that he was still owed money. In order to recoup his lost commissions from Douglas Aircraft, Bert filed a lawsuit in the same Consulate Courts that had sent him to prison – this time a civil action against Julian I. S. Laing. He convinced Floyd Shumaker to join him on the filing. The case paperwork was filed in the spring of 1937 but did not gain much traction.[11]

The problem was that the US Consulate Courts lacked the jurisdiction to try Chinese officials unless they were willing to submit to the courts – and Laing was not. Worse yet, the US Consulate was placed in a quandary as to whether they wanted to support charges in an arms sales, especially one that had been filed by a man recently pleading guilty to stealing from the Chinese. The matter languished for weeks before finally dying. Bert was undeterred. If he and Shumaker could not get the Chinese to pay, he was willing to go after the Douglas Corporation. In March 1937, he filed a lawsuit against Douglas for $55,000 in commissions that he claimed was due. This was not just a lawsuit for money. If Bert won, it would help redeem some of the damage his reputation suffered.

Hall pulled out all of the stops when it came the lawsuit. He produced letters from Minister of Finance, T. V. Soong, detailing the purse of the ten Douglas bombers. Bert had Floyd Shumaker took to the stand to detail the numerous meetings and nuances of the deal. Bert even had his son Norman take the stand to detail the suffering that the family had endured as a result of Hall not being paid.[12] The Los Angeles courtroom was packed everyday and Bert and his attorney played the press, making sure that the details of the trial were either on page one or two.

'I spent practically my entire time on the sale of Douglas airplanes,' Bert argued. He claimed that he laid out extensive funds to secure the deal. While he could not detail the exact amount, he assured the court it was 'Plenty!' As Bert put it while on the stand, 'I was under the impression that Douglas would take care of me.'[13]

Douglas Aircraft put up a fight, but the way the press covered it, it was a case of David (Hall) vs. Goliath (Douglas) and the media sided with Hall. Donald W. Douglas as President of the corporation was called to the stand. According to his account, Hall was never in the employ of Douglas in securing the deal. Bert was an independent contractor working for Floyd Shumaker. If anyone owed Hall money, it was Shumaker, not Douglas.[14]

Donald Douglas painted Shumaker as a failure in terms of securing the deal. 'He was persona non grata,' Douglas claimed. Superior Judge Henry Willis drilled into this point wanting to understand fully if Shumaker was such a failure, why/how did Douglas secure the sale?[15] Douglas' response was that this entire trial was about securing 'squeeze money'. The fact that the sale took place hurt their case the most. Douglas claimed that they had sent Hall 9,000 dollars for his contribution to the sale, which only eroded their case further. If Bert was not a licensed sales agent why pay him at all? How could Douglas claim that Bert was not owed the money as a sales commission when they had already made a payment to him. Douglas attempted vainly to refute the charge, claiming that the payment for Hall was intended to compensate Shumaker as well – and at best, Bert was owed only $3,000 of that amount. Instead of helping their case, it only served to make it worse. The final nail in the coffin against Douglas was their admission that they did eventually deliver the aircraft and were paid in full for them.

While the courtroom proceedings ended in April 1937, it took over a year for the final settlement. The jury awarded Bert the victory but it took months to schedule the award portion of the trail. When it became clear that Bert was going to win at least some of the amount that he was owed, Douglas entered into negotiations in the hope to sweeten the deal. They had no idea what they were up against. For Bert, the art of the deal was the same as betting on bridge or poker and he was a master. On 28 May 1938, the announcement was made that Bert Hall would be awarded $40,000 in settlement of his case. The press, in their zeal to get a story, seemed to confuse Hall's lawsuit with his imprisonment – so the settlement seemed to clear Bert's time in jail. The public was most likely confused as well. What they knew was that the wily old soldier of fortune had been exonerated. More importantly, his victory was portrayed as a lone man having won against a large powerful corporation that had taken advantage of his work.[16] Other than Douglas aircraft, the only other person likely to take Bert's victory as a loss was Paul Rockwell. Hall, the only surviving original member of the Lafayette Escadrille was staying in the press and worse, was redeemed in the public eye.

With the outbreak of war in Europe in 1939, Bert was quick to grant interviews with the newspapers. As America's leading aviation mercenary, Bert offered his opinions of the Japanese.

We'll never beat them with air power,' to affairs in Europe; 'The man Chinese known as General Chan turned his face today toward Europe and predicted war. It's coming this summer. Mussolini and his Italian legions will see Franco through in Spain. When the last snows have melted, Hitler will start the Germans marching on the Russian Ukraine. They can't stop the war from coming. It will show, for one thing, that the Russian army's power is greatly exaggerated. The Russians look impressive in their big reviews. But their mechanised units won't stand up. They haven't been building machines that will stand the gaff. And more than half their air force is obsolete.

The time to be careful is when you're young. I'll be fifty-two next November, the age when you can take a chance.[17]

This from a man whose entire life was built on taking chances.

By March 1940, rumours circulated that Bert was on his way to Finland to join the fighting there. For Bert and his sons, this was a surprise given that he had never even hinted at such an action.[18]

Paul Rockwell, in a bid to rekindle the spirit of the Lafayette Escadrille, went to France prior to the German invasion in May 1940. He connected with Georges Thénault in hopes that they might once more reform the escadrille in the hour of France's greatest need. It was idealistic and foolhardy. America in 1940 was isolationist, even more so prior to the First World War. The German blitzkrieg was so rapid there was no hope of France holding out. Rockwell fled France on one of the last boats for civilians to England. His dream of a new Lafayette Escadrille with him as its grand architect evaporated even before it began.

On 19 April 1940, Hall was a featured guest on Robert Ripley's national radio programme and was featured in his 'Believe it or Not!' newspaper column. Hall was billed as 'The World's Greatest Soldier of Fortune' and appeared with Edith Ogilvie, the first woman to fly in an aeroplane. 'Ripley led into his short interview with Bert talking about his flying for the Sultan of Turkey, an obvious reference to Nile's book, *One Man's War*. Bert embraced the altered history as fact. Hall wove an entertaining tale about being in Italy and meeting Benito Mussolini in Rome... Purely a tale from Bert's fertile imagination. When he spoke about his time in China, he painted an even a greater picture of his contribution. 'I received a whole Chinese province, and a completely equipped army of 350,000 men as an outright gift.' The energetic Ripley played along with his own positioning of such a boast. 'That's quite a gift, Bert. You know – that's more than the size of the standing Army of the United States.'[19]

Bert, for his part, moved to Sandusky, Ohio, with Elizabeth as she had family from that city on Lake Eerie. Bert was working at the Union Chain Company.[20] It was a far cry from co-ordinating operations for the Chinese Air Force just a decade earlier. Just when it appeared as if Bert might be settling back and letting the next war pass without his involvement, he left Elizabeth and set out once more for China.

Travel to China in 1940 was a risky business. Europe was under Nazi rule and China had been under siege by Japan for years. Plans were underway to establish an American volunteer squadron, the Flying Tigers, in China to fight Japan – much like his beloved Lafayette Escadrille of old. The world had become a dangerous place to travel, but that did not deter Hall. Checks of ship manifests do not show how Bert got to China, but somehow he did.

Bert contacted the State Department in Shanghai with intelligence information he felt they should be aware of. The report was forwarded onto Washington as '...from a highly reliable source'. Bert wrote:

> For your knowledge and information a certain Emmanuel F. Yannoulatos now acting as Greek Consul General, unbeknown to his intends to visit and later open offices, and continue his operations of selling and shipping goods ammunition saundries [sic] to German and Japan, act as intelligent bureau for these countries as he is now doing here. At the present moment he is shipping tyres and ammunition to Dairen, from there to Kennigsburg, Germany. His first great success from today was the change of the Greek Flag for the Panama Flag, through our Consulate, and under his own firm name of EMM. P. YANNOULATOS AND CO.
>
> Hoping this will be useful information as the intended trip is for November or there abuts [sic], my humble opinion is that we have enough of these sort of people there at the present moment with these anxious time, I remain, Bert Hall.[21]

Bert was clearly involved with the arms trade again in China and oddly enough, the State Department that he had clashed with so often during his career, now viewed him as a trusted source of intelligence. They launched an investigation into Yannoulatos lasting two years, probing into his arms sales, sources, etc. Bert often told the media that he was always working for the US Government throughout his career. In this particular case, he was definitely providing intelligence tips to the State Department – that much cannot be refuted. Bert's trip to China caused some strain with Elizabeth. In August 1941, she filed for divorce.[22] She charged him with cruelty, which was a generic divorce wording that covered any number of possible indiscretions. Hall had most likely taken off on her just as he had with Helen and his other wives. Her having the divorce covered nationally in newspapers seemed to have had the desired effect. Bert returned to Ohio and his wife and they reconciled. His days of running off to wars seemed over. This new war, the Second World War, at least for a short time, looked as if it would be devoid of having a member of the Hall family fighting it in. That changed with Bert's son, Donald Jordan Hall.

America was not at war but Britain was fighting for her very life alone. Many young American men signed up to go and fight for the Royal Air Force. Most were assigned to 'The Eagle Squadrons', American volunteer units similar to those of the Lafayette Escadrille. In June 1940, Donald signed up for flight training and applied for a commission in the Royal Canadian Air Corps for eventual transfer into the RAF.

Donald was supposed to be eighteen to enlist but lied about his age to get into action quickly. He went through the local offices of the Clayton Knight Committee, a volunteer American group that facilitated would-be aviators into flying for the defence of the Commonwealth. Clayton Knight was an old friend of Bert's who had flown in the First World War for Britain. In Donald Hall, they saw a public relations boon. Here was the son of an original member of the Lafayette Escadrille and the Lafayette Flying Corps. The press loved the story, photographing Donald with his father's certificate from the Lafayette Flying Corps, proudly joining up to get into the war.[23] Don was off to Canada for advanced flight training and was soon named a pilot/observer. While most American volunteers were transferred into the Eagle Squadrons, Donald did not – he was posted to a British RAF squadron, the 73rd Squadron. Instead of commenting on his son, Bert sent along his wings from his time flying for N 124. The British, sensing a good press moment, announced that Donald would be allowed to wear his father's wings along with the ones he earned on his own.[24] Where Paul Rockwell had failed to get the Lafayette Escadrille into the fight against Germany, the Hall family had succeeded.

Pearl Harbor happened four months after Don's enlistment – propelling the US into the war. But like his father, Don Hall was already there before the rest of the nation. Like his father, his exploits made the newspapers back home. Don was apparently motivated more out of revenge than anything else. In one newspaper account, he described his service.

His pal, Pilot Officer Bill Johnson, Denver, Colo., was shot down several months ago while on Spitfire patrol over Britain and Don is going to make the Axis airmen pay for that. Hall arrived in the desert several weeks ago and is now flying a four-cannon Hurricane fighter. He has made as many as three operational flights a day. Those flights, to use Hall's description were, 'mostly Stuka-chasing parties. So far I haven't had the luck to tangle with the Hun. But when I do, I'm going to do a double job – I'm going to get in a few shots for Bill and a few with myself. The desert isn't exactly like home but I'm pleased to be here and flying. In the last few days I think we've pushed the Hun some and we're going to rock him on his heels.'[25]

Like the long line of men in the Hall family, Don was no coward and was often in the thick of combat.

On July 22 my squadron was patrolling the El Alamein area. Suddenly out of the sun came nine Messerschmitts. A dogfight started. We turned toward them again and again. I was going to squirt at a Messerschmitt 109 in front of me when I noticed two Jerries on my tail. The men I was after weaved frantically from side to side. Just then there were four loud thuds. My plane was hit. Almost immediately it went out of control.

I stayed with the plane, trying to gain control for 12,000 feet. At last I decided to jump. I undid my harness, stripped off my helmet and went over the side. As I flew out I struck my head and back on parts of the spinning plane. My leg caught the radio aerial wire. Then I suddenly was flung free.

At once, I pulled the ring and my chute plumped open. I saw my plane crash and explode. Then as I got closer to the earth things began to move faster. I hit the ground and was surrounded by New Zealanders. I had landed 500 yards on our side of the lines. A brigadier had me over for lunch then I made my way to the rear in an ambulance.[26]

Don's injuries were apparently severe enough to have to him sent home. His service was outstanding and he had more combat experience than most American pilots by 1942.

Don logged over 400 combat hours, with two and a half victories to his credit. He was injured from three parachute jumps and two crashes. His hair mussed and his sky-blue RAF uniform somewhat awry, Don pointed to the stripe on his sleeve and remarked candidly, 'I would have had more of these only I believed it was a short life and tried to make it sweet.' 'Those ____knocked me down three times' he grinned. [...] On a subsequent jump he hit the silk because his controls were shot away. Don landed in a native village, rested a few days and spent a week in Alexandria before reporting to his squadron. One thing he wants to do – write a book.'[27]

Don's father did not grant interviews about his son or his service. Perhaps Bert realised just how much risk his son was facing. Bert secured some work in Dayton, Ohio, most likely doing war work. Hall portrayed his work as test flying and developing new engines for the Army Air Force. What is known is that he was not on the employment of the Army Air Force as a civilian employee at the time. There were plenty of small plants and manufacturers which made parts and components that were vital to the war effort. It is probable that Bert was working for one of those subsidiary producers.

In 1941, his good friend Fred Zinn arranged for a small reunion of sorts in Dayton. Zinn convinced Paul Rockwell and Dudley Hill to go with him to meet Bert. While the gathering of these men was noted in a local newspaper, the context of the meeting was never discovered.[28] Given the history between Paul Rockwell and Bert Hall, this meeting had to have been entertaining if nothing else. One thing is certain, it did not dull Rockwell's disdain for Hall. And despite this being their last meeting together, Rockwell was poised to get in the last word in his bitterness towards Bert.

CHAPTER THIRTEEN

The Final Days

...he was a lovable old rogue, and no one would have questioned him had he declared that he had guided Dr. Frederick A. Cook to the north pole in 1908.[1]

Bert settled into life in Castalia, Ohio, outside of Sandusky. It was an unlikely place for the one-time aviation mercenary. Castalia on the flat Ohio plains bordered with farm fields framed by guardian oak trees. The population of Castalia numbered in the hundreds, most of which were farmers in 1944. The tiny town's only claim to fame was the Castalia Pond, a duck pond that was spring-fed and never froze, even in the most bitter of Ohio winters. Poised near Lake Erie, Castalia was the kind of quaint, quiet little town that people drove through on their way to someplace interesting.

Bert and Elizabeth settled there in 1944 and Bert took on the ownership and management of a strange project for him – a toy company. The Bert Hall Sturdy Toy Company was a small operation. They made two key products for children. The first was the Sling-A-Plane, a red-painted balsa airplane that was launched by a slingshot device. The other was the Sturdy Robot Catapult. This toy consisted of an aluminium gun-like device that the child would slide, launching a balsa airplane with aluminium wings into the air. The Sturdy Robot Catapult would never have been created in this day and age – it had a half-dozen places where someone could be injured and was more like a metal tool than a toy. Even the wings were sharp enough to cut in the right circumstances. Bert sold the toys in Cleveland, Toledo and Detroit for the department store Highbee's and Toy Mart. At its peak, the Sturdy Toy Company employed less than ten people.

Aside from making toys, Bert's little company also manufactured small air compressors which they sold commercially and under contract to the US Navy. The business had a small laboratory, a tiny foundry for casting aluminium, and an assortment of other tools which had been purchased at war surplus sales. His business partner, G. A. Chisholm, helped finance the business along with the Castalia Bank. The company was only marginally profitable, hardly enough to merit the work and effort that went into it. On at least two occasions, the company was successfully sued for outstanding bills.[2]

Of all of the ventures in Bert Hall's incredible life this one is by and large the most puzzling. He was not embezzling money from the business. He was not using it as a platform to launch a larger and more lavish scheme. It was simply a small toy company.

Hall tried to settle in with the business community in the Sandusky/Castalia area but it was an awkward relationship at best. The last two years of his life he tried to fit in with his peers, but what they wanted to hear were the stories of his past. He attended luncheons with the Rotary Club of Sandusky where the crowd was little more than thirty people.[3] He tried to talk about world affairs at events at the Elmira YMCA, but the small group of businessmen had no interest in his now-dated view of the Far East.[4] The local Lion's Club only wanted to see the old pilot in their meetings when Bert wanted to talk about Russia.[5] The Sandusky Yacht Club brought in only twenty or so attendees to hear Hall's tales of adventure.[6] The Lake Erie Chapter, Ohio Society of Professional Engineers, wanted to hear about his exploits in Turkey. While that tale was nothing more than a lie, it was one of the few things he could cling to in the last years of his life.

As much as he was hoping to promote his toy company, the good people of Erie County did not want to hear about toys. They wanted the Bert Hall of myth, the ace of the Lafayette Escadrille, the Chinese General, the adventurous aviation mercenary. Even then, the stories he told were the ones he had told thousands of times before. With the Second World War over, people looked towards a new generation of pilots for their war-hero tales. Bert's exploits had been eclipsed by a world that was rapidly passing him by. The aeroplanes that Hall flew in the First World War seemed antiquated and primitive to the new jet technology and a world of missiles and rockets. Almost once a month, Bert managed to secure a free lunch or dinner speaking. It was a far cry from the adventuresome lifestyle he had lived only a decade earlier.

Bert had always been the master of reinventing himself, but time and history outpaced him. On 6 December 1948 at the age of sixty-three, he suffered a massive heart attack on his way to Chicago two miles west of Fremont, Ohio. His car veered into a utility pole and fence. Bert was found slumped on the floor only a few minutes after the crash. Bert finally went west to join the rest of his friends from the Lafayette Escadrille. Given his lifestyle and profession, his survival up to this point had been as incredible as the life he led.

Elizabeth found herself alone and facing national media attention. *Time Magazine*, the *New York Times* and most of the large metropolitan newspapers covered Hall's death. Elizabeth was notified by Arlington National Cemetery that space would be provided for Bert. Given that Bert had never served in the armed forces of the United States, this announcement was incredible and accompanied news of Bert's death nationally. Elizabeth made arrangements to have Bert cremated and to be buried on 14 December 1948 at 3:00 pm at Arlington with full military honors.[7]

Two days later, Arlington contacted Elizabeth and informed her they were reversing their decision. Since Bert had not fought for the US, it was seen as inappropriate for him to be buried there. Obviously someone complained to Arlington after the press announcement. While it could have been any of the surviving members of the Lafayette Escadrille that joined later in the war, it is no difficult to comprehend who might have led this blocking manoeuvre. Elizabeth then contacted Henri Bonnet, France's Ambassador, to ask if Bert could join his comrades at the Lafayette Escadrille and Flying Corps memorial outside of Paris. There were open crypts that Bert's remains could have used and it was only fitting that, despite the public snubbing at the hands of Paul Rockwell and Dr Gros, that Bert join his comrades back in France. Bonnet contacted the Minister of Foreign Affairs who in turn suggested she contact Lafayette Flying Corps pilot Charles Gray who was with the American embassy staff in Paris. Gray reached out to the current president of the memorial: Paul Rockwell. He immediately rejected her request on the grounds that Bert had not engaged in battle over France. This was a completely arbitrary ruling.[8] A number of Lafayette Escadrille and Lafayette Flying Corps personnel who died after the war were offered internment in the crypt. Bill Thaw's family had been granted that opportunity after his burial in Pennsylvania. Rockwell's decision was completely arbitrary. It was his final revenge on Bert Hall for the perceived injustices Hall had been accused of when Kiffin had died. Sadly, it was not the last act of bitterness on Rockwell's part in the saga of the Lafayette Escadrille.

On 13 December 1948, Elizabeth held a public ceremony at a funeral home in Sandusky for her beloved Bert. The only member of the French Air Service to attend was Frederick Zinn.[9] Perhaps it was because Zinn lived in the next state (Michigan) and was easy to make the trip. Perhaps the members of the escadrille and flying corps simply wished to put Bert behind them and pray that he ended up nothing more than a footnote in the history of the unit.

It would be another year before Bert's ashes were finally scattered. Elizabeth had made one more impassioned plea to the French government to attempt to circumvent Paul Rockwell and have Bert entombed in the arch at the Lafayette Escadrille Memorial (as opposed to the burial crypt) outside Paris. The French government informed her that the arch had been damaged during the Second World War and her request was impossible to fulfil. The message from the memorial was clear: Bert Hall was not welcome there. Blocked at every avenue to have Bert honoured, Elizabeth opted for his friend to scatter his ashes over Higginsville, Missouri. Elizabeth reached out to Billy Parker, a friend of Hall's from Bartlesville, Ohio, who was the aviation director of Phillips Petroleum Corporation.

On 20 January 1950, Billy Parker angled his aeroplane over Higginsville to return Bert home for the final time. Most of the 4,000 residents in the town came out to watch the aerial ceremony. At 3,000 feet at approximately 11:45 am, Parker opened the cockpit of his aeroplane and Bert was scattered into the wind. Parker wagged the wings of his aeroplane and turned away from Higginsville, leaving its favourite son drifting downwards towards a home he only rarely admitted as his own.[10]

It took Elizabeth another year to fully settle Bert's estate. She had remarried during that period of time. Liquidating the Sturdy Toy Company and trying to sort through the complexities of Bert's business agreements took time, effort and money. He had left her a substantial (for 1948) insurance policy of $10,000, but also saddled her with the Sturdy Toy Company which, when fully sold off, barely covered the outstanding debts.

Bert had left money to five of his children. Thelma Reed, his first recorded child; his three children from his marriage to Helen: Weston, Donald and Norman; and Bert Hall Jr from his marriage to Della. When all was said and done there was little money for Bert's offspring to split up amongst themselves. After his death, one of his children continued on with his legacy of an adventuresome lifestyle: his son Norman. Norman had been drawn into car racing at an early age. Like his father who had raced in his youth, Norman was drawn to the excitement and dangers that car racing offered. For two decades, Norman Hall worked as an insurance agent during the week and a race car driver on the weekends. He raced with the likes of A. J. Foyt and others in the early 1960s. Norman Hall ranked eighth in the 1964 USAC National Championship standings. He made the top ten in the Indianapolis 500, trying out for the race seven times and making the illustrious list of racers twice. He was a fierce competitor, so determined to drive fast that in one accident in 1965 he lost his foot as a result of a crash.[11] What daring his brother Don showed in the skies over Africa, Norman demonstrated in the brickyard of the Indianapolis 500 years later.

One has to believe that Bert would have been proud.

Epilogue

Bert Hall—we never were sure his real name was Bert Hall. Don't know where he really came from. According to his mood, he gave various birthplaces. Sometimes he said he was born at Bowling Green, Kentucky, at other times Higginsville, Missouri, and yet other times Eagle Pass, Texas. Bert was a man of mystery. He was older than the other boys. He did some very good work in the early days of the Escadrille, but his ardour cooled down after Victor Chapman was killed and Balsley was wounded. [...] He still turns up though. He's dead now. He had some qualities, but he did a lot of harm. He and this fellow Hill who deserted in 1914 were the two real black sheep of the several hundred Americans who volunteered to fly for France. Those two fellows did more harm to the good reputation of our country than anyone else. [...] Almost all the American fliers who volunteered for France in the war of 1914-18 were boys of excellent family and high moral standards. I would say that 95 percent of them were college graduates. They represented the cream of our country.[1]

– Paul Rockwell

Throughout his career, Bert's biggest detractor was Paul Rockwell. Rockwell's obsession with preserving an idolised vision of his brother and other members of the Lafayette Escadrille bordered on lunacy. His self-appointed role as historian came with it the power to alter the history of the unit. What he did to Bert, attempting to erase him from the unit history and tainting historians and public image of the man, was both sick and sad. For his part, Bert never said anything bad about Rockwell. If anything, Hall was probably amused with the effort and energy that Rockwell expended attempting to alter history. Bert only seemed to carry a grudge when money was involved. I am quite confident he chuckled to himself at how much he irritated Rockwell by simply being alive.

Rockwell made the perfect whetstone for Hall to sharpen himself against. The fact that Rockwell worked so hard to exclude and eradicate Bert from the unit only seems to make Hall more appealing and endearing. Rockwell never relented in attempting to purge Bert out of the history of N 124. His efforts to attempt to enshrine Kiffin in history knew few bounds. When the movie *The Lafayette Escadrille* was released in 1958, Rockwell rallied the surviving pilots behind him against the film. He typed long letters to *Time*, *Newsweek*, *New York Times* and *Atlanta Constitution* – anyone that would listen to him. The movie was horribly inaccurate. It portrayed the men of the unit as hard drinkers. 'The men of the Lafayette Escadrille were not drinkers.' [...] 'The main character frequents a brothel to meet the woman of his dreams. This is inaccurate, the men of the Lafayette Escadrille never frequented houses of ill repute.' The root issue was even more blatant in the letters – Paul Rockwell, self-declared historian of the escadrille had not been hired as a consultant for the film – and in his mind and words, he was '...the only person qualified to accurately portray the unit in the correct light'.[2]

Not only did they have a lion cub named Whiskey, they also secured a companion later in the history of the unit named Soda. Rockwell was the man that spread the story of Bert Hall frequenting bordellos, so his claim did not hold water. The now aging pilots of the escadrille's later years supported his efforts. Their letter writing had little effect. The film failed on its own accord thanks to an underdeveloped script and weak plot.

Rockwell died in 1985 in Asheville, North Carolina, having failed to effectively eradicate Bert Hall from the history of the Lafayette Escadrille.

Bert Hall was the product of an America that has since disappeared. Writing about him was a challenge to say the very least. I am convinced that as soon as this book is published, new details about his life will emerge. Aviation has always represented the pinnacle of technology and Hall lived through a period when this technology was dramatically changing. Bert was in the midst of this, starting in the First World War and spanning into the 1930s. His association was this burgeoning field only added to his prestige and image.

I have been asked what Bert's contribution was to aviation and I have to admit not a great deal. Yes, he flew with the Lafayette Escadrille and was in the thick of combat many times with great men like Bill Thaw and Raoul Lufbery. He was not one of the legendary aces of the war. His work in China was that of a mercenary more than a Chinese warlord. Hall's contribution to aviation was not so much in achievements of merit, but rather by the fact that he was *there*. *There* was wherever the action was over a four-decade period spanning two world wars.

Bert did not make history, he cut a swath across it. He was there at the founding of the Lafayette Escadrille, the iconic image of First World War aviation in the American psyche. He served on both the Western and Eastern

Fronts. His knack for being in the right place at the right time in history is almost uncanny. He lived by his wits, often operating without a plan... How many of us could make that claim? Bert came to define what a mercenary – an aerial soldier of fortune – was in the eyes of many people. Hall was unabashed about rushing off to a new conflict anywhere on the globe and inserting himself into the middle of it. If you were a young boy, how could you not idolise this daring adventurer?

At the same time, Hall was filled with human faults. He was an adulterer, a bigamist, most certainly a liar and exaggerator, and a thief... when it fit his needs. He put the women in his life through a great deal of strain, stress and financial burden. Hall drove one wife to attempt suicide. To look at him he seemed so casual, dishevelled and ordinary. One must assume that he had a silver tongue when it came to the ladies. Most assuredly he was able to talk the pants off them.

Bert did not try and correct his personal flaws, he simply reinvented himself. From pilot to Chinese General, from gun-runner to businessman, from bestselling author to movie producer, Bert always found a niche for himself and step into it. Bert personified being his own brand and he knew how to manipulate the press to his advantage. Even at his lowest moments in prison, Bert was able to rekindle his image. He lived his life always moving forwards, rarely looking back. It was not out of character for him to pack up and head off across the globe if he sensed an opportunity to make money out of a conflict. He did this without regards to his wives, children or the security of assured employment. How many of us could do the same?

It is safe to assume that Bert would hate our times. Abandoning so many women was easy back in the early twentieth century, but now he would be found and laden with support payments for wives and children. Hall's 'borrowing' of a Chinese General's identity would be spotted quickly and rectified swiftly in the digital age we live in. His mercenary lifestyle would draw fire from intelligence communities around the world and the State Department. Hall would find the world of the early twenty-first century as smothering and dull. And compared to the life he led, he was right.

We simply do not produce men like Bert Hall any more. There are many pretenders to his throne, but none that are worthy of his wings. For everyone that admires Bert Hall, there is a counterpart who attempts to write him off as a braggart, liar and cad. He was all of these things, but so much more. For those that respect him they need to take him in his entirety, both good and bad. In the end, when I think of the men of the Lafayette Escadrille, I have questions for them all and would enjoy meeting and talking to almost all of them. But meeting them would be the end of it. Bert Hall is the only one that I would want to sit down and get ripping drunk with. Imagine the stories he could and would tell.

Acknowledgements

I have had the privilege of working with a large number of people in pulling together this book. This list is far from exhaustive and any omissions are purely by mistake.

Jean Armstrong who undertook this journey three years ago and did a great deal of research to help with this project; Erin E. Foley, Archivist, Circus World Museum; Ann Robson, Interlibrary Loans, Culpeper County Library; Vaughan Stanley, Archivist, Washington and Lee University (The Paul Rockwell Collection); Brett Stolle, Manuscript Curator, National Museum of the US Air Force, Research Division/MUA; Amy Heidrick, Photo Archivist, The Museum of Flight, Seattle, WA; John L. Little, Assistant Curator & Research Team Leader, The Museum of Flight, Seattle WA; Edward Meyer – VP Exhibits & Archives, Ripley Entertainment; Rosemary Hanes, Reference Librarian, Moving Image Section, Library of Congress; Heather Riser, Special Collections; James McConnell Collection, University of Virginia; Charles Gosse, Smithsonian Air and Space Museum Udvar Hazy Center; Jon Guttman, a First World War aviation historian who has forgotten more than I remember about this era; Dennis Gordon, Dennis did excellent work in the 1980s crafting much of Hall's story; Tab Lewis, NARA Archivist, Civilian Records, Textual Archives Services Division; John Vernon, NARA Archives II Reference Section (NWCT2R) Textual Archives Services Division; Karen Billman, Reference Asst. Sandusky Library; Kimberly Harper, Reference Specialist, State Historical Society of Missouri; Burling Library Grinnell College; Yale University Library; Ann Robson, Interlibrary Loans, Culpeper County Library; Alan Renga, Assistant Archivist, San Diego Air and Space Museum; Mary Baumann, US Senate Historical Office; Vaughan Stanley, Special Collections Librarian, Washington and Lee University; Elizabeth C. Borja, CA, Reference Services Archivist, National Air and Space Museum Archives Division; Tom Darcey who put me in contact with surviving members of the Hall family; Murray and Alma Jeane Wheeler; Bill Jackson who is working on a book on the immortal Lufbery; Iulian Macreanu, LTC / RoAF, Chief of the International Relations Office – Romanian Air Force; Maj. Cristian Solea, Chief of Secretariat Office, ROU AF Staff; Carl J. Bobrow, Museum Specialist, Collections Processing Unit, National Air and Space Museum/Smithsonian Institution, Paul E. Garber Facility; Stephanie Gamache, The College of William and Mary, who assisted with some French language translations for me; Terry Harbin, Ithaca New York Film historian; Frank Stanger, Special Collections Library, Margaret I King Library, University of Kentucky; Aaron Pichel in Ithaca, New York; Amber Paranick, Library of Congress, Reference Specialist, Newspaper & Current Periodical Reading Room; Edward Meyer, VP Exhibits & Archives, Ripley's Entertainment; Willis Lamm, for his courteous use of photographs from the W. B. Haviland Collection; Charlie Woolley, First World War aviation historian, for his generous use of photographs in this book; Alan Toelle, First World War aviation historian; Frank Dalton, for his invaluable insights into Bert and Norman Hall.

Bibliography

Books:

Bailey, Frank W., *Chronology of the French Air Service* (London, Grub Street, 2001)

Brown, Ezra, *Knights of the Air* (Alexandria, Time-Life Books, 1980)

Chapman, John Jay, *Victor Chapman's Letters from France* (New York, The MacMillan Company, 1917)

Christensen, Lawrence O., *Dictionary of Missouri Biography* (Columbia, MO, University of Missouri Press, 1999)

Churchill, Winston S., *The World Crisis, 1914-1918* (Oxford, The Clarendon Press, 1934)

Clark, Alan, *Aces High: The Air War Over the Western Front 1914-1918* (London, Bloomsbury Publishing, 2011)

Cooksley, Peter, *Nieuport Fighters In Action* (Carrollton, TX, Squadron/Signal, 1997)

Davilla, James J. Dr., Soltan, Arthur, M., *French Aircraft of the First World War* (Marceline, MO, Flying Machines Press, 1997)

Driggs, Laurence La Tourette *Heroes of Aviation* (Boston, Little Brown and Company, 1934)

Edwards, John, *Shelby's Expedition to Mexico, An Unwritten Leave of the War* (Fayetteville, AK, The University of Arkansas Press, 2002)

Edwards, John. N. *Shelby and his Men: or, The War in the West* (Cincinnati, Miami Printing and Publishing Co., 1867) p. 233

Ferro, Marc, *La Grande Guerre* (Paris, Edmond Gallimard, 1969)

Flammer, Philip M. *The Vivid Air* (Athens, GA, The University of Georgia Press, 2008)

Franks Norman, Baily Frank and Duiven Rick, *Casualties of the German Air Service* (London, Grub Street, 1999)

Gordon, Dennis, *The Lafayette Flying Corps Biographies* (Atglen, PA, Schiffer Military History, 2000)

Guttman, Jon, *SPA 124 Lafayette Escadrille* (Wellingsborough, UK, Osprey Publishing, 2004)

Guttman, Jon, *The Origin of Fighter Aircraft* (Yardley, Pennsylvania, Westholme, 2009)

Hall, Bert, and Niles, John Jacob, *One Man's War* (London, John Hamilton Publishing, 1929)

Hall, Bert, *En L'Air!* (New York, New Library, 1918)

Hall, James Norman, *High Adventure, A Narrative of Air Fighting In France* (Toronto, Thomas Allan, 1918)

Hall, James Norman, *The Lafayette Flying Corps Volume I* (New York, Houghton Mifflin Company, 1920)

Hudson, James J. *Hostile Skies* (Syracuse, NY, Syracuse University Press, 1968)

Jablonski, Edward, *Warriors With Wings* (New York, The Bobbs-Merrill Company, 1983)

Johnson, Robert, *Battles and Leaders of the Civil War IV* (Edison, NJ, Castle Books, 1989) p. 375

King, David, *Ten Thousand Shall Fall* (New York, Duffold and Company, 1927)

Mason Jr., Herbert Molly, *The Lafayette Escadrille* (New York, Random House, 1964)

McConnell, James, *Flying for France* (New York, Grosset & Dunlap, 1916)

Morlae, Edward, *A Soldier of the Legion* (New York, Houghton Mifflin, 1916)

Mott, Colonel Bentley T., *Myron T. Herrick: Friend of France* (New York, Baltzell, 2007)

O'Balance, Edgar, *The Story of the Foreign Legion* (London, White Lion, 1961)

Parsons, Edwin C. *I Flew With the Lafayette Escadrille* (Indianapolis, IN, E. C. Seale & Company, 1963)

Parsons, Ted, *I Flew with the Lafayette Escadrille* (Indianapolis, Indiana, E. C. Seale & Company, 1963)

Pen, Ron, *I Wonder as I Wander: The Life of John Jacob Niles* (Lexington, Kentucky, The University of Kentucky Press, 2010)

Rockwell, Paul, *American Fighters in the Foreign Legion 1914-1918* (New York, Houghton Mifflin, 1930)

Rockwell, Paul, *American Fighters in the Foreign Legion 1914-1918* (New York, Houghton Mifflin, 1930)

Rockwell, Paul, *War Letters of Kiffin Yates Rockwell* (New York, The Country Life Press, 1925)

Rolle, Andrew, *The Lost Cause, The Confederate Exodus to Mexico* (Norman, OK, The University of Oklahoma Press, 1965)

Savas, Theodore and Dameron, David J. *A Guidebook to the Battles of the American Revolution* (New York, Savas Beatie LLC, 2010)

Sengupta, Narayan, *The Lafayette Escadrille* (self-published, 2010)

SHAA, *Les escadrilles de l' aeronautique militaire francaise 1912-1920*

The Indianapolis 500 Yearbook, Norman Hall Racing With the Big Boys, 1983

Thenault, Georges Captain, *The Story of the Lafayette Escadrille* (Boston, Small, Maynard Company, 1921)

Whitehouse, Arch, *Legion of Lafayette* (New York, Doubleday, 1962)

Wood, W. J., Eisenhower, John S. D. *Battles of the Revolutionary War, 1775-1781* (Cambridge, MA, Da Capo Press, 2003)

Xu, Guangqiu, *War Wings* (Westport, Connecticut, Greenwood Press, 2001)

Young, William, *History of Lafayette County Missouri Volume II* (Indianapolis, B B Bowen & Company, 1910)

Periodicals:

'Heroic Exploits of Aviation,' *Model Airplane News*, September 1937

'The Diary of H. Clyde Balsley,' *Cross and Cockade*, Vol. 18, No. 2, Summer 1977

'Who's Who in China,' *The China Weekly Review*, 23 April 1932

Barton, Charles, 'Wings of the Dragon,' *Air Classics*, Vol. 35, No. 3, September 1999

Connell, Dennis and Bailey, Frank W. 'Victory Logs of the Lafayette Escadrille and the Lafayette Flying Corps,' *Cross and Cockade Journal*, Vol. 21, No. 4, Winter 1980

Farber, James, 'The Adventurous Bert Hall,' *Popular Aviation*, May 1936

Hall, Bert, 'Fighting and Narrow Escapes in the Air,' *The American Magazine*, Vol. 86, July 1918

Lewis, Latané, 'He Fought the Hun! The Story of Bert Hall,' *Tiger Magazine*, July 1957, Vol. II, No. 3

Robinson, Dr. Douglas H., 'Old Ithaca Airport, 1914-1965,' *Journal of the American Aviation Historical Society*, Vol. 15, No. 1, 1st Quarter 1970

Rockwell, Paul A., 'L'Escadrille La Fayette,' *Le Guerre Aérienne*, September 1916, p. 562

Rockwell, Paul A., 'Writings of the American Pilots In The Lafayette Escadrille,' *Ex Libris*, Vol. 1, Number 5, November 1923

The China Weekly Review, Vol. 62, #3

Toelle, Alan, 'A White Faced Cow – The Operational History of the Escadrille Américaine N.124 to September 1916,' *Over the Front*, Vol. 24, No. 4, Winter 2009

Truby, David J., 'America's Bad boy Ace,' *Air Classics*, March 1978

Truby, David J. 'America's First Flier of Fortune, Bert Hall, was Roguish Adventure Personified,' *Aviation Heritage*, March 1992

Truby, David J., 'America's First Flier of Fortune,' *Flight Journal*, June 2010

Truby, David J., 'The First Airborne Mercenary,' *Gung-Ho Magazine*, November 1984

Van Gorder, E. R., 'Bert Hall, Soldier or Scoundrel?' *Cross and Cockade*, Summer 1963

Wagner, Ray, 'The Chinese Air Force,' *Journal of the American Aviation Historical Society,* Vol. 19, No. 3

Wynne, Hugh H., 'Escadrille Lafayette,' *Cross and Cockade*, Vol. 2, No. 1, Summer 1961

Newspapers:

'"En l'air!" In The Making,' *The Ithaca Journal,* 6 August 1918

'Ace Hall Will Lecture Here,' *The Estherville Enterprise*, 12 December 1917

'Airmen Losses Heavy,' *The Daily Independent*, Ashland Kentucky, 24 December 1915

'American Airmen in French Service To Carry US Flag,' *The Atlanta Constitution*, 12 April 1917

'American Flyer Gives Black Eye to Objector,' *The Oakland Tribune*, 2 December 1917

'American Flyers with the French,' *The Ogden Standard*, Ogden Utah, 8 October 1915

'American Sent to the Romanian Front,' *New Castle News*, 27 December 1916

'An American With The Allies,' *Chicago Daily Tribune*, 21 February 1915

'Average Life of Aviator, 17 Hours In the Air, Lafayette Escadrille survivor tells of wiping out aerial crew,' *Schenectady Gazette*, 4 November 1918

'Aviation 'Stunts' and How to Do Them,' *The Los Angeles Times*, 18 May 1918

'Aviator Falls From Dizzying Heights,' *The California Weekly*, The Oakland Tribune, 16 September 1917

'Aviators Fear Only Fire In the Air,' *The Boston Daily Globe*, 7 January 1919

'Bert Hall Held as a Gun Runner,' *Jefferson City Post Tribune*, 18 October 1933

'Bert Hall Is To Join War Fliers,' *The Piqua (Ohio) Daily Call*, 26 February 1932

'Bert Hall of Castailia,' *The Sandusky Register-Star News*, 10 December 1946

'Bert Hall,' *The Sandusky Register-Star News*, 5 September 1946

'Bert' Hall of Lafayette Escadrille Dies,' *The Washington Post*, 8 December 1948

'Bert Hall of Los Angeles Relates His Experience As A Flyer In Lafayette Escadrille,' *The Los Angeles Times*, 16 March 1918

'Bold Feats by Yankee Flyers,' *Boston Daily Globe*, 6 June 1916

'Californians Plan 24-Day Flight Around the World,' *The Oakland Tribune*, 6 April 1928

'Chapman Is Killed in Aeroplane Fight,' *New York Times*, 25 June 1916

'China Air Chief Is An American,' *New York Telegram*, 28 July 1930

'China Plane Deals Told,' *The Los Angeles Times*, 18 March 1937

'China Turns to Air in Building Defense,' *The Tyrone Herald*, 14 June 1934

'Chinese Air Commander Adventurer of Kentucky,' *The Circleville (Ohio) Herald*, 8 February 1932

'Conqueror of Nine Germans In Air To Fly Here Today,' *Oakland Tribune*, 8 June 1919

'Court House,' *The Sandusky Register-Star News*, 15 October 1948

'Douglas Replies to Hall's Claims,' *The Berkley Daily Gazette*, 15 March 1937

'Famed Flier's Child a Pauper,' *The Charleston Gazette*, 22 January 1933

'Famed Pilot's Son Volunteers For Canadian Air Corps,' *The Los Angeles Times*, 19 June 1941

'Famous Pioneer Aviator is Dead,' *The Altoona Mirror*, 23 April 1934

'Famous War Ace Arrested in Airplane Plot,' *The Reno Evening Gazette*, 2 September 1931

'Fights Three Aeroes, Then Feels Fourth,' *The Washington Post*, 25 May 1916

'First Flying Ace Visits America,' *Evening Public Ledger (Philadelphia)*, 30 January 1918

'Flier's Wife Tries Suicide,' *The Washington Daily News*, 22 March 1933

'Flyer Describes Narrow Escape From Hit Plane,' *The Los Angeles Times*, 4 August 1942

'Flying Corps to Aid America,' *The Los Angeles Times*, 31 October 1915

'Flying in France Is Great Sport,' *The Washington Post*, 9 February 1918

'Former Galveston Chauffer Making Good as Aeroplane Scout with the French Army,' *Galveston Daily News*, 22 May 1916

'Former World War Ace is Involved in Law Suit on the Coast,' *The Jefferson City Post-Tribune*, 9 September 1931

'France Honors Dead Air Aces of World War,' *The Kokomo Daily Tribune*, 4 July 1928

'France Honors Her American Fliers,' *New York Times*, 4 September 1927

'Freelance Fighter Pines in Prison, War's a Business to General Hall Who Made Chinese Pay; Explains Arrest,' *The Morning Avalanche*, 13 April 1934

'Friend of E. P. Woman Joins China Air Force,' *El Paso Herald Post*, 23 February 1933

'General Chan (That's Bert Hall) Flies to Asia To Get In A War,' *New York Evening Post*, 21 May 1929

'General Chan of China Calls Missouri Home – Aviation leader in Orient once drove motor car in State,' *The Southwest Missourian*, 2 February 1932

'General Chan of China is Just American Chin,' *Chicago Daily Tribune*, 4 February 1932

'General Chan Predicts War,' *The Jefferson Post-Tribune*, 14 April 1938

'Hall Forgery Charge Dismissed,' *The Jefferson City Post Tribune*, 21 September 1931

'Hall Says Allies Safer Without Russia,' *The Des Moines Morning News*, 7 December 1917

'Hall Will Fight for US,' *Higginsville Advance*, 28 May 1917

'High Tribute Paid By Lieutenant Hall to Kiffin Rockwell,' *The Atlanta Constitution*, 25 March 1919

'Hollywood Gives Him a Pain In the Neck,' *Morning Avalanche*, Lubbock, Texas, 1 June 1937

'Jailed Ace's Bonds Cut,' *The Los Angeles Times*, 6 June 1935

'Lafayette Emblem to Fly,' *New York Times*, 22 September 1941

'Leading Woman of Musical Comedy To Star In Film Here,' *The Ithaca Journal*, 5 August 1918

'Lee Side 'L.A.,'' *The Los Angeles Times*, 27 March 1940

'Lieut. Bert Hall, American Aviator, Writes of Thrills of Air Fighting,' *St. Louis Post*, 9 April 1918

'Lieut. Bert Hall at the Rex,' *Higginsville Advance*, 4 July 1919

'Lieut. Hall Will Fly From Cost to Tokyo,' *The Washington Post*, 8 June 1927

'Lieut. Thaw May Command Lafayette Escadrille,' *The Evening Record*, Greenville, PA, 31 October 1917

'Lieutenant Hall Tells Highly Interesting War Experiences,' *The Cedar Falls Record*, 6 December 1917

'Lieutenant Hall Tells Highly Interesting War Stories,' *Cedar Falls Record*, 6 December 1917

'Los Angeles R.A.F. Pilot Laughs and Cries at War,' *The Los Angeles Times*, 7 September 1943

'Memorial In France Will Honor Lafayette Airmen,' *The Washington Post*, 17 February 1924

'Narrative of the War,' *The Chester Times*, 30 January 1918

'On the Screen, Lieutenant Bert Hall Tells of His Experiences at the Rivoili,' *New York Tribune*, 11 November 1918

'Physically Disqualified!' *The Oakland Tribune*, 4 December 1917

'Pilots Free, Await Plane Deal Action,' *The Bakersfield Californian*, 3 September 1931

'Plane Sellers Again in Cells,' *The Los Angeles Times*, 16 October 1931

'Planting Spies Via Airplane Hazardous,' *The Fort Wayne Sentinel*, 6 July 1917

'Poilus and Tommies Need Devil-May Care Sammies,' *Atlanta Constitution*, 22 July 1917

'Puts Sons Through the School of Hard Knocks,' *The Jefferson City Post-Tribune*, 11 November 1936

'Real D'Artagnans Who Seek Peril Afar,' *New York Times*, 27 April 1930

'Rotarians Told of Situation in China,' *The Sandusky Register-Star News*, 6 November 1946

'Sandusky Yacht Club Luncheon,' *The Sandusky Register-Star News*, 13 February 1947

'Scathing Remarks Made By Purdy in Sentencing Hall,' *The North China Star*, 16 November 1933

'Seeks Arrest of Aviators,' *New York Times*, 25 December 1915

'Selling of Planes to China Described in Flyer's Suit,' *The Los Angeles Times*, 19 March 1937

'Soldier Airman Is Here,' *The Pittsburgh Press*, 27 December 1915

'Soldier of Fortune Prepares for War,' *The Logansport Pharos-Tribune*, 9 February 1932

'Son of Bert Hall Eager to Bag Nazi Plane to Avenge Dead Pal,' *The Los Angeles Times*, 20 July 1942

'Southern Aviators Do Daring Work in France,' *The Cordele Dispatch (Paris)*, 21 May 1916

'Tells of Fights in Air,' *Higginsville Advance*, 12 October 1917

'Terrible Conditions in War Torn Rumania,' *The Fort Wayne Sentinel*, 18 June 1917

'The Swashbucklers Carry On In China,' *The Sun*, 8 April 1934

'Third Arrested in Plane Deal,' *The Los Angeles Times*, 13 September 1931

'Three American John French Flying Corps,' *New York Times*, 3 January 1915

'Three Months in the Trenches,' *New York Times*, 14 February 1915

'To Scatter Pilot's Ashes Over Town,' *Jefferson Post-Tribune*, 20 January 1950

'Tribune-Kimena News Weekly Welcomed on First Showing,' *Oakland Tribune*, 9 June 1919

'War Flier Plans To Try for the Pulitzer Trophy,' *St. Louis Post*, 10 June 1916

'War Flyer Loose From Law's Grip,' *The Los Angeles Times*, 2 March 1932

'Warrior Gets New Call,' *The Los Angeles Times*, 1 September 1936

'What the Critics Say, The Book Review Pages,' *The Oak Parker*, 31 May 1929

'Will Not Intern Aviators,' *The Fort Wayne Journal Gazette*, 28 December 1915

'Wins $40,000 in Plane Deal,' *New York Times*, 29 May 1938

'World War Hero Sued For Divorce,' *The Oakland Tribune*, 28 August 1941

'US Fliers in a Trap,' *The Washington Post*, 25 July 1916

Archives:

USAFHA United States Air Force Historical, Oral History, Interview with Paul Rockwell, Interview #550, 1962

US National Archives, Enlistment Records of the Revolutionary War

US National Archives, Enlistment Records of the Civil War

US National Archives, Census Records

US National Archives, Gorrell's History of the American Expeditionary Forces Air Service, 1917-1919, Publication M990, History of the Lafayette Flying Corps

US National Archives, Records Group 59, State Department Records

Circus World Museum, Records of the Sells-Floto Circus

Washington and Lee University, The Paul Rockwell Collection

Yale University Library, Lafayette Escadrille Memorial Association, Microfilm MISC 611, Records of the Franco-American Flying Corps

University of Virginia, The James McConnell Collection, 2104

Smithsonian National Air and Space Museum, *Journal des Marches et Operations, Escadrille N.124*, Library

Grinnell College Archives, James Norman Hall Collection

The Romanian Air Force Archives, 'Le general Berthelot et l'action de la France en Roumanie et en Rusie Meridionale 1916-1918'

Ripley Entertainment

The Lafayette Foundation
Wings Over The Rockies Museum
The Kalamazoo Air Zoo

Other Sources:

Major Jesse T. Pearson, *The Failure of British Strategy during the Southern Campaign of the American Revolutionary War, 1780-81*, US Army Command and General Staff College, 27 July 2005
League of WWI Aviation Historians, Presentation at the Smithsonian Air and Space Museum, January 2012, Charles Gosse, Uniforms of the Lafayette Escadrille
Oral History, Interview with Colonel Paul Rockwell by Dr Louis D. Silveri, 22 July 1976, Southern Highlands Research Center, The University of North Carolina at Asheville

Endnotes

Introduction

1. Bert Hall Last Will and Testament, Case No. 8086A, 14 December 1948, p. 27.
2. Death Certificate of Weston Birch Hall and Flier's Last Wish Executed By Friend, *The Higginsville Advance*, 27 January 1950.
3. Rockwell, *American Fighters in the Foreign Legion 1914-1918* (New York, Houghton Mifflin, 1930). p. 20-41.
4. Whitehouse, *Legion of Lafayette* (New York, Doubleday, 1962). p. 50-51.
5. Higginsville MO Historical Society, File on Weston Birch Bert Hall.

Chapter One

1. Edwards, *Shelby's Expedition to Mexico, An Unwritten Leave of the War.* (Fayetteville, AK, The University of Arkansas Press, 2002). p. 8.
2. Ancestry.com. Family records of the Hall family.
3. US National Archives, Revolutionary War Pensions, William Hall.
4. Pearson, *The Failure of British Strategy during the Southern Campaign of the American Revolutionary War, 1780-81*, US Army Command and General Staff College, 27 July 2005.
5. Savas and Dameron , *A Guidebook to the Battles of the American Revolution* (New York, Savas Beatie LLC, 2010). p. 216.
6. US National Archives, Enlistment Papers, George Hall.
7. Ibid.
8. Ibid.
9. Wood and Eisenhower, *Battles of the Revolutionary War, 1775-1781* (Cambridge, MA, Da Capo Press, 2003). p. 184.

10. US National Archives, Pension Application, George Hall.

11. Savas and Dameron, *A Guidebook*, p. 285.

12. US National Archives, Pension Application, George Hall.

13. Ibid.

14. Higginsville Historical Society, Of Lafayette and Saline Counties, Portraits and Biographical Sketches, George Hall. p. 603.

15. Ancestry.com. Family records of the Hall family.

16. Young, *History of Lafayette County Missouri Volume II* (Indianapolis, B B Bowen & Company, 1910). p. 689-690.

17. Ibid.

18. US National Archives, Enlistment Papers, George Hall.

19. Edwards, *Shelby and his men: or, The War in the West* (Cincinnati, Miami Printing and Publishing Co., 1867). p. 233.

20. US National Archives, Enlistment Papers, George Hall.

21. Ibid.

22. Johnson, *Battles and Leaders of the Civil War IV* (Edison, NJ, Castle Books, 1989). p. 375.

23. Rolle, *The Lost Cause, The Confederate Exodus to Mexico* (Norman, OK, The University of Oklahoma Press, 1965). p. 18.

24. Ibid p. 19.

25. Ibid p. 58.

26. Edwards, *Shelby's Expedition*, p. 76.

27. Rolle, *The Lost Cause*, p. 99.

28. Edwards, *Shelby's Expedition*, p. 158-159.

29. Ibid, p. 159.

30. Rolle, *The Lost Cause*, p. 201-202.

Chapter Two

1. 'Friend of E. P. Woman Joins China Air Force,' *El Paso Herald Post*, 23 February 1933. p. 8.

2. Gorder, 'Bert Hall, Soldier or Scoundrel?' *Cross and Cockade*, Summer 1963. p. 274.

3. Higginsville Historical Society, Hall Family History.

4. Higginsville Historical Society, Of Lafayette and Saline Counties, Portraits and Biographical Sketches, George Hall. p. 603-604.

5. Higginsville Historical Society Hall Family History.

6. 'General Shelby is Dead,' *Empora Gazette*, 15 February 1897. p. 1.

7. Higginsville Historical Society, Of Lafayette and Saline Counties, Portraits and Biographical Sketches, George Hall. p. 603.

8. Higginsville Historical Society Hall Family History, And US National Archives, 1880 Census.

9. USAFHA – Oral History, Interview with Paul Rockwell, Interview #550, 1962, p. 8.

10. US National Archives, 1890 Census and validated on Bert's death certificate. Other references to Bert's birth year come from J. David Truby, 'Americas First Flier of Fortune,' *Flight Journal*, June 2010, p. 41.

11. Higginsville Historical Society, Of Lafayette and Saline Counties, Portraits and Biographical Sketches, George Hall. p. 603.

12. Washington and Lee University, Paul Rockwell Collection, Box 4, Clipping in Bert Hall file.

13. 'Hollywood Gives Him a Pain In the Neck,' *Morning Avalanche*, Lubbock, Texas, 1 June 1937, p. 8.

14. Higginsville Historical Society File on Bert Hall.

15. Gordon, *The Lafayette Flying Corps Biographies* (Atglen, PA, Schiffer Military History, 2000). p. 202. A check with the archives of the Rock Island Railroad do not have Bert Hall listed as an employee, but their records are incomplete.

16. Gorder, 'Bert Hall, Soldier or Scoundrel?' *Cross and Cockade*, Summer 1963. p. 274. No reference is given to the source but this is certainly substantiated by various other interviews.

17. Gordon, *The Lafayette Flying Corps Biographies* (Atglen, PA, Schiffer Military History, 2000). p. 202-203.

18. Circus World Museum, Records of the Sells-Floto Circus, Billboard pay records 1906.

19. Truby, 'Americas First Flier of Fortune,' *Flight Journal*, June 2010, p. 41.

20. Ibid.

21. Higginsville Historical Society, Bert Hall Files.

22. Truby, 'America's Bad boy Ace,' *Air Classics*, March 1978, p. 61.

23. Gorder, 'Bert Hall, Soldier or Scoundrel?' *Cross and Cockade*, Summer 1963. p. 274.

24. Higginsville Historical Society File on Bert Hall.

25. Ancestry.com – Marriage Certificate – Weston B. Hall and Opal McColloch.

26. Higginsville Historical Society File on Bert Hall.

27. US National Archives, 1910 Census.

28. US National Archives, 1920 Census. Opal married Ira M. Reed and both she and her daughter took the Reed surname.

29. US National Archives, 1910 Census.

30. Christensen, *Dictionary of Missouri Biography* (Columbia, MO, University of Missouri Press) 1999. p. 787.

31. Ibid.

32. 'General Chan of China Calls Missouri Home – Aviation leader in Orient once drove motor car in State,' *The Southwest Missourian*, 2 February 1932. p. 6. The dates of Bert's employment are based on the details of the car that he drove. While the article references a one/two-cylinder Moon Motor Car, it was most likely the first true production car from the Moon Motor Company which was in 1905.

33. Higginsville Historical Society File on Bert Hall *The Higginsville Advance*, Hall will fight for US, Clipping from 1917 (no date specified).

34. Ancestry.com. Marriage Certificate for Bert Hall, 1 October 1910.

35. 'Former Galveston Chauffer Making Good as Aeroplane Scout with the French Army,' *Galveston Daily News*, 22 May 1916. p1.

36. Higginsville Historical Society File on Bert Hall, *The Higginsville Advance,* Hall will fight for US, Clipping from 1917 (no date specified).

37. Washington and Lee University, The Paul Rockwell Collection. File on Bert Hall.

38. Truby, 'America's Bad boy Ace,' *Air Classics*, March 1978, p. 61.

39. 'Former Galveston Chauffer Making Good as Aeroplane Scout with the French Army,' *Galveston Daily News*, 22 May 1916. p. 1.

40. Washington and Lee University, The Paul Rockwell Collection. File on Bert Hall.

Chapter Three

1. King, *Ten Thousand Shall Fall* (New York, Duffold and Company, 1927). p. 24.

2. Rockwell, *American Fighters in the Foreign Legion 1914-1918* (New York, Houghton Mifflin, 1930). p.iii-44.

3. 'Colonel Thaw, War Ace, Dies After a Week's Illness,' *Pittsburgh-Post Gazette*, 23 April 1934. p. 4.

4. Gordon, *The Lafayette Flying Corps Biographies* (Atglen, PA, Schiffer Military History, 2000). p. 39.

5. Oral History, Interview with Colonel Paul Rockwell by Dr Louis D. Silveri, 22 July 1976, Southern Highlands Research Center, The University of North Carolina at Asheville.

6. Hall, *The Lafayette Flying Corps Volume I* (New York, Houghton Mifflin Company, 1920). p. 407.

7. Rockwell, *American Fighters*, p. 8.

8. Mott, *Myron T. Herrick: Friend of France* (New York, Baltzell, 2007). p. 144.

9. O'Balance, *The Story of the Foreign Legion* (London, White Lion, 1961). p. 146-221.

10. Rockwell, *American Fighters*, p. 13-14.

11. Ibid. p. 9.

12. Hall, 'Three Months in the Trenches', *New York Times*, 14 February 1915, p.SM1.

13. Hall, *En L'Air!* (New York, New Library, 1918). p. 7.

14. King, *Ten Thousand*, p. 11-12.

15. Hall, *One Man's War* (London, John Hamilton Publishing, 1929). p. 49.

16. Hall, *Three Months*, p.SM1.

17. Ibid.

18. Hall, *En L'Air!*, p. 20.

19. Hall, *Three Months*, p.SM1.

20. Ibid.

21. King, *Ten Thousand*, p. 9.

22. Ibid., p. 40.

23. Hall, *En L'Air!*, p. 31.

24. Hall, *Three Months*, p.SM2.

25. Ibid.

26. Hall, *En L'Air!*, p. 30.

27. Hall, *Three Months*, p.SM2.

28. Ibid.

29. Ibid.

30. Ibid.

31. Hall, *En L'Air!*, p. 33-34.

32. Ibid. p. 36-37.

33. Ibid. p. 36.

34. 'Three American John French Flying Corps,' *New York Times*, 3 January 1915, p. 1.

35. Hall, *Three Months*, p.SM2.

Chapter Four

1. Hall, 'Three Months in the Trenches,' *New York Times*, 14 February 1915, p. SM1.

2. Flammer, *The Vivid Air* (Athens, GA, The University of Georgia Press, 2008). p. 8.

3. Ibid, p. 9.

4. Hall, *The Lafayette Flying Corps Volume I* (New York, Houghton Mifflin Company, 1920). p. 458.

5. Ibid. p. 458-459.

6. Hall, *En L'Air!* (New York, New Library, 1918). p. 44.

7. Thenault, *The Story of the Lafayette Escadrille* (Boston, Small Maynard Company, 1921). p. 8.

8. King, *Ten Thousand Shall Fall* (New York, Duffold and Company, 1927). p. 59-60.

9. Flammer, *The Vivid Air*, p. 15.

10. Mason Jr, *The Lafayette Escadrille* (New York, Random House, 1964). p. 43.

11. Ibid.

12. Hall, *En L'Air!*, p. 40.

13. League of WWI Aviation Historians, Presentation at the Smithsonian Air and Space Museum, January 2012, Charles Gosse, Uniforms of the Lafayette Escadrille.

14. Hall, 'Fast Fighting and Narrow Escapes in the Air,' *The American Magazine*, Vol. 86, July 1918, p. 45.

15. Guttman, *The Origin of Fighter Aircraft* (Yardley, Pennsylvania, Westholme, 2009). p. 20.

16. Flammer, *The Vivid Air*, p. 15.

17. Hall, *The Lafayette Flying Corps*, p. 455.

18. Gordon, *The Lafayette Flying Corps* (Atglen, Pennsylvania, Schiffler Military History, 2000). p. 117.

19. Hall, *The Lafayette Flying Corps*, p. 6.

20. Ibid. p. 7.

21. Gordon, *The Lafayette Flying Corps*, p. 117.

22. Hall, *The Lafayette Flying Corps*, p. 10.

23. Ibid. p. 10-11.

24. McConnell, *Flying for France* (New York, Grosset & Dunlap, 1916). p. 10.

25. SHAA, *Les escadrilles de l' aeronautique militaire francaise 1912-1920*, p. 103-104.

26. Hall, *The Lafayette Flying Corps*, p. 99.

27. Ibid. p. 100.

28. Ibid. p. 100-101.

29. http://albindenis.free.fr/Site_escadrille/escadrille038.htm.

30. Hall, *En L'Air!*, p. 61.

31. Hall, *The Lafayette Flying Corps*, p. 456.

32. Cooksley, *Nieuport Fighters In Action* (Carrollton, TX, Squadron/Signal, 1997). p. 7-8.

33. Hall, *En L'Air!*, p. 50.

34. Ibid. p. 57.

35. Ibid.

36. Ibid, p. 52.

37. Ibid.

38. Ibid. p. 59.

39. Parsons, *I Flew with the Lafayette Escadrille* (Indianapolis, Indiana, E. C. Seale & Company, 1963). p. 251-252.

40. O'Balance, *The Story of the Foreign Legion* (London, White Lion, 1961). p. 146-221.

41. Rockwell, *American Fighters in the Foreign Legion 1914-1918* (New York, Houghton Mifflin, 1930). p. 147.

42. Morlae, *A Soldier of the Legion* (New York, Houghton Mifflin, 1916). p. 11.

43. Lafayette Escadrille Memorial Association, Yale University Library, Microfilm MISC 611, Records of the Franco American Flying Corps, p. 1.

44. Ibid.

45. Ibid p. 3.

46. Ibid.

47. Hall, *En L'Air!*, p. 62.

Chapter Five

1. Clark, *Aces High: The Air War Over the Western Front 1914-1918* (London, Bloomsbury Publishing, 2011). (e-book) Chapter 8.

2. Hall, *The Lafayette Flying Corps Volume I* (New York, Houghton Mifflin Company, 1920). p. 12-13.

3. 'American Flyers with the French,' *The Ogden Standard*, Ogden Utah, 8 October 1915, p. 2.

4. Hall, *The Lafayette Flying Corps*, p. 8.

5. 'Airmen Losses Heavy,' *The Daily Independent*, Ashland Kentucky, 24 December 1915, p. 3.

6. Flammer, *The Vivid Air*, (Athens, Georgia, The University of Georgia Press, 1981). p. 25.

7. 'Seeks Arrest of Aviators,' *New York Times*, 25 December 1915, p. 1.

8. 'Soldier Airman Is Here,' *The Pittsburgh Press*, 27 December 1915, p. 1.

9. Ibid.

10. 'Will Not Intern Aviators,' *The Fort Wayne Journal Gazette*, 28 December 1915, p. 11.

11. Author interview, Nicholas Champetier 2009 and 2012. Also, details from the birth certificate of Nadine Hall, 1920.

12. Hall, *En L'Air!* (New York, New Library, 1918). p. 62.

13. Parsons, *I Flew With the Lafayette Escadrille* (Indianapolis, Indiana, E. C. Seale & Company, 1963). p. 103.

14. Hall, *The Lafayette Flying Corps,* p. 16.

15. Oral History, Interview with Colonel Paul Rockwell by Dr Louis D. Silveri, 22 July 1976, Southern Highlands Research Center, The University of North Carolina at Asheville.

16. McConnell, *Flying for France* (New York, Grosset & Dunlap, 1916). p. 23-24.

17. Rockwell, *War Letters of Kiffin Yates Rockwell* (New York, The Country Life Press, 1925). p. 119.

18. McConnell, *Flying for France,* p. 25.

19. Toelle, 'A White Faced Cow – The Operational History of the Escadrille Américaine N.124 to September 1916,' *Over the Front,* Vol. 24, No. 4, Winter 2009. p. 294.

20. Rockwell, *War Letters,* p. 123.

21. Ibid. p. 126-127.

22. Parsons, *I Flew With the Lafayette Escadrille,* p. 7.

23. Hall, *High Adventure, A Narrative of Air Fighting In France* (Toronto, Thomas Allan, 1918).

24. 'Southern Aviators Do Daring Work in France,' *The Cordele Dispatch (Paris),* 21 May 1916.

25. Toelle, 'A White Faced Cow', p. 294.

26. Churchill, *The World Crisis, 1914-1918* (Oxford, The Clarendon Press, 1934). p. 262.

27. McConnell, *Flying for France,* p. 67.

28. Hall, *En L'Air!,* p. 67-68.

29. McConnell, *Flying for France,* p. 55.

30. Rockwell, *War Letters,* p. 128.

31. Washington and Lee University, Paul Rockwell Collection, Box 4.

32. Rockwell, *War Letters,* p. 128.

33. Norman, Frank and Rick, *Casualties of the German Air Service* (London, Grub Street, 1999). p. 187. There were two Aviatiks downed in the range/vicinity of the escadrille. This one most mirrors the description provided.

34. 'Fights Three Aeroes, Then Feels Fourth,' *The Washington Post,* 25 May 1916, p. 2. A variant appears in Rockwell, *The War Letters of Kiffin Yates Rockwell* (New York, The Country Life Press, 1925). p. 127-128. Paul Rockwell edited his brother's letters extensively for publication.

35. Washington and Lee University, Paul Rockwell Collection, Box 3.

36. Rockwell, *War Letters,* p. 132.

37. University of Virginia, The James McConnell Collection, 2104 Box 1, Letter dated 28 May 1916.

38. Toelle, 'A White Faced Cow,' p. 295.

39. Hall, *En L'Air!*, p. 78.

40. Hall and Niles, *One Man's War* (London, John Hamilton Ltd., 1928). p. 156. While *One Man's War* is mostly a piece of fiction, this was confirmed in a photograph by Alan Toelle.

41. University of Virginia, The James McConnell Collection, 3 June 1916. Letter to Marcelle Guérin (available online).

42. 'Bold Feats by Yankee Flyers,' *Boston Daily Globe*, 6 June 1916, p. 4.

43. Rockwell, *War Letters,* p. 133-134.

44. Guttman, *SPA 124 Lafayette Escadrille* (Wellingsborough, UK, Osprey Publishing, 2004). p. 22.

45. McConnell, *Flying for France*, p. 38-39.

46. Hall, *The Lafayette Flying Corps*, p. 79-82. This portion was written by Clyde Balsley under the heading 'The Hospital'.

47. Ibid. p. 107-109.

48. Ibid. p. 80-85.

49. Guttman, *SPA 124*, p. 24-25.

50. Hall, *En L'Air!* (New York, New Library, 1918). p. 71.

51. Guttman, *SPA 124*, p. 25-26 and Flammer, *The Vivid Air*, p. 77.

52. Hall, *En L'Air!*, p. 73.

53. University of Virginia, The James McConnell Collection, 1 July 1916, misdated as 1 July 1915. Letter to Paul Rockwell.

54. University of Virginia, The James McConnell Collection, 2104 Box 1. Letter dated 1 July 1916.

55. Washington and Lee University, Paul Rockwell Collection, Box 5. The copy located was not the original, however. A subsequent check shows the same material used in Truby, David J. 'America's First Flier of Fortune, Bert Hall, was Roguish Adventure Personified,' *Aviation Heritage*, March 1992, p. 16.

56. University of Virginia, The James McConnell Collection, 2104 Box 1. Letter dated 16 July 1916.

57. Rockwell, *War Letters,* p. 144.

58. Washington and Lee University, Paul Rockwell Collection, Box 4. Copy of the letter dated 21 July 1916.

59. Truby, 'America's First Flier of Fortune, Bert Hall, Was Roguish Adventure Personified,' *Aviation Heritage*, March 1992, p. 20.

60. 'US Fliers in a Trap,' *The Washington Post*, 25 July, 1916, p. 1.

61. University of Virginia, The James McConnell Collection, 2104 Box 1. Letter dated 25 July 1916.

62. Hall, *En L'Air!*, p. 71.

63. Toelle, 'A White Faced Cow', p. 295 and Franks Baily and Duiven *Casualties of the German Air Service*, p. 190.

64. Rockwell, *War Letters,* p. 147.

65. Washington and Lee University, Paul Rockwell Collection, Box 4.

66. Washington and Lee University, Paul Rockwell Collection, Box 3 – partial letter from Kiffin Rockwell.

67. Hall, *En L'Air!*, p. 71.

68. Rockwell, *War Letters,* p. 149.

69. Hall, 'Fast Fighting and Narrow Escapes In The Air,' *The American Magazine*, Vol. 86, July 1918, p. 45.

70. Journal des Marches et Operations, Escadrille N.124, Library, National Air and Space Museum, Smithsonian Institution.

71. Thénault, *The Story of the Lafayette Escadrille* (Boston, Small Maynard and Company, 1921). p. 68-69.

72. Flammer, *The Vivid Air*, p. 54-55.

73. Ibid. p. 83-84.

74. Hall, 'Fast Fighting and Narrow Escapes In The Air,' *The American Magazine*, Vol. 86, July 1918, p. 45.

Chapter Six

1. Hall, *En L'Air!*, (New York, New Library, 1918). p. 142.

2. McConnell, *Flying for France*, (New York, Grosset & Dunlap, 1916). p. 98.

3. Hall, *The Lafayette Flying Corps Volume I* (New York, Houghton Mifflin Company, 1920). p. 408-409.

4. Guttman, *SPA 124 Lafayette Escadrille* (Wellingsborough, UK, Osprey Publishing, 2004). p. 49.

5. Washington and Lee University, Paul Rockwell Collection, Box 4, document typed by Paul Rockwell refuting Bert Hall's book, *One Man's War.*

6. Ibid.

7. Guttman, *SPA 124*, p. 49.

8. Rockwell, 'L'Escadrille La Fayette,' *Le Guerre Aérienne*, September 1916, p. 562. From Grinnell College Archives, James Norman Hall Collection.

9. Hall, *The Lafayette Flying Corps*, p. 408-409.

10. Ibid.

11. Rockwell, 'Writings of the American Pilots In The Lafayette Escadrille,' *Ex Libris*, Vol. 1, No. 5, November 1923, p. 135. From Grinnell College Archives, James Norman Hall Collection.

12. McConnell, *Flying for France*, p. 96.

13. Ibid. p. 138.

14. Washington and Lee University, Paul Rockwell Collection, Box 4, document typed by Paul Rockwell refuting Bert Hall's book, *One Man's War*.

15. Guttman, *SPA 124*, p. 50.

16. Flammer, *The Vivid Air* (Athens, Georgia, The University of Georgia Press, 1981). p. 90-91.

17. Washington and Lee University, Paul Rockwell Collection, Letter to Paul Rockwell from Paul Pavelka, 14 October 1916.

18. Gordon, *The Lafayette Flying Corps* (Atglen, PA, Schiffer Military History, 2000). p. 319-321.

19. Hall, *The Lafayette Flying Corps*, p. 34.

20. Flammer, *The Vivid Air*, p. 93.

21. Hall, *The Lafayette Flying Corps*, p. 34

22. McConnell, *Flying for France*, p. 115.

23. Ibid. p. 115-116.

24. Gorder, 'Bert Hall, Soldier or Scoundrel?' *Cross and Cockade*, Summer 1963.

25. Truby, 'America's Bad Boy Ace,' *Air Classics*, March 1998, p. 61.

26. Truby, David J. 'Americans First Flier of Fortune,' *Flight Journal*, June 2010, p. 42.

27. Chapman, *Victor Chapman's Letters From France* (New York, MacMillan Company, 1917). p. 178.

28. Truby, 'America's Bad Boy Ace,' p. 63.

29. Ibid. p. 63-64.

30. University of Virginia, The James McConnell Collection, 2104 Box 2, Letter dated 19 July 1916.

31. Truby, 'America's First Flier of Fortune, Bert Hall, Was Roguish Adventure Personified,' *Aviation Heritage*, March 1992, p. 20.

32. Ibid. p. 42.

33. Truby, 'The First Airborne Mercenary,' *Gung-Ho*, November 1984, p. 21.

34. 'Average Life of Aviator, 17 Hours In the Air, Lafayette Escadrille survivor tells of wiping out aerial crew,' *Schenectady Gazette*, 4 November 1918, p. 6.

35. Hall, 'Fast Fighting and Narrow Escapes In The Air,' *The American Magazine*, Vol. 86, July 1918, p. 43.

36. Truby, 'America's First Flier,' p. 18.

37. Washington and Lee University, Paul Rockwell Collection, Box 8.

38. Truby, 'The First Airborne Mercenary,' p. 22.

39. Washington and Lee University, Paul Rockwell Collection.

40. Author interview, Nicholas Champetier 2009 and 2012.

41. Truby, 'America's First Flier,' p. 18.

42. Washington and Lee University, Paul Rockwell Collection.

43. University of Virginia, The James McConnell Collection, 1 July 1916, misdated as 1 July 1915. Letter to Paul Rockwell.

44. University of Virginia, The James McConnell Collection, 1 July 1916, misdated as 1 July 1915. Letter to Paul Rockwell.

45. Washington and Lee University, Paul Rockwell Collection. Letter by Paul Rockwell refuting *One Man's War*.

46. Washington and Lee University, Paul Rockwell Collection. Letter by Paul Rockwell refuting *One Man's War*.

47. Rockwell, *American Fighters In the Foreign Legion, 1914-1918* (New York, Houghton Mifflin, 1930). p. 191.

48. 'Lieutenant Hall Tells Highly Interesting War Experiences,' *The Cedar Falls Record*, 6 December 1917, p. 6.

49. Toelle, 'A White Faced Cow – The Operational History of the Escadrille Américaine N.124 to September 1916,' *Over the Front*, Vol. 24, No. 4, Winter 2009, p. 335.

50. Guttman, *SPA 124*, p. 61.

51. Truby, 'The First Airborne Mercenary,' p. 23.

Chapter Seven

1. Hall, *En L'Air!* (New York, New Library, 1918). p. 96-97.

2. Bailey, *Chronology of the French Air Service* (London, Grub Street, 2001). p. 82. Supporting references were viewed in the Lafayette Foundation reference files, which are assumed to be from the Journal des Marches et Operations, Escadrille N.103. Also from Hall, *En L'Air!*, p. 91.

3. University of Virginia, The James McConnell Collection, Box 2, 19 November 1916. Letter to Paul Rockwell.

4. Hall, *The Lafayette Flying Corps Volume I* (New York, Houghton Mifflin Company, 1920). p. 255.

5. American Sent to the Romanian Front,. *New Castle News*, 27 December 1916, p. 2.

6. Pen, *I Wonder as I Wander: The Life of John Jacob Niles* (Lexington, Kentucky, The University of Kentucky Press, 2010). p. 56.

7. US National Archives, Gorrell's History of the American Expeditionary Forces Air Service, 1917-1919, Publication M990, History of the Lafayette Flying Corps, p. 5.

8. Flammer, *The Vivid Air* (Athens, Georgia, The University of Georgia Press, 1981). p. 103.

9. Ibid.

10. Thénault, *The Story of the Lafayette Escadrille* (Boston, Small, Maynard and Company, 1921). p. 105.

11. Ferro, *La Grande Guerre* (Paris, Edmond Gallimard, 1969). p. 86-88.

12. http://www.mapn.ro/smg/gmr/Engleza/Ultimul_nr/giurca-p. 177-185.pdf.

13. 'American Sent to the Romanian Front,' *New Castle News*, 27 December 1916, p. 2.

14. Sere, 7 N Carton, (457 G.Q.G.F. an M.G. 7/20 7 *Janvier 1917*) and The Romanian Air Force Archives, 'Le general Berthelot et l'action de la France en Roumanie et en Rusie Meridionale 1916-1918'.

15. 'Terrible Conditions in War Torn Rumania,' *The Fort Wayne Sentinel*, 13 June 1917, p. 16.

16. 'Ace Hall Will Lecture Here,' *The Estherville Enterprise*, 12 December 1917, p. 1.

17. Hall, *En L'Air!*, p. 115.

18. Ibid. p. 120.

19. Ibid, p. 116-117.

20. Ibid. p. 118.

21. 'Lieutenant Hall Tells Highly Interesting War Stories,' *Cedar Falls Record*, 6 December 1917, p. 4.

22. Romanian Air Force Archives, 'Le general Berthelot et l'action de la France en Roumanie et en Rusie Meridionale 1916-1918', p. 115.

23. 'Lieutenant Hall Tells Highly Interesting War Stories,' *Cedar Falls Record*, 6 December 1917, p. 4.

24. 'Ace Hall Will Lecture Here,' *The Estherville Enterprise*, 12 December 1917, p. 1.

25. Sere, 7 N Carton, (457 G.Q.G.F. an M.G. 7/20 7 *Janvier 1917*) and The Romanian Air Force Archives, 'Le general Berthelot et l'action de la France en Roumanie et en Rusie Meridionale 1916-1918'.

26. 'Lieutenant Hall Tells Highly Interesting War Stories,' *Cedar Falls Record*, 6 December 1917, p. 4.

27. Hall, *En L'Air!*, p. 136-137.

28. US National Archives, Record Group 59, Bert Hall File, 1917, Letter to Secretary of State Lansing.

29. US National Archives, Record Group 59, Bert Hall File, 1917, Receipt, Weston B. Hall.

30. Hall, *En L'Air!*, p. 140.

31. Ancestry.com: ships manifest for *Koren Maru* lists forty-year-old Bert Hall.

Chapter Eight

1. Library of Congress, files relating to *A Romance of the Air*. Stars and Name Should Get Business: Don't Promise That Film Is Good.

2. Hudson, *Hostile Skies* (Syracuse, NY, Syracuse University Press, 1968). p. 2-3.

3. Ibid. p. 3.

4. 'Hall Will Fight for US,' *Higginsville Advance*, 28 May 1917, p. 1.

5. 'Physically Disqualified!' *The Oakland Tribune*, 4 December 1917.

6. 'Planting Spies Via Airplane Hazardous,' *The Fort Wayne Sentinel*, 6 July 1917, p. 7.

7. 'Terrible Conditions in War Torn Rumania,' *The Fort Wayne Sentinel*, 18 June 1917, p. 16.

8. 'Aviator Falls From Dizzying Heights,' *The California Weekly*, The Oakland Tribune, 16 September 1917.

9. Ibid.

10. 'Hall Says Allies Safer Without Russia,' *The Des Moines Morning News*, 7 December 1917, p. 7.

11. 'Narrative of the War,' *The Chester Times*, 30 January 1918, p. 1.

12. 'Tells of Fights in Air,' *Higginsville Advance*, 12 October 1917, p. 1.

13. Ibid.

14. Ibid.

15. US National Archives, Record Group 59, Bert Hall File. Letter dated 16 September 1917 – State Department translation.

16. 'Lieut. Thaw May Command Lafayette Escadrille,' *The Evening Record*, Greenville, PA, 31 October 1917, p. 1.

17. 'American Flyer Gives Black Eye to Objector,' *The Oakland Tribune*, 2 December 2 1917, p. 1.

18. 'First Flying Ace Visits America,' *Evening Public Ledger (Philadelphia)*, 30 January 30 1918, p. 2.

19. 'Flying in France Is Great Sport,' *The Washington Post*, 9 February 1918, p. 7.

20. Ancestry.com, Passport applications, Bert Hall.

21. Gordon, *The Lafayette Flying Corps* (Atglen, PA, Schiffer Military History, 2000). p. 210.

22. US National Archives, FBI Case File, BERT HALL Impersonating a French Officer, 8 March 1918.

23. US National Archives, FBI Case File, BERT HALL Impersonating a French Officer, 8 March 1918.

24. 'Aviator Falls From Dizzying Heights,' *The California Weekly*, The Oakland Tribune, 16 September 1917.

25. Romanian Air Force's History Site: http://www.roaf.ro/en/istorie1_en.php.

26. Hall, 'Fast Fighting and Narrow Escapes In The Air,' *The American Magazine*, Vol. 86, July 1918, p. 43.

27. Hall, *En L'Air!* (New York, New Library, 1918)

28. Ibid. p. 148.

29. Guttman, *SPA 124 Lafayette Escadrille* (Wellingsborough, UK, Osprey Publishing, 2004). p. 112.

30. 'Aviators Fear Only Fire In the Air,' *The Boston Daily Globe*, 7 January 1919, p. 2.

31. '"En l'air!" In The Making,' *The Ithaca Journal,* 6 August 1918.

32. Library of Congress, files relating to *A Romance of the Air.*

33. 'Leading Woman of Musical Comedy To Star In Film Here,' *The Ithaca Journal,* 5 August 1918.

34 Author interview, Terry Harbin in March 2012 and his website: http://www.ithacamademovies.com.

35. Author interview, Terry Harbin in March 2012.

36. Library of Congress, files relating to *A Romance of the Air.* Clipping dated 23 November 1918.

37. Library of Congress, files relating to *A Romance of the Air.* Clipping dated 28 December 1918.

38. 'On the Screen, Lieutenant Bert Hall Tells of His Experiences at the Rivoili,' *New York Tribune,* 11 November 1918.

39. Library of Congress, files relating to *A Romance of the Air.* Clipping dated 11 January 1919.

40. Library of Congress, files relating to *A Romance of the Air.* Clipping dated 25 January 1919.

41. 'Aviators Fear Only Fire In the Air,' *The Boston Daily Globe*, 7 January 1919, p. 2.

42. Pen, *I Wonder as I Wander: The Life of John Jacob Niles* (Lexington, Kentucky, The University of Kentucky Press, 2010). p. 83-84.

43. Ibid. p. 84-86.

44. Ancestry.com – Marriage Application Records, Helen and Bert Hall, 11 March 1919.

45. Author interview with Nicolas Champetier, February 2009. Also Nadine Hall's birth certificate.

46. 'Conqueror of Nine Germans In Air To Fly Here Today,' *Oakland Tribune,* 8 June 1919, p. 4A.

47. 'Tribune-Kimena News Weekly Welcomed on First Showing,' *Oakland Tribune,* 9 June 1919, p. 4.

48. 'Lieut. Bert Hall at the Rex,' *Higginsville Advance,* 4 July 1919, p. 1.

49. Ancestry.com, 1920 US Census.

Chapter Nine

1. Latané Lewis, 'He Fought the Hun! The Story of Bert Hall,' *Tiger Magazine*, July 1957, Vol. II, No. 3, p. 13.
2. Gordon, *The Lafayette Flying Corps* (Atglen, PA, Schiffer Military History, 2000). p. 210. Verified by the author with 20th Century Fox's Personnel Department.
3. The Library of Congress, Motion Picture and Photography Group. Verified by the American Film Institute.
4. Ancestry.com. State Department Passports File, Weston Birch Hall 2 November 1922.
5. Washington and Lee University, Paul Rockwell Collection, Box 4. Clipping in Bert Hall file.
6. Higginsville Historical Society, Bert Hall File. Clipping from the Higginsville Advance, 5 January 1923.
7. 'Lieut. Hall Will Fly From Cost to Tokyo,' *The Washington Post*, 8 June 1927, p. 1.
8. 'War Flier Plans To Try for the Pulitzer Trophy,' *St. Louis Post*, 10 June 1916, p. 3.
9. 'War Flier Will Try Globe-Girdling Hop,' *New York Times*, 6 April 1928, p. 16.
10. Ibid.
11. 'Californians Plan 24-Day Flight Around the World,' *The Oakland Tribune*, 6 April 1928, p. 12.
12. Gordon, *The Lafayette Flying Corps,* p. 484.
13. Washington and Lee University, Paul Rockwell Collection, Box 8, Lafayette Memorial Materials.
14. 'France Honors Her American Fliers,' *New York Times*, 4 September 1927, p.SM8.
15. Washington and Lee University, Paul Rockwell Collection, Box 8, Lafayette Memorial Materials.
16. Washington and Lee University, Paul Rockwell Collection, Box 8, Lafayette Memorial Materials.
17. Author interview with Richard 'Bud' Zinn, son of Frederick Zinn, 2007. Frederick Zinn is said to have complained to Rockwell about the slighting of Bert Hall.
18. 'France Honors Dead Air Aces of World War,' *The Kokomo Daily Tribune*, 4 July 1928, p. 7.
19. Ancestry.com, Passport Application, Bert Hall, 25 September 1928.
20. 'General Chan of China Calls Missouri Home,' *The Southeast Missourian*, 2 February 1932, p. 6.

21. University of Kentucky, special Collections Library, John Jacob Niles Collection, Colliers letter dated 18 May 1928.

22. 'General Chan (That's Bert Hall) Flies to Asia To Get In A War,' *New York Evening Post*, 21 May 1929, p. 3.

23. University of Kentucky, special Collections Library, John Jacob Niles Collection, Copy of Bert Hall letter dated 28 September 1929.

24. University of Kentucky, special Collections Library, John Jacob Niles Collection, Copy of Henry Hold letter dated 26 October 1929.

25. 'What the Critics Say, The Book Review Pages,' *The Oak Parker*, 31 May 1929, p. 18.

26. Letter to author from the Turkish Air Force, 2008, confirming that Bert Hall never served in any aspect or role in their military. A similar check with Bulgaria's archives yielded a similar response – only with the proviso that their records are not complete from that time period.

27. Author interview, Nicholas Champetier 2009 and 2012.

28. Hall, *One Man's War* (London, John Hamilton Publishing, 1929). p. 89-90.

29. Washington and Lee University, Paul Rockwell Collection.

Chapter Ten

1. 'General Chan of China is Just American Chin,' *Chicago Daily Tribune*, 4 February 1932, p. 4.

2. US National Archives, Record Group 94, Records of the Adjutant General Files, 1926-1939, Box 481, Letter to Commanding General, Philippine Department, 27 October 1930.

3. Guangqiu, *War Wings* (Westport, Connecticut, Greenwood Press: 2001). p. 37-40.

4. Ibid. p. 44.

5. 'China Turns to Air in Building Defense,' *The Tyrone Herald*, 14 June 1934, p. 3.

6. Barton, 'Wings of the Dragon,' *Air Classics*, Vol. 35, No. 3, September 1999, p. 52.

7. 'General Chan (That's Bert Hall) Flies to Asia To Get In A War,' *New York Evening Post*, 21 May 1929, p. 3.

8. 'Who's Who in China,' *The China Weekly Review*, 23 April 1932, p. 18-9.

9. Pyle, 'China Air Chief Is An American,' *New York Telegram*, 28 July 1930, p. 2.

10. 'Chinese Air Commander Adventurer of Kentucky,' *The Circleville (Ohio) Herald*, 8 February 1932, p. 2.

11. US National Archives, Records Group 65, 893.11.3Quotation on Vought Corsair Planes, 8 October 1929.

12. Guangqiu, *War Wings* (Westport, Connecticut, Greenwood Press, 2001). p. 61.

13. US National Archives, Record Group 165, Report Number 7737, Lieutenant Colonel Nelson Margetts to the War Department, 4 July 1930.

14. US National Archives, Record Group 165, Bert Hall File, 1934 – Clipping from Shanghai newspaper (no date attributed).

15. Guangqiu, *War Wings* (Westport, Connecticut, Greenwood Press: 2001). p. 45.

16. 'Real D'Artagnans Who Seek Peril Afar,' *New York Times*, 27 April 1930, p. 89.

17. Ancestry.com, 1930 Census Records, Helen Hall.

18. Higginsville Historical Society, File on Bert Hall.

19. 'Plane Sellers Again in Cells,' *The Los Angeles Times*, 16 October 1931, p.A3.

20. 'Famous War Ace Arrested in Airplane Plot,' *The Reno Evening Gazette*, 2 September 1931, p. 1.

21. 'Pilots Free, Await Plane Deal Action,' *The Bakersfield Californian*, 3 September 1931, p. 1.

22. 'Plane Sellers Again in Cells,' *The Los Angeles Times*, 16 October 1931, p.A3.

23. 'Third Arrested in Plane Deal,' *The Los Angeles Times*, 13 September 1931, p.A8.

24. 'Former World War Ace is Involved in Law Suit on the Coast,' *The Jefferson City Post-Tribune*, 9 September 1931, p. 2.

25. 'Hall Forgery Charge Dismissed,' *The Jefferson City Post Tribune*, 21 September 1931, p. 1.

26. Gordon, *The Lafayette Flying Corps* (Atglen, PA, Schiffer Military History, 2000). p. 211.

27. 'War Flyer Loose From Law's Grip,' *The Los Angeles Times*, 2 March 1932, p.A2.

28. 'Soldier of Fortune Prepares for War,' *The Logansport Pharos-Tribune*, 9 February 1932, p. 4.

29. 'Bert Hall Is To Join War Fliers,' *The Piqua (Ohio) Daily Call*, 26 February 1932, p. 1. and the files of the Higginsville Historical Society.

30. Washington and Lee University, Paul Rockwell Collection, Box 4. Clipping in Bert Hall file.

31. Washington and Lee University, Paul Rockwell Collection, Box 4. Clipping in Bert Hall file.

32. Washington and Lee University, Paul Rockwell Collection, Box 4.
    Clipping in Bert Hall file.
33. 'Famed Flier's Child a Pauper,' *The Charleston Gazette*, 22 January 22
    1933, p. 5.
34. 'Flier's Wife Tries Suicide,' *The Washington Daily News*, 22 March
    1933, p. 3.

Chapter Eleven

1. 'Bert Hall Held as a Gun Runner,' *Jefferson City Post Tribune*, 18
   October 1933, p. 2.
2. Cleveland Williams, 'Freelance Fighter Pines in Prison, War's a Business
   to General Hall Who Made Chinese Pay; Explains Arrest,' *The Morning
   Avalanche*, 13 April 1934, p. 3.
3. Ancestry.com: ship's manifest, *SS President Hoover*.
4. Gilman, 'The Swashbucklers Carry On In China,' *The Sun*, 8 April 1934,
   p.MS4.
5. US National Archives, Records Group 65, File 171.6937- Hall, Bert/2,
   Letter from F. P. Lockhart.
6. Gordon, *The Lafayette Flying Corps* (Atglen, PA, Schiffer Military
   History, 2000). p. 212.
7. US National Archives, Records Group 165, File 171.6937- Hall, Bert/2.
   Letter 12 October 1933, Activities of Bert Hall.
8. US National Archives, Records Group 65, File 171.6937- Hall, Bert/2,
   Translation of Initial Contract, 12 August 1933.
9. Gordon, *The Lafayette Flying Corps*, p. 211.
10. US National Archives, Records Group 165, File 171.6937- Hall, Bert/2,
    Criminal Action No. 6, United States vs. Bert Hall, 14 October 1933.
11. US National Archives, Records Group 65, File 171.6937- Hall, Bert/2,
    Letter from F. P. Lockhart.
12. US National Archives, Records Group 65, File 171.6937- Hall, Bert/2,
    Criminal Action No. 6, Message to Secretary of State, 17 November
    1933.
13. US National Archives, Records Group 65, File 171.6937- Hall, Bert/2,
    Warrant for Arrest Details, 27 October 1933, pg.2.
14. 'Scathing Remarks Made By Purdy in Sentencing Hall,' *The North
    China Star*, 16 November 1933.
15. Ibid.
16. USAFHRA, Oral Interview with Leroy Prinz, p. 33.

17. Williams, 'Freelance Fighter Pines in Prison, War's a Business to General Hall Who Made Chinese Pay; Explains Arrest,' *The Morning Avalanche*, 13 April 1934, p. 3.

18. Ibid.

19. 'Famous Pioneer Aviator is Dead,' *The Altoona Mirror*, 23 April 1934, p. 1.

20. Washington and Lee University, Paul Rockwell Collection, Box 7, Correspondence of the Trench and Air Association.

21. 'Jailed Ace's Bonds Cut,' *The Los Angeles Times*, 6 June 1935, p.A3.

22. Ancestry.com, Parole Records, Bert Hall, McNeil Island, 11 November 1935.

Chapter Twelve

1. Ripley Entertainment, Transcript of 19 April 1940 radio programme used with permission.

2. 'Hollywood Gives Him a Pain in the Neck,' *The Morning Avalanche*, 1 June 1937, p. 10.

3. Ibid.

4. Ibid.

5. Ibid.

6. 'Puts Sons Through the School of Hard Knocks,' *The Jefferson City Post-Tribune*, 11 November 1936, p. 6.

7. 'Warrior Gets New Call,' *The Los Angeles Times*, 11 September 1936, p. 10.

8. *The Indianapolis 500 Yearbook*, Norman Hall Racing With the Big Boys, 1983, p. 199.

9. Ibid. p. 198.

10. 'Warrior Gets New Call,' *The Los Angeles Times*, 1 September 1936, p. 10.

11. *The China Weekly Review*, Vol. 62, #3, p. 122.

12. 'Selling of Planes to China Described in Flyer's Suit,' *The Los Angeles Times*, 19 March 1937, p.A2.

13. 'China Plane Deals Told,' *The Los Angeles Times*, 18 March 1937, p.A2.

14. 'Douglas Replies to Hall's Claims,' *The Berkley Daily Gazette*, 15 March 1937, p. 1.

15. Ibid.

16. 'Wins $40,000 in Plane Deal,' *New York Times*, 29 May 1938, p. 3.

17. 'General Chan Predicts War,' *The Jefferson Post-Tribune*, 14 April 1938, p. 3.

18. 'Lee Side 'L.A.',' *The Los Angeles Times*, 27 March 1940, p.A4.

19. Ripley Entertainment, Transcript of 19 April 1940 radio programme used with permission.

20. US National Archives, 1942 Draft Registration Card, Weston Birch Hall.

21. US National Archives, Record Group 159, 862.24/521, State Department Records, Shanghai, 22 October 1940.

22. 'World War Hero Sued For Divorce,' *The Oakland Tribune*, 28 August 1941, p.D9.

23. 'Famed Pilot's Son Volunteers For Canadian Air Corps,' *The Los Angeles Times*, 19 June 1941, p. 9.

24. 'Lafayette Emblem to Fly,' *New York Times*, 22 September 1941, p. 5.

25. 'Son of Bert Hall Eager to Bag Nazi Plane to Avenge Dead Pal,' *The Los Angeles Times*, 20 July 1942, p. 2.

26. 'Flyer Describes Narrow Escape From Hit Plane,' *The Los Angeles Times*, 4 August 1942, p. 3.

27. 'Los Angeles R.A.F. Pilot Laughs and Cries at War,' *The Los Angeles Times*, 7 September 1943, p. 3.

28. Museum of the United States Air Force, Frederick Zinn Collection, clipping maintained in files.

Chapter Thirteen

1. Whitehouse, *Legion of Lafayette* (New York, Doubleday, 1962). p. 50.

2. 'Court House,' *The Sandusky Register-Star News*, 15 October 1948, p. 12.

3. 'Bert Hall,' *The Sandusky Register-Star News*, 5 September 1946, p. 6.

4. 'Rotarians Told of Situation in China,' *The Sandusky Register-Star News*, 6 November 1946, p. 2.

5. 'Bert Hall of Castailia,' *The Sandusky Register-Star News*, 10 December 1946, p. 6.

6. 'Sandusky Yacht Club Luncheon,' *The Sandusky Register-Star News*, 13 February 1947, p. 8.

7. 'Bert Hall of Lafayette Escadrille Dies,' *The Washington Post*, 8 December 1948, p.B2.

8. Gordon, *The Lafayette Flying Corps* (Atglen, PA, Schiffer Military History, 2000). p. 214.

9. Museum of the United States Air Force, Frederick Zinn Collection, clipping maintained in files.

10. 'To Scatter Pilot's Ashes Over Town,' *Jefferson Post-Tribune*, 20 January 1950, p. 4, and The Higginsville Historical Society file on Bert Hall.

11. *The Indianapolis 500 Yearbook*, Norman Hall Racing With the Big Boys, 1983, p. 194-209.

Epilogue

1. USAFHA – Oral History, Interview with Paul Rockwell, interview #550, 1962, p. 4.
2. Washington and Lee University, Paul Rockwell Collection, Box 7, various letters by Paul Rockwell, 1958-59.

Index